DOING POSTGRADUATE RESEARCH

Second edition

Edited by Stephen Potter

The Open University

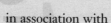

in association with

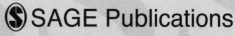

SAGE Publications

London ● Thousand Oaks ● New Delhi

The Open University
Walton Hall
Milton Keynes
MK7 6AA
United Kingdom
www.open.ac.uk

First edition published 2002
Second edition published 2006

 SAGE Publications Ltd
1 Oliver's Yard
55 City Road
London EC1Y 1SP

SAGE Publications Inc.
2455 Teller Road
Thousand Oaks, California 91320

SAGE Publications India Pvt Ltd
B-42, Panchsheel Enclave
Post Box 4109
New Delhi 110 017

British Library Cataloguing in Publication data

A catalogue record for this book is available
from the British Library

ISBN-10 1 4129 2404 9   ISBN-13 978 1 4129 2404 7
ISBN-10 1 4129 2405 7 (pbk)   ISBN-13 978 1 4129 2405 4 (pbk)

Library of Congress Control Number: 2005937983

Typeset by C&M Digitals (P) Ltd., Chennai, India
Printed in Great Britain by the Cromwell Press Ltd, Trowbridge, Wiltshire
Printed on paper from sustainable resources

Contents

List of Figures

List of Tables

Notes on Contributors

Stephen Potter is Professor of Transport Strategy at The Open University. Beginning his career in Social Sciences, he now works in the Faculty of Technology's Department of Design and Innovation. He has run interdisciplinary research training workshops since 1992 and contributed to a variety of research training programmes, courses and packs at the Open University and in other universities.

Martin Le Voi is a Senior Lecturer in Psychology in The Open University's Social Sciences Faculty. Together with Stephen Potter he chaired the team producing this book and has played a major role in developing the Open University's research training Master's programme.

Chris High is Lecturer in Systems Thinking and Practice at The Open University. As a PhD student, he was on the receiving end of an early version of this book's materials in 1997, and has contributed to postgraduate research training at the Open University and elsewhere.

Jane Montague is a Lecturer in Psychology at the University of Derby and has taught qualitative research methods; since 1998 she has run research training workshops in several universities.

Wendy Stainton-Rogers is a Professor at The Open University working on critical psychology. She is the Academic Co-ordinator for the Open University Research School.

Theresa Lillis is a Senior Lecturer in language and education in the Centre for Language and Communications at The Open University. She has published research on academic and student writing in higher education.

Sarah North is a Lecturer in The Open University's Centre for Language and Communications. She contributes to the OU's research student training programme, and has been involved in academic writing programmes both in the UK and overseas.

John Oates is a Senior Lecturer in Developmental Psychology, in The Centre for Childhood, Development and Learning at The Open University, and is Chair of the OU's Research Ethics Committee.

Trevor Collins is a Research Fellow in The Open University's Knowledge Media Institute (KMI), where he is Postgraduate Tutor and has run workshops with PhD students on developing presentation skills.

Ann Jones is a Senior Lecturer in The Open University's Institute of Educational Technology. She has contributed to The Open University's research training programme over a number of years and to developing and running the OU's research training Master's programme courses.

Verina Waights is a Lecturer in Professional Health Care Education in the Faculty of Health and Social Care at The Open University and has made a major contribution to The University's research student training programme.

Professor Steve Evans, this book's External Assessor, is head of the International Ecotechnology Research Centre at Cranfield University. He has a particular interest in the organization of co-operation and innovation, and integrating environmental and social sustainability into design.

Meridian managed the writing team.

Acknowledgements

The authors are grateful to the following for permission to reproduce copyright material: Gordon Rugg and Marian Petre, *The Unwritten Rules of PhD Research* (offprints); Martin Terre Blanche and Kevin Durrheim, *Research in Practice* (photo and text for "Miss Lovely Legs"); David Goldblatt, photographer of "Miss Lovely Legs"; Judith Bell, *Doing Your Research Project: A Guide for First-Time Researchers in Education and Social Science* (offprint); The UK GRAD Programme, *Joint Statement of the Research Councils'/AHRB Skills Training Requirements for Research Students* (Appendix, Chapter 1); Brigitte Thomas, photographer of "Crazy paving path through flowerbed"; The Garden Picture Library/Alamy, for "Crazy paving path through flowerbed".

The authors also wish to thank the following who contributed in other ways to this second edition of the book: Alison Bailey-Calcutt, Sally Baker, Ben Lane, Geoff Mallory, Meridian, Marie Morris, Sue Oreszczyn, Carina Paine, John Smith, Professor John Swift, Peter Taylor, Jackie Topp, Professor Dave Wield and Piers Worth.

1 Introduction

Martin Le Voi and Stephen Potter

Welcome to the second edition of *Doing Postgraduate Research*. This book is intended to help both full- and part-time research students and those undertaking a dissertation for a taught Master's to do their research projects better, quicker and with as little hassle as possible. The materials in this book have been produced by a team involved in postgraduate research training for many years. Earlier versions of the chapters in this book have been used since 1998 by hundreds of part- and full-time research students at the Open University (OU). The first edition of this book made these research training materials available outside the OU. This second, much enlarged, edition has been produced to cover expanding training requirements and, in particular, the specification provided by the HEFC Joint Skills Statement (more on that below).

1.1 The Evolution of Postgraduate Research Degrees

From the very beginning of the universities in the twelfth century, there have been 'doctors' teaching in them, although the title 'master' preceded that of doctor. Our modern PhD and Master's degrees stem from these two titles. However, the first PhD of modern times was instituted in Berlin in Germany, starting in 1810. It was Yale University in the USA that adopted this new degree from the early 1860s, and it wasn't long before the best English universities observed how American scholars went to Germany to obtain their doctorate. It is perhaps remarkable to note that, in the UK, doctorates have existed for less than a century. Oxford University began its DPhil programme in 1917, largely copying the American model. British universities were already on their way to introducing the PhD when Ernest Rutherford (physicist and Nobel prizewinner) said:

> It should be made clear that the new degree which many Universities propose is an entire innovation. ... It will involve ... introducing into Britain a system practically identical with that which obtains in America, and to a large extent in Canada also. ... It will be a real and

very great departure in English education – the greatest revolution, in my opinion, of modern times.

(Quoted in Simpson, 1983, p. 155)

What, therefore, is a PhD? The largely mythical view is that it is some kind of a magnum opus which a student writes in order to astound the world with his or her mighty intellect. This probably was never really the case. A good way to familiarize yourself with the work that goes into a PhD is to go to a library and read a thesis or two. You'll soon find it isn't the magnum opus of the myth, but that it is a practical piece of work which has advanced the boundaries of your discipline. People who have done them are not superhuman, and they have not done them alone. There is support from all directions, not just from a student's supervisors, so it is fortunately rare for anyone to fail.

In the last 20 years, the purpose and function of the PhD have come under close scrutiny, especially in the UK. Nowadays it is seen not just as a thesis which contains some original material (see Section 2.2 for discussion of the requirements for each research degree), it is also a *programme* of study in which the student learns a wide variety of skills not only necessary for him or her to do the research, but also useful in any kind of employment they may take up after their research degree. This is a crucial theme that runs throughout this book. The concept that a PhD produces not only a thesis that represents a contribution to knowledge, but also develops transferable generic skills, applies also to the MPhil degree and taught Master's with a dissertation, although with modifications allowing for the more restricted research that is undertaken compared to a PhD. Taught Master's, particularly those in research methods, put a particular emphasis on training in such transferable generic research skills.

The concept that a PhD is a programme of study in which a student develops transferable generic skills has now been formally incorporated into the UK Higher Education system. In 2001, the Higher Education Funding Council for England and the research councils (including the Arts and Humanities Research Board) produced a joint statement which specified the generic skills they expect a research student to master during the course of their PhD programme. This statement (reproduced in the Appendix to this chapter) is now embedded in the UK Quality Assurance Agency (QAA) Code of Practice (QAA, 2004) and so is used by British universities to define part of the training provided to research students in their programme. The training requirements fall into seven sections:

- **research skills and techniques;**

- **research environment;**

- **research management;**

- **personal effectiveness;**

- **communication skills;**

- **networking and teamworking;**

- **career management.**

Doing Postgraduate Research is designed to address this current and developing concept that a research degree needs to generate both a piece of research work (a thesis or dissertation) and provide training in the skills required to produce that research work. The aim of *Doing Postgraduate Research* and its associated materials is therefore to provide resources which will enable you, as a research student, under the guidance of your supervisors, to acquire these skills as you proceed through your Master's or PhD programme. In planning *Doing Postgraduate Research*, an audit of the Joint Skills Statement was used, together with best practice training across the UK, to develop the Learning Objectives for each of this book's 12 chapters.

1.2 A Practical Generic Pack

Training by doing

A key rationale of *Doing Postgraduate Research* is 'training by doing'. The materials in this book provide research training in conjunction with you, the student, doing your own research work and in particular link into tasks that your supervisors will require you to do anyway (for example, developing a viable research plan and timetable, and doing a review of your topic area).

This is all part of a central ethos in this book of not teaching research skills separately and in abstract. A crucial part of this are the **Activities** that feature throughout the book, which are designed to help you apply what you learn to your own research project. Most of the Activities take the form of 'now the above has told you about X, work on applying this to your own research work'. You should not skip over the Activities to 'get on to the next bit of training', because they are a core part of your training. These Activities will ensure that you can actually apply and work through what is being taught, and as such will form part of your record of training, Research Portfolio and Personal Development Plan. The Activities are also the key link between the generic research processes that are the main subject of this book and your subject-specific training needs.

All this links into the key point discussed above that a research degree is now recognized as much more than producing a learned thesis. In order to have evidence of the skills you acquire and your progress in research, you need to keep records of what you are doing. You will probably begin by doing what is known as a 'skills analysis'. In this you look at the skills you need to acquire, and compare this to the skills you already have acquired, perhaps from your employment. Having done that, you can construct a map of what you need to do to acquire (or update) the missing skills during your research degree. At various points in this book, the Activities will help you to identify where you need to develop research skills. As well as keeping a record of your research, probably in a research journal (see Chapter 2), you should keep a record of the skills training you feel you need and the evidence you build as you learn the skills, to show you have acquired them. This record, grandiosely known as a Personal Development Plan, will help you keep track of your progress through your degree work. All the chapters in this book refer to the kind of evidence you can put in your Personal Development Plan, and give you tips as to how to keep it up to date. For more on Personal Development Planning, see the links from this book's website.

For supervisors, you should find the Activities helpful in tutorials and can draw upon them to structure and set tasks for your students. The book has very much been designed to support your role as a supervisor and to help you to fulfil the training requirements that are now required in a research degree programme. Its contents and the Activities have been written to work for part-time as well as full-time research students and can be undertaken individually or in group workshops. The materials in this book are very flexible and can work across a range of situations – from the isolated student studying at a distance through to a departmental workshop for full-timers. Indeed, in an OU context, earlier versions of these materials have been successfully used across this whole range of student and teaching circumstances.

A core resource pack

One implication of the growing training requirements for research degrees is that, today, one book cannot of itself be adequate for any individual's postgraduate training needs. You, the student, will need to draw upon a range of materials and resources. So what this book seeks to do is to provide a flexible core 'study pack' to guide and help you and your supervisor access materials that are best suited to your own research training needs. Thus this book acts as a core resource that complements other training guides and helps you sort out how to use a whole range of research training materials.

This 'study pack' approach is emphasized by the way in which the book is integrated with its own multimedia resources. As well as, at various points, referring you to other books and offprints to explore issues in more depth, contained with this book is a DVD. The DVD contains a set of audio and video training programmes. The book also has a website, which is **http://www.sagepub.co.uk/potter**. On this website you will find a host of materials that support the chapters, links to a number of important research training websites where updating material will be placed. So, in using *Doing Postgraduate Research*, you get far more than a book. You are getting a multimedia research training pack.

Following on from the 'research pack' design for this book, as well as providing multi-media resources and links to other generic research training resources, *Doing Postgraduate Research* also provides a core framework around which subject-specific training can be added. As noted above, the Activities in each chapter are the main link into your identifying subject-specific training materials. If you are doing a research degree, your supervisors are the key link for training in subjects specific to your topic, such as subject-specific literature indices, research methods, data and information sources and analysis methods. If you are studying a Master's course, then you will also be undertaking topic-specific modules and will need to demonstrate your mastery of them in your dissertation.

However, sometimes much less formal avenues turn out to be really helpful. Chatting to someone on an online conference or meeting someone in the library can result in new ideas which may help you enormously. Always keep your eyes and ears open for any new ideas that may come your way. At several places in this book suggestions are made that will help you to identify and develop the less formal side of your research training.

1.3 How Research REALLY Happens

Before moving on to examine the practicalities of how this pack is organized, it is worthwhile thinking a little about the nature of an academic research project, be it a Master's dissertation or a PhD. Quite often textbooks on research suggest that a research project is made up of a series of straightforward tasks, each of which is tackled in sequence. First, there is a review of a subject area from which a research question is selected; then an appropriate research method is chosen, data are gathered and analysed, and the results are written up. In structuring a research report, a thesis or a research article, authors tend to present their research in this sort of logical manner. Although this may be useful for presenting results, in truth research is never as straightforward as this. Boxes 1.1 and 1.2 are two brief accounts by Ben Lane, who undertook his PhD as a part-time research student. Box 1.1 is how it was written up; Box 1.2 is how it happened ... .

Box 1.1   My PhD

Background

Even as a physics undergraduate in the 1980s, I was concerned about environmental and energy use issues. These included the topic of climate change, which was just appearing on the political agenda. Although I was aware that sources of renewable energy were being developed, I was unconvinced that much thought had gone into planning the transition of shifting from a fossil fuel to a renewable paradigm.

Research area

As the transport sector is one of the largest consumers of energy in the UK, I decided to focus on road vehicles for my PhD. In particular, I had come across previous work looking at the use of hydrogen and fuel cells for mobile applications. Knowing that, in principle, the use of these technologies could reduce the environmental impacts of road transport, I wanted to investigate the optimum scenarios that could lead to a sustainable transport system.

Focusing

Although the goal is well defined, the path of the transition to a fuel cell future is highly uncertain. This is due to the method of fuel delivery, many aspects of which remain undecided, and also to the social and economic implications posed by a change to a new energy infrastructure. Therefore, as part of the process of investigating the introduction of fuel cell vehicles within the existing oil-based/ internal combustion engine regime, I needed to consider non-technological issues in parallel with technological developments. It was the socio-technical transition, rather than the fuel cell technology *per se*, that formed the focus of my thesis.

Methodology

To inform the required socio-technical analysis, I employed the approach of *Strategic Niche Management* (SNM). This includes analysis of environmental impacts, user attitudes, market acceptance, social learning, regulatory framework and government policy. Applied as a management tool, it can be used to encourage innovations by designing protection measures that enable new technologies to develop their potential before being exposed to prevailing market forces.

Box 1.1   (Continued)

Extension of the methodology

Essentially SNM is a qualitative management tool. As part of my analysis and comparison of different transition scenarios, I needed to extend the methodology to include quantitative measures. This was achieved by the use of the Lifetime Evaluation of Alternative Fuels (LEAF) model, which was designed to assess cleaner fuels and technologies on economic and environmental grounds. Using the new *Quantitative SNM* approach, I was able to fully compare the most significant implementation strategies for fuel cell vehicles in the UK.

Overall results

The thesis identified the need for a number of non-economic protection measures with which to support the emerging UK niche in order to accelerate technology diffusion and made a case for the development of new transport innovations that could synergistically promote fuel cell vehicle technology. Through the application of the LEAF model, the research quantified a number of economic protection measures that would assist the introduction of fuel cell vehicles and, most importantly, identified a protection measure exit-strategy to enable market forces to play their role in technology selection.

If you were to read Ben's thesis, you would get the impression of a purely linear development of ideas, aims, methods, analysis and application, leading neatly from the objective to the conclusion. This linearity of development is, of course, entirely fictional, and, in fact, his research degree developed entirely differently … .

Box 1.2   The Reality …

Before I started my PhD in 1992 as a part-time external student, I was well aware of the environmental and technological debates concerning energy use and climate change. I also had some experience working as a junior researcher at a wind energy company. It was then clear to me that the introduction of renewables was a difficult process dependent on a large number of technical, political, regulatory and economic factors. At that time, I also came across the Pure Energy Trust, a small

(Continued)

Box 1.2 (Continued)

organization dedicated to promoting the use of hydrogen and fuel cells for sustainable transport applications. I quickly became very interested in these technologies, and decided that this was the area in which I wanted to conduct research.

By the time I enrolled as a postgraduate at the Open University I was working as a science teacher in secondary and further education. In what spare time I had (i.e. very little!) I found out as much as I could about the use of hydrogen and fuel cells, their production, use, applications and environmental impacts. Strange as it may seem to those in the field now, even in 1992 little research had been done in this area and I was able to get up to speed very quickly. Although I was fortunate that the field was wide open, this obviously meant that I had little data to go on and had to base my ideas on dated research from around the world, not all of which was applicable to the UK.

Early on I had two lucky breaks. My supervisor found some funding for me to attend a conference in the United States (where I happened to be going on holiday). While there, I also plucked up the courage to go and visit a research group at a university in California where they were building fuel cell demonstration vehicles. This was invaluable as it allowed me to see at first hand technologies I had only read about or seen on video. However, although I was now over a year into my PhD, I still had no idea how to get a handle on transition issues regarding a technology that was then only in its infancy.

It was about this time that I found some paid contract work (again through my supervisor) on an EU project entitled *Strategic Niche Management as a Tool for a Transition to a Sustainable Transport System*. This involved visiting UK projects that were demonstrating cleaner vehicles, such as the Coventry Electric Vehicle Project. Although there were no fuel cell vehicles in any of the UK projects, I was able to learn a great deal about other alternative vehicle fuels and technologies, and also about the analytical approach employed by Strategic Niche Management, one that was completely new to me at the time.

In was only by 1996 (four years into my part-time PhD), therefore, that I had the analytical tools and enough data with which to really start to address the aims of my thesis. I now also realized that to understand the potential of hydrogen and fuel cells, I had to analyse all the alternative fuels as these provided learning pathways through which a hydrogen-based future could be reached. The SNM methodology also provided the theoretical framework within which I could analyse non-technical issues and design protection measures that would assist the emerging fuel cell vehicle niche markets. This research itself took around two years (part-time), the work being done in parallel with my continuing teaching responsibilities.

Box 1.2   (Continued)

There came a point in 1999, however, where I almost ran out of steam. Not only had I exhausted the existing data sources (and myself in trying to balance paid work and research), I had taken the SNM approach as far as I could. Also, as it stood, the thesis had no clearly definable 'original' work that would make it eligible for submission. Then came my third lucky break. Through contacts I now had made within the vehicle industry, I was invited (in association with the Energy Saving Trust) to compile a report for the Cleaner Vehicle Task Force. Not only was this a great honour (and a lot of work!), it enabled me to leave my part-time teaching post and immerse myself in the issues at the cutting edge.

As part of the work, I was also involved in the development of the Lifetime Evaluation of Alternative Fuels (LEAF) model that compared the cleaner vehicle options. At last I now had a quantitative tool that I could use for my PhD, one that would extend the existing methodology. This did two things. First, it provided a more complete analysis of the transition scenarios so that I was able to quantitatively compare different transition pathways. Second, it meant that the thesis now contained an original element, one that would enable me to submit the thesis for a PhD.

All that was now left to do was write up the thesis. With my maximum deadline approaching fast, there was nothing to do but give up all my paid work and dedicate myself full time. Although I knew that I had enough data and a comprehensive methodology behind me, it was still a very daunting experience to put this all down on paper (despite having several sections of the thesis already complete). It also required a very understanding partner, a drop in salary and the forgoing of a social life for several months. However, I am pleased to report that the time spent was successful in securing the PhD and has led to many new career opportunities. This includes the establishment of a small transport and environment consultancy for which I now work.

One point of this example is to show how doing research is not a linear process. You will always be doing several things at the same time, which will all impinge upon each other. For example, although you will do a 'state of the art' literature review to focus on your research topic, you will also draw on what other researchers have done to plan your project, the method used, how data are gathered and analysed, how reports are written, and to relate your own findings and conclusions to the existing body of research. It is a continuous interaction – not a self-contained stage from which you move on. Most other research 'stages' similarly have feedback loops. Academic research may be better thought of as a flow diagram, around which you will go several times between key boxes, until you exit at the bottom (at least for the purpose of your degree).

Note also how Ben developed his skills through the first four years of his studentship (remember he was a part-time PhD student). Over this time he followed up a number of seemingly serendipitous contacts, which all pulled together so that, when he did embark upon his own research project, he was able to complete it pretty quickly. In actual fact those contacts were not as serendipitous as they may have seemed. They actually reflected a mixture of his supervisor's experience and of Ben building up his own network of contacts in his research field.

Note Ben's 1999 danger point when he 'almost ran out of steam' and felt disillusioned. Most research degrees have a low point like this (usually about a third to half way through a research degree). But Ben had learned so much about organizing and doing research that he could rapidly adapt his plans and exploit opportunities. Planning your research, reviewing your plans, and coping with change and problems are all part of the research process. Your research will *not* go smoothly. There will be problems and difficulties, and this has been recognized by the authors of this book. There is a lot here about organizing and planning your research project, not because this is a simple mechanistic process, but because you do need to be organized and learn how to be flexible and adapt, so that you can take the knocks and still win through, just as Ben did.

Like many a part-time student, Ben also had difficult decisions about blending his PhD research with his work and home life. In the end this was resolved as his research led him into a new career which was much more fulfilling than the one he'd had before he started his part-time PhD.

1.4 Organization of This Book

We have organized this book to reflect the fact that, as already noted, research requires you to do several things at once, and involves an 'iterative' process of feedback loops. Each activity affects and is affected by another. Consequently, the chapters are not intended to form a simple linear sequence; rather, you should go to each chapter for insight and advice as the need arises. Nevertheless, we had to establish a starting-off point (Chapter 2, rather obviously entitled 'Getting Going'). Some chapters are of most relevance early on in your research project (for example, 'Planning and organizing your research'), while others mainly fit in later (particularly 'The examination process and the viva'). But even these contain material and issues of relevance throughout your research. For example, Chapter 2, 'Getting going', describes the competencies you have to demonstrate in your research degree; Chapter 11, 'The examination process and the viva', notes things that you should plan early (such as building up experience of answering questions on your research); and Chapter 12, 'Developing your career', identifies things (such as skills development and keeping a portfolio of training) that need to be built into your research plan. Consequently these two chapters should not be left unread until after you have handed in your thesis.

The 12 chapters are summarized below, together with an estimate of the amount of time it may take to study them. The timings refer to roughly how long it will take to go through the chapter's materials and associated activities. Of course, in practice you are unlikely to simply work your way through an individual chapter but will use it together with links and contacts on the book's website, further training and also subject-specific training associated with these chapters.

Chapter 1: Introduction
Here you are! This chapter is broadly intended to give you an understanding of how to use the pack and how it is organized.

Chapter 2: Getting going
This chapter acts as a starting-off point for your work and has two major aims:

1 **To work through what you want to achieve in your research degree or Master's dissertation.**

2 **To help you develop the first steps involved in starting a research project.**

More specifically this will involve:

- **finding out the standards expected;**

- **exploring what are realistic expectations of your degree;**

- **relating your research to your motivations for taking a higher degree;**

- **working through the initial steps of doing your research;**

- **exploring the support provided by your supervisors and your university.**

It would take about 10 hours to complete this chapter, including exercises.

Chapter 3: Scoping your research
This chapter takes you through how to focus your research ideas into a manageable project. After you have completed it, you should be able to do the following:

1 **Demonstrate your ability to plan and focus your research.**

2 **Set boundaries for your project and draw upon/use sources of support as appropriate.**

3 **Demonstrate original, independent and critical thinking in the design of your project.**

4 **Demonstrate flexibility and open-mindedness in planning and focusing your project.**

It would take about 7 hours to complete this chapter, including exercises.

Chapter 4: Logics of enquiry

This chapter allows you to place your research in some broad philosophical traditions. After reading this chapter and working on its associated activities you should be able to:

1 **Define objectivist and interpretivist approaches to research, list the ways in which they are similar to or different from each other, locate your research in one or other approach, and say why.**

2 **Explain what is meant by a 'logic of enquiry', describe three forms of enquiry adopted in social research – induction, deduction and abduction – explicate the differences between them (and say how explicating is different from explaining!).**

3 **Identify an example of each of the three logics of enquiry in your own field of research, and locate them in different historical periods, schools or paradigms.**

4 **Explore your plans for the approaches and methods you will use in your research, and provide a reflexive justification for the one(s) you expect to pursue.**

This is a chapter that is particularly worth returning to as your research develops, especially when you wish to analyse the research approaches used by others and in deciding your own research and plan. It will take about 10 hours to work through this chapter.

Chapter 5: Planning and organizing your research

This chapter contains a wealth of material on research project design and planning. Again this is a chapter that you will need to return to several times as you design, implement and revise your research plans. Key tasks covered in this chapter are to:

1 **Identify key tasks and scheduling your time.**

2 **Draw up a work plan for the project development phase of your research and an outline plan to completion.**

3 **Identify funding needs and sources.**

4 **Identify training needs to fulfil your work plan.**

5 **Develop and maintain co-operative networks and working relationships with supervisors, colleagues and peers, within the institution and the wider research community.**

This is a substantial and important part of the book and you should allow 15 hours to complete it.

Chapter 6: Academic writing

Writing is obviously a vital part of doing any postgraduate degree and it is important that you should get into the habit of writing as soon as you start. There is more to writing than just using the correct academic style; writing a research thesis is a major undertaking, which can easily result in grief. This chapter advises you how to approach writing consistently and professionally. You cannot develop good writing habits too early!

This chapter covers:

1 **Understanding the role of writing as part of the research process.**

2 **Learning how to adapt writing style according to purpose and audience.**

3 **Learning how to revise drafts of a thesis and sharpen their focus and coherence.**

4 **How to elicit and respond effectively to feedback on writing.**

5 **How to structure a thesis coherently.**

6 **Understanding the way in which conference abstracts and journal articles are typically structured, and being able to write in the same format.**

7 **Developing an awareness of the typical features of writing in your own discipline by reading from a range of academic texts.**

Again this is a chapter you will need to return to as your writing tasks develop throughout your studies. You will probably spend about 15 hours on this chapter and its activities.

Chapter 7: Undertaking a literature review

A 'topic' or 'literature' review is a crucial part of any research project. The main focus of this chapter is on planning your information search and the research purposes of doing such a review in your subject area. In particular, this chapter aims to assist you to:

1 **Establish the purposes for which you are doing a literature review.**

2 **Plan and organize your literature review.**

3 **Identify and document sources of information and relevant research methodologies and techniques within your research field.**

4 **Learn the basics of information searching and identify training needs.**

5 **Write up your literature review in a creative, innovative and original manner.**

Depending on your experience of literature or information searching, you should allow around 10 hours for this section, although doing the searches for your review is in addition to this.

Chapter 8: Doing the right thing

Academic research is a major undertaking and needs to be taken very seriously. This is even more important when the product of the research is going to be a public document, such as a report or a thesis which will be available to the public in a library. This chapter takes you through the moral, ethical and legal standards in research, as our society currently sets them. It then moves on to consider intellectual property rights. First, this looks at when, as well as acknowledging sources, you are legally required to seek permission to use them; second, in conducting research you will have generated your own intellectual property, which you will need to know how to protect.

Specifically, this chapter will cover:

1 **Attributing ideas correctly without plagiarism.**

2 **Understanding the need for commercial and personal confidentiality.**

3 **Understanding the importance of security with computer use.**

4 **Understanding the repercussions of the Data Protection Act on your research.**

5 **Understanding basic intellectual property rights constraints.**

Study time for this chapter and its activities is about 8 hours.

Chapter 9: Ethical frameworks for research with human participants

Some research can be intrusive or potentially harmful to other living beings or the environment. If your work involves this, you need to be aware of the ethical issues.

After having studied this chapter you should be able to:

1 **Give an account of why ethical conduct has become an increasingly important element of the design and conduct of research with people.**

2   Describe the main areas of ethical concern associated with research with humans.

3   Discuss the issue of balancing research benefits with risks and harm.

4   Critically evaluate an ethical protocol.

5   Draft an application for ethical approval for a research project that you propose to conduct.

Study time for this chapter and its activities is about 8 hours.

Chapter 10: Research presentations
This chapter considers what research presentations should achieve, the common fears that presenters experience and the steps that can be taken to alleviate such fears. Specifically, the chapter will address the concerns people have about the audience, their material and their performance.

After reading this chapter you will be able to:

1   Identify the purposes of different types of presentation and the audiences involved.

2   Identify what makes a good and bad presentation.

3   Work through the common fears that presenters experience.

4   Use appropriate visual materials, including the use of presentation software tools.

5   Structure and deliver an articulate and coherently argued presentation that summarizes and reflects on your progress and results.

6   Defend your research outcomes constructively in answering questions and receive feedback effectively.

There is a DVD programme associated with this chapter.

Study time will vary depending on your previous experience in giving presentations. This chapter and its activities will take about 10 hours, plus preparing a short presentation for your supervisor.

Chapter 11: The examination process and the viva
You may think that you do not need to consider your viva until after you have submitted your thesis, but think again. If you make sure the design of your thesis

is clear and easy for your examiners to understand, then you will have a much better viva than might be the case. The viva is a research planning issue. This chapter looks at:

1 **Demonstrating that you have fulfilled the core competencies required for your research degree.**

2 **Effectively preparing for your viva.**

3 **Understanding how your examiners are appointed and what they are required to do.**

4 **Understanding what is involved in evaluating Master's and PhD research.**

5 **Defending your research outcome constructively and being able to listen, receive feedback and respond perceptively.**

There is a DVD track associated with this chapter, which is a discussion between recently examined research students and their external examiners.

Study time is about 6 hours, plus any additional preparation work arranged with your supervisors (e.g. a mock viva).

Chapter 12: Developing your career
Career planning is something that needs to be considered throughout your research degree studies, and this chapter particularly links into issue such as maintaining a skills portfolio and identifying and developing transferable skills that are now sought by employers. The second part of the chapter concentrates on the practicalities of job applications, the production of a good CV and preparing for interviews.

The chapter helps you to:

1 **Explore opportunities to develop your career.**

2 **Identify the skills that you can offer a prospective employer.**

3 **Write job applications and CVs that promote your knowledge, experience and suitability.**

4 **Prepare for interviews effectively.**

This chapter will take 6–8 hours to study, although you will obviously spend more time in actually applying for jobs.

1.5 And Finally ...

Your schooldays are said to be the best years of your life. But nothing can quite match doing your own research. If you are lucky enough to be studying for a research degree, it is a time when you can do research relatively free of the hassle of writing interim reports for research councils, when you can pursue a research programme with a single-mindedness and dedication to purpose few can achieve after finishing. So enjoy it, *relish* it, and you can be sure of a unique and sometimes exhilarating experience.

References

Quality Assurance Agency for Higher Education (2004) *Code of Practice for the Assurance of Academic Quality and Standards in Higher Education*, Mansfield: QAA, September.

Simpson, R. (1983) *How the PhD Came to Britain*; Guildford: Society for Research into Higher Education.

Appendix: HEFC Joint Skills Statement

Introduction

The Research Councils and the Arts and Humanities Research Board play an important role in setting standards and identifying best practice in research training. This document sets out a joint statement of the skills that doctoral research students funded by the Research Councils/AHRB would be expected to develop during their research training.

These skills may be present on commencement, explicitly taught, or developed during the course of the research. It is expected that different mechanisms will be used to support learning as appropriate, including self-direction, supervisor support and mentoring, departmental support, workshops, conferences, elective training courses, formally assessed courses and informal opportunities.

The Research Councils and the AHRB would also want to re-emphasise their belief that training in research skills and techniques is the key element in the development of a research student, and that PhD students are expected to make a substantial, original contribution to knowledge in their area, normally leading to published work. The development of wider employment-related skills should not detract from that core objective.

The purpose of this statement is to give a common view of the skills and experience of a typical research student thereby providing universities with a clear and consistent message aimed at helping them to ensure that all research training was of the highest standard, across all disciplines. It is not the intention of this document to provide assessment criteria for research training.

It is expected that each Council/Board will have additional requirements specific to their field of interest and will continue to have their own measures for the evaluation of research training within institutions.

(A) Research Skills and Techniques – to be able to demonstrate:

1 the ability to recognise and validate problems
2 original, independent and critical thinking, and the ability to develop theoretical concepts
3 a knowledge of recent advances within one's field and in related areas
4 an understanding of relevant research methodologies and techniques and their appropriate application within one's research field
5 the ability to critically analyse and evaluate one's findings and those of others
6 an ability to summarise, document, report and reflect on progress

(B) Research Environment – to be able to:

1 show a broad understanding of the context, at the national and international level, in which research takes place
2 demonstrate awareness of issues relating to the rights of other researchers, of research subjects, and of others who may be affected by the research, e.g. confidentiality, ethical issues, attribution, copyright, malpractice, ownership of data and the requirements of the Data Protection Act
3 demonstrate appreciation of standards of good research practice in their institution and/or discipline
4 understand relevant health and safety issues and demonstrate responsible working practices
5 understand the processes for funding and evaluation of research
6 justify the principles and experimental techniques used in one's own research
7 understand the process of academic or commercial exploitation of research results

(C) Research Management – to be able to:

1 apply effective project management through the setting of research goals, intermediate milestones and prioritisation of activities
2 design and execute systems for the acquisition and collation of information through the effective use of appropriate resources and equipment
3 identify and access appropriate bibliographical resources, archives, and other sources of relevant information
4 use information technology appropriately for database management, recording and presenting information

(D) Personal Effectiveness – to be able to:

1 demonstrate a willingness and ability to learn and acquire knowledge
2 be creative, innovative and original in one's approach to research
3 demonstrate flexibility and open-mindedness
4 demonstrate self-awareness and the ability to identify own training needs
5 demonstrate self-discipline, motivation, and thoroughness
6 recognise boundaries and draw upon/use sources of support as appropriate
7 show initiative, work independently and be self-reliant

(E) Communication Skills – to be able to:

1 write clearly and in a style appropriate to purpose, e.g. progress reports, published documents, thesis
2 construct coherent arguments and articulate ideas clearly to a range of audiences, formally and informally through a variety of techniques
3 constructively defend research outcomes at seminars and viva examination
4 contribute to promoting the public understanding of one's research field
5 effectively support the learning of others when involved in teaching, mentoring or demonstrating activities

(F) Networking and Teamworking – to be able to:

1 develop and maintain co-operative networks and working relationships with supervisors, colleagues and peers, within the institution and the wider research community
2 understand one's behaviours and impact on others when working in and contributing to the success of formal and informal teams
3 listen, give and receive feedback and respond perceptively to others

(G) Career Management – to be able to:

1 appreciate the need for and show commitment to continued professional development
2 take ownership for and manage one's career progression, set realistic and achievable career goals, and identify and develop ways to improve employability
3 demonstrate an insight into the transferable nature of research skills to other work environments and the range of career opportunities within and outside academia
4 present one's skills, personal attributes and experiences through effective CVs, applications and interviews.

2 Getting Going

Stephen Potter

INTRODUCTION AND LEARNING OUTCOMES

This chapter considers the initial steps in starting a postgraduate research project. Other chapters of this book will develop these initial steps in more detail; however, it is worthwhile getting a strategic overview first. After reading this chapter and working on its associated activities, you should be able to:

- Relate your research to your motivations for taking a research degree, and identify how this links to any career goals you have and improving your employability.
- Explore what are realistic expectations of your research degree.
- Find out the standards expected and what constitutes good research.
- Work through the initial steps of undertaking your research degree.
- Begin to develop co-operative networks and working relationships with supervisors, colleagues and peers, within the institution and the wider research community.
- Effectively support the learning of others.
- Start identifying your own training needs.

This chapter will also contribute towards you:

- Demonstrating a willingness and ability to learn and acquire knowledge.
- Understanding the need to show initiative, work independently and be self-reliant.
- Developing your ability to recognize and validate problems.

A number of activities are suggested. One idea that is strongly recommended in this book is to keep a 'research journal' in which you note ideas and thoughts on the development of your project (this is detailed in Chapter 3). It would be useful to keep the notes on these activities in your research journal.

This chapter obviously deals with the initial stages of a research project, but you will probably need to refer to this chapter frequently as your research progresses. For example, the part on demonstrating what is expected of a research degree is of relevance to writing your thesis and preparing for your viva.

2.1 Why Am I Doing This?

Activity 2.1

First, simply write down why you want to do a research degree or Master's. Try to be as specific as possible.

Second, note down what you expect to have come out of your work when you have finished in terms of:

1 results
2 you personally
3 what you will be able to do that you could not do before.

There can be a whole range of reasons why a person wishes to undertake a research degree. When supervising and training both Master's and PhD students, I have come across strong career, aspirational, ethical and other personal reasons for people wishing to do a research degree. Career advancement is a very obvious motivation and this links closely into the function of higher education to advance people's skills, thinking and capabilities.

In other cases the primary motivation has been that the student, in some way or another, wishes to contribute to knowledge, or advance understanding. I have known students who have had strong environmental concerns and wanted to undertake research to explore and highlight challenging issues and policy options. Another student was trying to sort out why parents are so frustratingly indifferent to school governing structures seeking their involvement.

It is very unlikely that you simply wrote down 'advancement of knowledge' as a reason for undertaking your studies, but something that represented a mixture of your motivations and interests. For example, the following quotation is from an Open University research degree student, Piers Worth, who undertook a PhD in the Institute for Educational Technology, looking at the relationship between creativity and age. This is a subject that spans cognitive psychology and adult development. Piers started as a part-time student and then moved on to full-time study.

> I had a very demanding full-time job, and was struggling as a part-time OU student. Generally I do what I do well – and yet I knew that was becoming increasingly likely to be untrue if I kept on the way I was as a part-time student. Jane Henry [his internal supervisor] helped incredibly by setting me a VERY specific schedule, and I was responding, yet I think that danger of failure was still there.

So I was facing the question what to do. I knew I loved what I was studying. Passionate about it is not too strong a word. I knew I didn't want to get 'old' and find I had not done this – I knew I could not NOT do the study. So that prompted me into asking and asking about applying for a full-time place. And when I took the decision to try, so many things just seemed to fall into place to help me do it.

Undoubtedly I was doing a PhD with future work/career in mind. Yet as I have moved through, I am staggered by what I am learning about ME, and finding me changing as a result. I think this may be made 'easier' or more likely in that I am working with people on biographies and their own work processes, so I am prompted into looking at myself as this unfolds.

Note how Piers has found his motivations deepen and develop through his PhD.

In commenting on an earlier version of this chapter, a member of our academic staff reflected on what motivated her to undertake a PhD:

In my own case, career progression was probably a key driver. I was working in an administrative job (in the NHS) but wanted to become more involved in policy making or consultancy. Experience in job applications suggested that 'an administrator' was not regarded as having the right skills for such work! Doing a PhD enabled me to become more expert both in terms of subject matter and transferable research skills. It also enabled me to use concepts and theories I had become interested in through OU undergraduate studies which were more difficult to apply in my everyday work. (As it turned out I ended up staying at the OU but that's another story!)

In her book, *The Research Student's Guide to Success*, Pat Cryer makes a distinction between what she calls 'essential' reasons for undertaking a research degree and 'supporting' reasons. She defines 'essential' reasons as follows:

Motivations which are essential for success are almost certainly intellectual ones: developing a trained mind; satisfying intellectual curiosity; finding a challenge when one feels 'in a rut'; experiencing an academic community; contributing to knowledge; fulfilling a lifelong ambition etc.

(Cryer, 2000, pp. 12–14)

Cryer considers other motivations to be 'supporting' reasons. These are perfectly valid reasons, but ones that on their own will not keep a student going through a research degree. She does note that many students may start out with only 'supporting' reasons, but then 'essential' ones develop as the research progresses and students get caught up in their research subject. Interestingly she views career advancement as only a 'supporting' reason, as may be reasons such as dissatisfaction with a current job (or lack of job) or a personal situation. I think that career advancement could be an essential reason if you have a burning ambition for a certain career path, but not if it is simply to enhance kudos or get a bit more money. In a similar discussion on motivations, Phillips and Pugh (2000, pp. 23–4) mention one student whose girlfriend lived in Finland. He tried to get a job there, but could not get a work permit and, as he was unable to get a job in the UK, went for a PhD studentship instead. They say this may not have been the best of reasons to start a PhD, but (like Cryer) note that motivations can develop and change as a student progresses through their studies.

Activity 2.2

Make a list of what you consider to be 'essential' and 'supporting' reasons for someone undertaking a research degree or dissertation topic. Draw upon the text above to make up your list together with any experiences and thoughts of your own.

Essential reasons might include:

1 **Personal development.**

2 **To be able to make a difference – for example, a desire to change practice in work or to learn more about a 'condition' that a student or members of their family have experienced.**

3 **To follow a new or better career.**

4 **Burning interest in a topic (intellectual curiosity).**

5 **To keep one's mind active.**

For example, one external student I supervised, when he retired, undertook a part-time PhD to apply some work he had done in his job (the development of fuel cells) to a topic that deeply interested him – pollution from road traffic. Another student doing an MA at Brunel University recognized that he was not cut out for teaching schoolchildren and sought a career change to become a design manager in industry – something that had come to interest him greatly. Following a work placement associated with his MA, he secured a very satisfying job with that company.

Another research student developed a strong interest in Roman social history during her first degree. She was unable to follow this up at the time but, finding herself at home with small children, she felt she had to do something to keep her mind active and registered for a research degree. Another student undertook a very specific PhD study into the properties of new composite materials specifically with the aim of pursuing an industrial career in a closely related job.

Supporting reasons might include:

1 **Current job is a dead end.**

2 **For the experience.**

3 **Employer sponsorship is available.**

Personal circumstances can play an important part and constrain your choices. A mature student with a family may purposefully constrain their choice of where to study. I know full well that personal circumstances affected my decision to accept a studentship at the OU, in that my girlfriend and I had just got engaged. Sorting out if, after we were married, living in Milton Keynes would be compatible with my wife commuting to London was a pretty important thing to take into account. Nonetheless, just because the studentship fitted well with our developing relationship, it was not in itself an essential reason to undertake the PhD topic that I chose. I suspect situations like ours arise pretty often.

The boundary between 'wrong' and 'right' reasons can be blurred. For example, as noted above, the career/job aspect can fall between categories. Perhaps the difference is whether someone is simply trying to escape from one job or situation, or is positively running towards another. My wife, for example, was stuck with a dead-end job until an MA at the Royal College of Art provided her with the opportunity to shift to a new career that really excited her. She was not looking for something to help her run away, but something to run to. The example above of the MA student who wanted to leave teaching also falls into this category, as he had a clear idea of where he wanted to go.

Activity 2.3

Return to what you wrote down in Activity 2.1. How do your own reasons relate to your categories of essential and supporting reasons for doing a research degree?

Discussion

In her book, Cryer says that research students need to have, at least in part, motives that are intellectual. I would add that it is perfectly acceptable to have a core motivation that is not intellectual, but can be fulfilled in an intellectual way. For example, an environmental campaigner may find a research degree a good way to work through a strongly held ethical belief. Others do this by organizing campaigns or political action, but researching a key issue and publicizing the results is a perfectly valid way of working through such a motivation.

This raises the question of whether a research degree is the right way to work through your motivations. A research degree is not, for example, a suitable way to simply campaign for a particular environmental or ethical stance, although academic research can perfectly well take place within such a context. In some cases I have advised students against registering for a research degree because it would not satisfy their core motivations. In one case, a part-time student realized this after being registered for a year for a PhD, and instead did a full-time vocational taught Master's, which suited his needs much better.

Overall, do not be apologetic about what motivates you to undertake your research. Even if you need to be a little more realistic about what you can achieve (more on that below), your motivations are still what started you out on this work – and what will keep you going. You are bound to have days (possibly weeks) when things are really tough. When this happens, perhaps turning back to your notes on the first activity of this chapter might help.

Chapter 12 of this book, which looks at career development, will return to this issue of motivations and develop further some of the points raised in this chapter.

2.2   Research Degree Requirements

What is achievable in a research degree

Having thought about motivations for undertaking a research degree it is worthwhile noting that, even if you are doing your research for the 'best' intellectual reasons, you need to have a clear idea of what can or cannot be achieved in a research degree. Much of the rest of this chapter is intended to help you to explore this question.

First, when thinking about PhD research (as opposed to an MPhil or taught Master's dissertation), it is important to note that this book covers the concept of a PhD degree that exists in the UK, North America, Australasia and most of Asia. This is that a PhD is a training qualification showing that you are capable of formulating, designing, undertaking and reporting upon your own academic research project. A PhD demonstrates that the recipient is a fully professional researcher in his or her field.

Although this concept of a PhD is shared by the education systems of many other countries, it is important to emphasize that what constitutes a PhD does vary. In some places (for example Germany and certain other northern European countries), the education system is different and PhDs are seen not as a training qualification but as proof by experts of their leading position in a field of study. As a result, these sorts of PhD take much longer to complete than in the UK (in Germany there are, for example 'double doctorates'). In the USA PhDs can also take longer than in the UK, but there is less standardization. In general, US PhDs are also seen as a training qualification, but they can involve a long route through taught postgraduate classes, together with a written thesis. However, in some US universities it can be acceptable for the thesis to be an applied research project with no theoretical or conceptual contribution. Such a research project would be considered unacceptable for a PhD in the UK.

Quite apart from these differing concepts of a PhD, students do have a tendency to be overambitious. This applies to Master's as well as PhD students and is a crucial problem in the early stages of virtually all research degrees. Even a PhD cannot accommodate a life's work. If you think that your research project is going to result in you producing the ultimate in your topic area, or shift the whole way in which your subject is studied (a so-called 'paradigm shift'), then you will have real problems. Even the continental concept of a PhD does not go that far!

Many students start off by viewing their research degree in this way ('my life's work'). This is an unreal expectation. In *How to Get a PhD*, Phillips and Pugh point out that Einstein's theory of relativity was

> ... not [his] PhD thesis (that was a sensible contribution to Brownian motion theory). *Das Kapital* was not Marx's PhD (that was on the theories of two little-known Greek philosophers). Of course, while doing their PhDs Einstein and Marx were undoubtedly preparing themselves for the great questionings that led to the big shifts, but they were also demonstrating their fully professional mastery of the established paradigms.
>
> (Phillips and Pugh, 2000, p. 36)

Although your research degree will show that you know what you are doing in your topic area, it is not a requirement that you prove yourself to be the best in the world. Your research degree can be part of your own lifelong learning, but it will be something after which you will continue to learn and grow. On the other hand, your research degree should be able to produce something that is useful and fulfilling in terms of your core motivations. You can add a few pieces to a jigsaw that were not there before.

Doing too little is also a problem, but this is usually a misunderstanding about the academic nature of a research degree. This issue is explored further in Chapters 3 and 5, but it is worth mentioning here, if only to juxtapose it to the 'life's work' misconception of a research degree.

There is also an issue of not understanding the sort of research that is required. This can be a real danger for part-time students who work, for example, in journalism, marketing or some types of applied industrial research. Their experience in these areas, although very valuable, can lead to a research approach that is inadequately rigorous for an academic qualification. This can also be true for people from a campaigning/pressure group background. While representing valuable experience, the methods of gathering and using evidence in such a 'political' context may not be appropriate for a research degree.

One academic had a salutary experience as an external examiner for a PhD in another university where the student, from overseas, seemed to have been sent to the UK to do a PhD that would solve a problem that his government had about installing new computer systems. Unfortunately, the resulting thesis was theory-free and descriptive (and hence not a PhD – or at least not yet). He would have been better off with a taught MSc in computer science with a relevant dissertation.

So, central to the UK-style research degrees is that they are about training in your area, and that through them you should demonstrate that you are a competent researcher – be it to the level required for a Master's dissertation, MPhil or PhD. If you think of your research degree as essentially a training qualification, then you are likely to hit the right standard for your own research degree.

> If you have any concerns emerging from what you have done and read in this chapter, make sure you discuss them with your supervisor.

What is expected of a research degree

This section looks at what is expected of a research degree and a dissertation that is part of a taught Master's degree. Although all of these involve undertaking a research project, there are differences in what you have to demonstrate in your research, and the competencies required. It is therefore useful to have an overview of what competencies you need to show for each type of degree. This should help you to pitch your research at the right level for the degree you are taking.

This part uses as its basis the Open University's regulations and criteria for its MPhil and PhD research degrees, although reference will be made to the guidance and regulations from other UK universities. The research degree regulations of all UK universities are required to meet nationally agreed standards, so it is appropriate to structure this part of Chapter 2 around the OU regulations. However, details of the regulations do vary between UK universities, so you should check up on the wording used in your own regulations and discuss with your supervisor(s) any important differences from those detailed below.[1]

Under the QAA Qualifications Framework, UK universities offer two levels of research degrees, MPhil and PhD. Some universities also offer a DPhil which, without wishing to get into too many arguments, for practical purposes can be taken as a variation on a PhD. What do these two levels of research degrees involve? To explore this question, it is useful to look at the OU award regulations to see what is required of these two degrees. In the written report that the examiners make after reading a thesis and undertaking a viva, they are required to state how the student has (or has not) fulfilled these requirements (see Chapter 11 on the examination and viva).

MPhil (Master of Philosophy)

This involves a research programme that must show evidence of:

1   **your proficiency in the methods and techniques of research;**

2   **good style and presentation;**

3   **an adequate knowledge and discussion of the literature in your specific field of study;**

4   **initiative and independence of thought;**

5   **a distinct contribution to scholarship.**

    (Maximum 60,000 words)

A dissertation as part of a taught Master's course is at this level. The taught modules in a Master's will have covered these competencies and the dissertation is intended to show that the student is able to apply them. The dissertation is, of course, much shorter than an entire Master's degree by research. This will be set by the course, but it is typically under 20,000 words.

PhD (Doctor of Philosophy)

This involves a research programme that must show evidence of:

1   **good presentation and style;**

2   **a significant contribution to knowledge;**

---

1 If you are registered for a research degree in an institution where the OU validates degrees (through OU Validation Services), the regulations are the same as if you were directly registered with the OU.

3   **your capacity to pursue further research without supervision;**

4   **a significant amount of material worthy of publication.**

   (Maximum 100,000 words)

You should note that one thing that does vary between institutions is the specified maximum length of a thesis. For example, De Montfort University's regulations specify the following as the 'normal' maximum length:

- **In Science and Engineering and Art and Design for PhD 40,000 words.**

- **In Science and Engineering and Art and Design for MPhil 20,000 words.**

- **In Arts, Social Sciences and Education for PhD 80,000 words.**

- **In Arts, Social Sciences and Education for MPhil 40,000 words.**

However, this limit does exclude 'ancillary data' that would appear in an appendix.

There is a specified range where the presentation or submission consists substantially of material in other than written form, which is:

- **For PhD 10,000–12,000 words.**

- **For MPhil 6,000–8,000 words.**

Sometimes the maximum length is specified in terms of pages rather than words. A 250-page limit is one example I have come across.

When considering maximum word limits or page numbers, you should realize that this is not a target to aim for! Word limits exist for several reasons. They are for the examiners' benefit, in that it would be unreasonable to require an examiner to wade through a 300,000-word text. However, given that, in your research degree, you are proving your capability as a researcher, the central rationale is that you should be able to produce a reasonable-sized research report on your project. An overlength thesis or dissertation would suggest that you still have much to learn about organizing and writing a research report.

The OU word limits allow for research methodologies that require a lot of written information to be reported (for example, discourse analysis, literature studies or where detailed case examples are involved), and so most research degrees should be well below the maximum limits given. This particularly applies to scientific research degrees, which can be considerably shorter than those in the humanities and social sciences. The regulations for De Montfort University reflect this difference between disciplines, and their guidelines where non-written presentations are involved show by how much a thesis may be shortened. The OU regulations take a different approach in that they specify a higher, but generic, word limit.

Competencies required for a research degree

It is worthwhile exploring the competencies required for the Master's and doctorate research degrees. As well as the PhD student attempting to take on too much (the 'last word in ... life's work' view of a PhD), there is also a danger of those undertaking a Master's dissertation trying to do a PhD project. Beside the universal requirement for 'good style and presentation', the requirements are cumulative: a higher-level degree will also require a demonstration of the skills and competencies of the degree below it. So, I will start by looking at what is expected to be demonstrated at the Master's level, and then move on to what in addition is required of a Doctorate.

Competencies required for all research degrees

Good presentation
Good presentation and style is expected of all research degree theses and dissertations. Sometimes the regulations of a university imply rather than explicitly state the need for good presentation and style. However, writing well and coherently is a fundamental competence needed for any research degree. Academic writing is covered in Chapter 6 of this book. However, the following activity can be useful in terms of thinking about how the writings of others succeed (or not) in getting their message across.

Activity 2.4

When you review a piece of written work in your area, instead of considering its content and method, look at it in terms of presentation. How well does it communicate the research to you?

Pick out two or three examples that you feel are the best at doing this and two or three you feel are bad. Make a list of what makes the good ones good and the bad ones bad. (This activity can be combined with your work on 'Familiarizing yourself with research standards', later in this section).

Critically reviewing existing knowledge

Critically reviewing existing research in your subject area is needed for all research degrees. Such a review is then expected to be a springboard for further original research. The MPhil and PhD research degree regulations for De Montfort University develop this requirement a little further, specifying 'a critical investigation and evaluation of the topic of research'. All other university regulations contain some similar phrase.

Chapter 7 of this book deals with undertaking a literature review and how this links into other research tasks, so it will not be discussed here. However, at this point it is worthwhile looking at what such a review should achieve. A literature review must demonstrate:

1 **your ability to investigate critically a specific field of study (i.e. to evaluate what has been done);**

2 **an adequate knowledge and discussion of the literature of that field.**

The key phrase in the first criterion is the term 'investigate critically'. It is not just about producing a list of what others have done in your topic area; it is about demonstrating that you understand it, showing, for example, if you can say whether a particular contribution makes sense, fits in or disagrees with what others have said, and is important or not. The wording of the De Montfort regulations, using the word 'evaluation', puts emphasis on demonstrating your critical abilities.

This links into the second criterion for a literature review, to demonstrate an adequate knowledge and discussion of the literature. Demonstrating 'adequate knowledge' does not mean following up every minor piece of work, but making sure that you cover the major writers and their work. This is very much about discernment – that you do not miss out anything important, but equally that you do not become side-tracked by following up every triviality.

Adequate knowledge also includes your ability to discern where the literature is thin, or where there are gaps in knowledge and also that you can identify the boundaries of your specific area, and draw out from the wider literature lessons that are of importance to your more tightly defined topic. An analogy might be of an explorer writing a guidebook about a new country they have discovered, which is to be used by others who are planning to visit. The guidebook would therefore have to identify the major places worth visiting, how to get to them, how important they are and how they relate to each other. A series of unrelated photographs with simple captions is no guidebook.

Proficiency in research methods

The thesis is required to demonstrate your 'proficiency in the methods and techniques of research'. Some research degree regulations word this a little differently. For example, one says 'demonstrate an understanding of research methods appropriate to the field of study' and another (Brunel University) specifies this as 'knowledge and understanding of his/her discipline and of associated research techniques'. In other words you do not have to be proficient in all research methods, just those of relevance to your topic area (which, of course, makes eminent sense). So you need to show not only a critical understanding of the results of research undertaken in your field of study, but also *the methods and techniques used to obtain those results*. Furthermore, you need to show that you can apply those methods and techniques yourself (the Brunel regulations include the phrase 'and to show that they [the research techniques] have been successfully applied'). This does not mean that you have to use every technique in the book, but that you must be able to show that you know about them and have chosen and justified one or more methods that are most appropriate for your particular research project.

This, and the other additional criteria discussed below, also applies to a dissertation as part of a taught Master's course, although a dissertation is obviously far shorter than an entire Master's by thesis. Even so, it should be to the same standard and so display the same competencies. There also may be very specific requirements, for example applying competencies and techniques that were part of the taught component of the course. If this is so, such requirements should be specified.

Initiative and independence of thought

This point follows on from the issues raised with respect to the topic review. It is about showing that you have an understanding of what you are investigating and are not treating research as a mechanistic process – even though it may involve a lot of routine work.

It is very important to show HOW you did your research – warts and all. Things always go wrong in any research project. How you overcame challenges and problems shows your initiative and independence.

Originality

The OU regulations say that a Master's should make 'a distinct contribution to scholarship', which may sound a rather daunting prospect. It is really about showing that you have the astuteness to sort out where you can make a useful contribution. For a PhD, the OU regulations use the term 'a significant contribution to knowledge'. De Montfort regulations require a PhD to 'constitute an independent and original contribution to knowledge'. Brunel University's regulations are similar: 'a distinct and original contribution to knowledge of the subject'. These are both a step up from the Master's requirement. This does not mean that the *whole* of a PhD thesis must be original and every bit of it is a contribution to knowledge, just that there is something original somewhere in it.

Behind both these phrases there is the concept of originality in research. There are many ways to fulfil the originality criterion, which can vary according to topic area. It is also worth noting that some of the originality categories below may only be achievable in a larger research project rather than, for example, in a Master's dissertation.

Originality categories
1 A new product.

Just making something new is not academically adequate – it has to be made as the result of a research process (e.g. analysing the way in which an existing product or component undertakes a task and then demonstrating how it could be improved; scientific and engineering PhDs are often of this nature).

2 Providing something new for the first time.

This can be anything from new material, new case studies of an industry, new data or an archaeologist digging a new site. Again, the provision of something new must be linked to a research process. Just digging up a load of bones or discovering a new form of social behaviour will not do; it needs to be set in the context of a particular archaeological or sociological debate and shown how this discovery advances understanding.

3 A development of or an improvement on something which already exists.

Originality can be developing further a previously original piece of work. James Watt did not invent the steam engine; he improved it.

4 A new theory or perspective.

This can include a synthesis of existing information using the new theory/perspective by way of verification.

5 A reinterpretation of an existing theory.

This can involve an original exposition of another's work – for example, suggesting that an alternative theoretical interpretation of data is possible that provides a better understanding of the system under study.

6 Applying an existing idea or theory to a new field or a set of data.

For example, taking a model that was developed under test conditions and seeing if it works with field data.

7 A new research tool or technique.

For example, in one PhD, the student applied a psychology methodology to a transport planning issue (traffic calming) and did fieldwork to test its viability. This had never been done before and the thesis established both the concept and the feasibility of doing this.

8 A new model or perspective.

This can be anything from a new mathematical model, to a new way of understanding how businesses develop innovative products, or a new commentary on a classical Latin poem.

9 A new in-depth study.

This could add to knowledge (for example, by detailing a process already known in outline), without necessarily developing a new perspective. Many arts and social research degrees take this form.

10 A critical analysis.

Showing originality in testing somebody else's idea and/or developing an original critique. Art and literature research can often take this form.

11 A portfolio of work based on research.

In some art research degrees in particular, a portfolio can demonstrate the student's competence in their subject. A PhD by publications (usually available only to staff of a university) also involves the use of an existing portfolio of research.

12 A collection of generalizable findings or conclusions.

In this case originality is in the generalizations made. My own thesis was of this type; it pulled together existing primary information on the land use/transport design of Britain's new towns and drew comparative and generalizable conclusions about their efficiency in providing personal mobility to their residents.

13 Carrying out original work within a project designed by others.

Laboratory and experimental PhD projects can take place within a larger team research project. The scope and design of the PhD project are thus largely predetermined. This is quite common and is accepted, but you need to ensure that your own originality plays a part as well.

These categories are not exclusive; indeed, there are quite a few overlaps. However, it is useful to develop a list like this in order to think through what constitutes originality. In many cases originality does not necessarily require generating new data or material, but is about utilizing existing material in an original way. Remember that originality does not apply to the whole thesis or dissertation; it means that the thesis or dissertation contains something original. For example, one student commented:

> I think what my examiners felt was original in my own PhD was that I applied systems theories to a particular area of NHS activity which had not really been investigated systematically before (performance measurement systems), and included a development of an existing process (being debated among systems academics at the time) for choosing appropriate methodologies for investigating different types of problems. A consequence of this interdisciplinarity was I needed three examiners – one expert on the performance measurement issues, one on NHS policy with a bit of systems background, and one expert on the systems approaches I'd applied!

In this case the originality was in both applying an existing method to a new area and developing the method further.

Activity 2.5

In which of the above ways do you expect your research to be original? Or will it be original in another way? You may have only a vague or preliminary idea of this at the moment, but suggest what you can.

Discuss this with your supervisor as well as making your own notes in your Research Journal.

Other PhD-level competencies

Phillips and Pugh (2000, chap. 3) argue that a PhD essentially needs to demonstrate that:

1 **You have a command of your subject and demonstrate this by having 'something to say'.**

2 **You have the astuteness to sort out where you can make a useful contribution.**

3 **You know the methods and techniques of investigation (and their limitations).**

4 **You can communicate the results effectively.**

5 **Overall, you are a professional in your field.**

As well as the requirement to make an original contribution to knowledge, which has already been considered above, Phillips and Pugh say that the key hallmark of a PhD is to demonstrate that you are a 'fully professional researcher'. This returns us to the point noted in Section 2.1 above about the nature of the PhD qualification.

This point features in all UK university regulations, which contain some phrase indicating that a PhD should demonstrate your capacity to pursue further research without supervision. This is about arriving as a professional in your field. A PhD should show that you know how to design a research project, organize it, carry it out and report the results. In consequence it is important in your PhD to:

1   Show HOW you did your research as well as WHAT you found out (theses are often thin on the crucial HOW side).

2   Show warts and all – how you overcame problems (things always go wrong in even the best organized research project).

3   Show how, even if the results are negative, they can still represent an original contribution, particularly if you display a professional use of the research methods in your field. One way you could make these points very clear in your thesis is to have a short 'postscript' at the end reflecting on what you have learned about doing research in undertaking your degree.

There is a further criterion, which is that a PhD should contain *material worthy of publication*. This is one way of demonstrating that you have arrived in your field of research. It should be emphasized that such a criterion does not mean that the whole thesis is worthy of publication, just that it contains something in it that is. An indisputable way to prove this is to publish papers based on your thesis work. However, do check with your supervisor or research office as some institutions do not permit the publication of thesis chapters before a viva. Editing the material may get you around this.

What will the examiner be looking for?

There is a separate chapter in this book on the examination process and viva. An examiner will specifically be asked to report on how the candidate fulfilled the specific requirements for each research degree. In summary, your examiner will be looking for the following key indicators that reflect whether you have demonstrated the competencies expected of a research degree.

For all research degrees, examiners will be looking for:

1   a clear focus;

2   a good grasp of the nature of the situation addressed;

3 a coherent rationale for undertaking the research;

4 good connections made with existing work on the topic;

5 the results and conclusions displayed in a scholarly and creative manner;

6 a method appropriate to the topic of investigation;

7 appropriate level of originality;

8 (for a PhD) evidence that you have arrived as a professional in your field.

Activity 2.6

How would you know whether your thesis has fulfilled the core academic criteria listed for your research degree?

It would be useful to discuss your responses with your supervisor.

Familiarizing yourself with research standards

Having given some thought to the criteria for your research degree, you would find it useful to look at some publications in your intended field of study in terms of how they represent good research. This could be of particular use for previously inexperienced researchers or part-time external research students. This is probably best done as part of your literature review when you need to be working through key publications in any case. Part of looking at the research in your field is to get an idea of the standards expected.

It is very useful indeed to look at successful relevant dissertations or theses in your field. This should help focus on what are the standards expected. Even in a very specific topic area, theses can take varied and diverse forms, utilizing different research approaches and methods. Your supervisor should be able to suggest some for you to see. You will need to read some quite thoroughly, but for others at least skim through them to get a general feel.

Remember that specific subject areas have traditions and styles of their own that cannot be covered in this book. Talk to your supervisor about this.

2.3 Progressing from MPhil to PhD

Before leaving the subject of competencies required for a research degree, mention needs to be made of transferring between an MPhil and a PhD. In many universities, PhD research students are initially registered for an MPhil and then, towards the end of their first year's study,[2] are required to submit a 'Transfer' or 'Probation' Report to be upgraded to a PhD. This Transfer Report is typically 5,000–10,000 words in length and involves:

1   **the completion of an initial review of the subject;**

2   **the identification of the research problem to be addressed;**

3   **the development of a research plan.**

One example comes from De Montfort University, whose regulations for a Transfer Report indicate that the research plan should 'include details of the original contribution to knowledge which is likely to emerge.' This indicates the key criterion that you need to demonstrate in a Transfer Report, and this is that you have demonstrated the potential to achieve PhD-level competencies. In a number of universities, students are also expected to give a presentation as part of the transfer process, and be questioned on their research plan. The form of the transfer report can vary substantially between universities, so you should check carefully what is required in your own case.

The Transfer Report is not just a bit of bureaucracy (although the danger is that it can be). It is useful to have a formal check on progress when you are about a third into your PhD work. If there are any serious problems they need to be picked up before it is too late – a third into a PhD project is about right for such a check. As Rugg and Petre (2004, pp. 15–16) note, this is when 'you should have done enough work for The System to have a fair idea of your ability. ... The transfer is therefore an important stage, which normally involves genuine academic assessment of how you are doing, rather than an administrative convenience.'

Activity 2.7

If you are expecting to undertake a PhD, find out how you have to prepare a Transfer Report, or what other form of review will take place. Note down the criteria that need to be met.

Ensure that you will have completed all that is needed in time for when your transfer report is due.

The tasks that a Transfer Report contains (topic review, focusing on a research question and developing a research plan) are all in this book, so whatever your regulations may be, the following chapters will equip you to face them.

---

2 Or about 18 months in for part-time PhD.

2.4 Starting Off

Having considered what constitutes a research degree or dissertation and the criteria involved, the obvious question is then how to get going. Chapter 5 of this book, 'Planning and organizing your research', looks at the initial stages of the research process in more detail, but the following may be useful in the first instance. Even if you alter your plans, it is worthwhile starting to sort out a rough project structure now. Begin by focusing on the immediate work that needs to be done and then sketch out what might be the big tasks in the longer term. This forms the basis of Activity 2.8.

Activity 2.8

What do you see as the key tasks to be done in the first few months of your project?

Why are these tasks so important?

How do you propose to set about these tasks?

How will you measure your success?

Sketch out a work programme of the crucial tasks you think will be involved in:

1   over the next three months;
2   producing the thesis as a whole.

This would be a useful activity to discuss with your supervisor.

2.5 Support for Research

A research degree or a Master's dissertation is not undertaken in total isolation. It is your research project, but you will undertake it with support and guidance from your supervisor, institution and a wider network of institutional and personal contacts.

Working with your supervisor

In terms of support for your studies, the relationship you have with your supervisor(s) is utterly crucial for your whole postgraduate work and experience. This is particularly so for part-time students, as your main contact will be through your supervisor(s). A number of authors of research training books have commented on the importance of a good working relationship between a student and their supervisor. There is an offprint at the end of this chapter from Rugg and Petre's book *The Unwritten Rules of PhD Research*, but this issue is also covered well in Cryer (2000) and Phillips and Pugh (2000).

Activity 2.9

Read the offprint from Rugg and Petre. This deals with the practicalities of establishing a good relationship with your supervisor. After reading this, make a set of notes of the main points that you feel apply to your situation, highlighting any that you feel to be of particular relevance to you and that you need to tackle.

Training needs analysis

In particular, it is worth noting what Rugg and Petre say about training needs (p. 38 of the offprint). It is worthwhile undertaking a *Training Needs Analysis* and Activity 2.10 provides some guidance on how to do this. This is part of your ongoing project planning. Once you have (as in Activity 2.8) identified the activities and tasks that you need to undertake, you should then consider if you need any form of training (or simply whether you need advice or to see an example) to undertake that task. It is fairly obvious that if you plan to use a particular statistical or analytical technique, then you may need training in that. However, other training needs may not be so apparent. You may include on your list of tasks giving a seminar on your research plans – so if you are not experienced in presentations, then some training or ways to build up experience would be useful. If you've never presented in public, you need this on your list of training needs, but if (for example) you are a school or FE teacher, then you probably have this skill anyway. Another example is that you may be setting out on your literature review. How do you intend to record this, and do you need training in methods of data/literature recording (such as the use of a bibliographical package)? This book covers the basic generic research skills, but you (and your supervisor) should identify and decide if you need further training on these subjects as well as training in any methods or skills that are more specific to your research subject. Rugg and Petre also note that you may benefit from training in less obvious areas like assertiveness and relaxation, to which might be added skills such as teamworking, network development and self-discipline. These three are among the more generic skills mentioned in the HEFC skills statement.

Activity 2.10

1 Check your list of key tasks from Activity 2.8 and identify if you consequently have any specific training needs.
2 Prepare an agenda for your next tutorial based upon the guidance in the Rugg and Petre reading (including your Training Needs Analysis).

Activity 2.10 (Continued)

You could use the following grid to undertake your Training Needs Analysis. For each of the skills you identify as needed in order to fulfil your key tasks, rate your ability with a score of A–E, where A means a high capability at handling this skill, and E means a low capability. Then note how you know you have that level of skill. You can then decide (or discuss with your supervisor) whether developing this skill is a high priority and then what needs to be done about improving things. This may involve formal training, reading up on a subject/skill area, or other ways of building up experience in a skill.

Skill	My current level A–E	How do I know?	Improvement priority (High, Moderate, Low)	What might I do about it?

Departmental support

It is worth going through the support provided for students by your university and department and sorting out what are the general facilities and services that are provided. Establish who knows how to get hold of things (so you don't need to pester your supervisor with requests like how to get stationery or what is the internal extension number for the library help desk). For example, your departmental secretary, administrator or your supervisor's secretary are likely to be people who will know how 'The System' operates, where the photocopier is, who to go to if your PC is on the blink, and so forth. Such matters should be covered in your departmental induction.

There will also be other academic members of your department and faculty/school who may well have research student support responsibilities. Many universities have a supervisory team or groups and a system of mentoring to back up supervisors. These systems can often provide additional help and support to you.

So, as well as your supervisor(s), key people to get to know are therefore:

1 **The person in charge of administrative support (departmental secretary or administrator).**

2 **Your supervisor's secretary.**

3   **Any person or group with an 'overview' role for students (e.g. a research subdean or supervisory team).**

4   **The head of your research group (if you are in one).**

5   **Departmental research student mentor.**

There may be others with particular research student support roles. Check with your supervisor who they are and find out how to contact them. For a number of research areas it is also important to know the person responsible for health and safety (a subject covered in Section 2.6 of this chapter).

Departmental research training

As was mentioned in Chapter 1, this book covers only generic research training aspects. For training in, for example, methods specific to your subject area, your supervisor or department should advise you on what is available. Your department may well run a seminar series and there could be relevant taught courses in your topic area.

Do keep in touch with other research students in your department or even others doing similar work in other institutions. You can learn many of 'the ropes' from each other. I did my PhD full-time at the Open University in its pioneering years and I was the only research student in the Social Sciences Faculty. To some extent I was facing problems of isolation similar to those of a part-time student. In consequence, my supervisor encouraged me to network with students and other researchers elsewhere, which I found to be very helpful and encouraging.

The latter raises the wider issue of developing a personal support network, which is considered in Chapter 5 of this book.

Other support for your studies

Library and computing access

Full-time students will have library and computing access, but the procedures to obtain these, and the rules of use, will obviously vary between institutions. It is likely that each faculty/school/department will also have its own specialist computing and information technology (IT) facilitator. University computing departments will also run their own training courses for both staff and students. Contact the 'help desk' (or whatever it is called in your university) and find out what is available.

For part-time external research degree students, find out what library and computing support is available.

Assistance in research funding

A very important area to sort out is what money is available to support your research. Students on a Research Council grant have monies provided to their departments for research expenses and training. Make sure you know how much is available to you and how to claim this. You may also be able to apply for support for specific expenses (for example, an overseas conference or a field trip) from your grant funder. Internal departmental or faculty/school funds may also be available through your supervisor, who should be able to advise you on all these aspects.

The situation for external part-time research degree students is very different. They are normally expected to be self-funding. It is thus important to make allowances in designing your research programme for any additional costs that are a consequence of your research methods (this is considered in Chapters 3 and 5). This is also true for full-time students if your research is likely to involve costs beyond those routinely provided.

In some cases, part-time external students can apply for a limited amount of departmental or faculty/school funds through their internal supervisor, but, even when they exist, resources are very limited. Of perhaps wider relevance, several bursary schemes are offered by educational charities, the British Council or industry. Sometimes conferences provide bursaries for student attendance. It is very worthwhile having an initial talk about the financial aspects of your research with your supervisor, who may know of such schemes.

Your Research Office

Finally, there is always a Research Office, Centre or School that is responsible for administering research degree studies. Sometimes this office goes beyond an administration role and provides useful support facilities for students and may also organise research training sessions.

Activity 2.11

Find out the following (if available):

1 Who provides administrative support in your department.
2 Who is responsible for providing information on training in your department.
3 Who provides specialist research methods training courses.
4 The programme of departmental seminars.
5 A list of computer training courses.
6 A list of library training courses.
7 Activities of your research/graduate school.
8 Guidance notes for research students.
9 If there is a mentoring system, who your mentor is and guidance on complaints procedures.

2.6 Health and Safety

A final area that you need to consider early on in your work is your own health and safety in undertaking your research project. Health and safety considerations are very much to the fore in some areas of research, for example in laboratories or when travel to hazardous places is involved. However, all research has some health and safety implications, which may not be immediately apparent, so it is very worthwhile thinking these through with respect to your own project.

Working at home

Many research students work from home as well as at their universities and, of course, part-time students will mainly base their research work from home. We tend to be more aware of health and safety considerations in the workplace than at home, but it is as important to make sure that working from home is safe and healthy. Your university may provide home working guidance on Health and Safety, so as well as working through this section, do check up on any homeworking guidelines or rules.

There are a number of basics which you should consider.[3]

1 Fire safety
How would you escape in a fire? You should have a smoke alarm, test it weekly and replace the battery annually. Keep your work area tidy and do not allow waste paper to accumulate. Further information is available from the Firekills link on this book's website.

2 Electrical equipment
You need to check that your electrical equipment, plugs, leads, etc., are in good working order and in good condition. Avoid overloading sockets and do not use an adaptor with equipment that uses a lot of power, such as electric fires, kettle and toasters.

Your university is responsible for the safety of equipment that is supplied to you for use at home. It should be portable applicant tested (PAT) before you take it. You also have a duty to report faults which may be a hazard to your own or anyone else's safety.

3 Slips, trips and falls
Slips, trips and falls are the biggest cause of workplace accidents. Make sure that at home your floor coverings are sound and that there are no trailing cables in areas where you need to walk.

---

3 List and checklist based on homeworking guidance from the Open University's Occupational Health and Safety Department and advice from the OU's *Student website*.

4 Working environment
Provide yourself adequate heating, ventilation and lighting.

5 Manual handling
Some research activities can involve manual handling. If so, there must be a risk assessment for the tasks and you will need to have training.

6 Display screen equipment
This is perhaps the most important aspect of health and safety for research students working from home. It is also a major issue of working at your university. The use of display
screen equipment (DSE), like personal computers, has been associated with a range of
symptoms related to the visual system and working posture. These are often reflected in
various types of body fatigue. Applying simple ergonomic principles to the layout of your
work area and the way in which you study can easily and readily prevent them. The
following guidance applies to the use of DSE both at home and at your university.

Try to position the monitor to minimize glare and reflections on the screen. Suitable
lighting is important. Remember that glare can occur either directly or by reflection
from the screen. Glare from windows can usually be eliminated by using curtains or
blinds, or by adjusting the orientation of the screen.

As with any task which involves working in one position for a length of time, it is
important that you make yourself as comfortable as possible to use your computer.
Place the monitor in front of you and at a comfortable viewing distance. Try to position
the top of the display slightly below eye level when you are sitting at the keyboard
(accepting that this is sometimes not possible with a laptop). Adjust the positions of the
screen, the keyboard, the mouse and the documents from which you are working, so as
to achieve the most comfortable arrangement (check if you are having to constantly
move your eyes around which can cause problems).

Adjust the position of your chair so as to sit squarely in front of your computer and to
achieve a comfortable viewing distance and posture. As a broad guide, your forearms
should be approximately horizontal and your elbows level with the keyboard or the
mouse. Ensure you have enough space to use your mouse comfortably, and to rest your
wrists in front of the keyboard when not typing. Equipment such as a footrest or
document holder can be helpful.

Whenever possible, try to arrange your studies to consist of a mix of screen-based and
non-screen-based work to prevent fatigue and to vary visual and mental demands.
Breaks should be taken before the onset of fatigue, not in order to recuperate. So try to

break up long spells of intensive display screen work with periods of non-intensive, non-display screen activities. Short, frequent breaks are more satisfactory than occasional, longer breaks, e.g. a 5–10 minute break every 2 hours.

8 Children

If you are a parent you will know full well that children, particularly if young, affect how you organize your research work. You should also take them into account in assessing the health and safety of your work area in the home.

9 Security

If your research will involve obtaining confidential information, this needs to be kept secure and locked away when not in use.

Activity 2.12

This book's website contains two checklists: (a) A general Homeworking Self Assessment Checklist and (b) a Display Screen Equipment Checklist.

1   First find out if your university provides guidance on safe homeworking and use of display screen equipment. If so, work through your own guidance materials. Otherwise print off a copy of the two checklists provided on the book's website.
2   Go to the Healthy Computing website. There is a link to this from this book's website. Open the page on 'Office Ergonomics' and go through the set-up and positioning advice contained there. Identify what improvements you need to make to the layout of your workspace (computer layout, chair, lighting, etc.) in your office and/or home.
3   Go through the Display Screen Equipment Checklist to ensure that there are not any other important aspects that you have missed.
4   Now go through the Homeworking Self Assessment Checklist. You may have covered some aspects in the DSE Checklist, but the Homeworking Checklist covers other health and safety aspects of working from home.

If you are unable to address any health and safety issue, then discuss this with your supervisor or your department's Health and Safety officer (see also Activity 2.13 below).

Health and safety at work

The above discussion of the safe use of computers applies both to working at home and at your university. Universities have a legal obligation, under the Management of .

Health and Safety at Work Regulations 1999, to assess risks to health and safety to their staff and others (including students). This requires suitable and sufficient assessments of the risks to health and safety arising from work activities. Trivial risks can usually be ignored, as can risks arising from routine activities associated with life in general, unless the work activity compounds those risks. The above has covered DSE safety and office layout, but there are a number of other workplace safety aspects that particularly affect research students.

If working in your department involves particular health and safety risks, then other, specific legal requirements and procedures will be involved. For example there are regulations covering the Control of Substances Hazardous to Health (COSHH), display screen equipment (as mentioned above) and manual handling, which also require risk assessments to be made which specifically address the hazards concerned.

Your department will have a health and safety officer, who is someone appointed to ensure that legal obligations to assess risks to health and safety are in place and appropriate procedures are carried out. So, as well as conducting a check on your home studying area, you should contact your department's health and safety officer to check if there are any particular health and safety issues that you need to take into account in planning your research. The safe layout of an office will affect all research students, but if your research involves laboratory work or working with potentially hazardous equipment, you should ensure that your are fully briefed on this, and seek specific training if needed.

Activity 2.13

Make an appointment with your department's health and safety officer to:

(a) Check the layout of your office area (particularly if you identified issues in Activity 2.12).
(b) Discuss if your research plans have aspects that require any further risk analysis.

This book's website contains some links to sites that provide further advice on health and safety and risk analysis.

Fieldwork

Fieldwork also needs risk analysis. If you are engaged in technical activities in the field (e.g. operating data gathering equipment or collecting samples), you need to get specialist advice for your risk analysis. However, risks in data gathering do not just apply to people operating equipment, collecting rock samples from active volcanoes or travelling to places where you might catch a tropical disease. If you are interviewing participants, there are some research methods that involve more risks than others. For example, there is an inherent risk in stopping strangers in the street to talk to them, or going into the homes of strangers. Some interviewers are reluctant to enter unknown homes by themselves because of potential dangers. There is an example in the next chapter of a student who needed to interview people with a history of mental health issues and drug abuse, and she had to think carefully about how to ensure her own safety in this situation. If you identify such a situation, you should explore ways that reduce your risk. This may be to use a different data collecting method, or to use procedures that reduce the risk of a particular method (e.g. instead of interviewing a participant on your own, ensure that you are accompanied or interview them in a safer environment). This issue is explored further in Chapter 9 (section 9.6) of this book, which also looks at the issue of the health and safety of participants in your research.

When you discuss with your supervisor the method(s) you plan to use to gather data, ensure that you cover your own health and safety. If you feel there are important health and safety issues you should arrange to undertake a formal risk assessment.

References

Cryer, P. (2000) *The Research Student's Guide to Success* (2nd edn). Buckingham: Open University Press.

Phillips, E. and Pugh, D. (2000) *How to Get a PhD*. Buckingham: Open University Press.

Rugg, G. and Petre, M. (2004) *The Unwritten Rules of PhD Research*. Buckingham: Open University Press.

Offprint

Practical ways of establishing a good relationship with your supervisor
As usual, try looking at it from the other person's point of view – most of the answers will then become pretty obvious. Supervisors are research-active academics and research-active academics are hideously overworked. PhD students take up time, which is the supervisor's scarcest resource, and are in that sense a liability. A sensible student will reduce their liability rating; a good student will find ways of being a positive asset.

Reducing the liability rating mainly involves basic professional courtesies. It's your PhD, not the supervisor's; if you can't be bothered to work on making it happen, why should they? Making it happen includes making supervision meetings work: you should take the initiative in setting up the meetings, circulating relevant information in advance, drafting an agenda and coming with a clear set of things to report and questions to ask. Something which is easily overlooked is that you should also minute the meeting, recording decisions and actions, and circulate those minutes afterwards, then check that the actions are in fact done. A related issue in many organizations is keeping logs of meetings for The System.

Running meetings properly is a rare skill, so we've summarized the key points here – this particular skill is valuable in most walks of life.

Several days before the meeting, the organizer of the meeting should:

- circulate the agenda;
- check that the venue is still available, if it isn't the supervisor's office;
- remind people of the time and place of the meeting;
- circulate any briefing material, including minutes of the last meeting.

During the meeting, the chair of the meeting should:

- record the date and the parties present;
- check that everyone agrees with the minutes of the last meeting;
- check that actions from the last meeting have all been done;
- record any decisions made, including milestones and deliverables (and check that everyone agrees with this record);
- record any actions agreed (and check that everyone agrees with this record);
- fix the time and place of the next meeting.

After the meeting:

- the organizer should write up the minutes and distribute them;
- everyone should do what they have agreed to do.

There are different types of meeting, suitable for different purposes. The description above relates to formal meetings, but PhDs also require informal meetings when you explore ideas or discuss your longer term career plans, or work through a problem which is bothering you. These usually take place over the legendary cup of coffee.

Some classic irritating habits which students often show in relation to meetings include the following:

- failing to take deadlines seriously;
- failing to respect the supervisor's time pressures (you are but one demand among many);
- dumping demands on the supervisor at the last minute instead of allowing them time for reading, thanking, enquiring etc.;
- expecting the supervisor to read every draft, usually by the next day;

- expecting the supervisor to organize everything;
- organizing things without consulting the supervisor (independence is good up to a point; but you need to check you're being independent in the right way).

Dealing with your supervisor

There are various strategies which students can use to make life better for all parties in the PhD, but which are not as widely used as they should be. These include:

- exchanging favours, such as tracking down an obscure reference for your supervisor in exchange for some advice about a job application (but make sure that the exchange is agreed explicitly, so you both know where you stand);
- showing explicitly that you value your supervisor's knowledge and experience;
- trying to do something the supervisor's way, but setting criteria and a date for evaluation of the success of it (especially if you're reluctant);
- not just refusing to do something you don't like, but offering an alternative instead;
- being scrupulous about giving credit where credit is due (e.g. when you publish papers);
- finding out about your supervisor's research – surprisingly few students do this, even though their supervisor's research is probably one of the most valuable resources available;
- allowing your supervisor to be human – tolerating human weaknesses, and making the most of your supervisor's strengths.

What to put in

The supervisory relationship is a two-way one; you are supposed to be actively learning, not passively waiting to be told all the answers.

At the most academic level, you should be actively finding things out and actively generating ideas. One sign that you're doing a proper PhD is that you are finding out things which are new to your supervisor; another is that your supervisor finds at least one of your ideas sufficiently interesting to merit genuine engagement and discussion. It's useful as well as courteous to give your supervisor a précis of what you've found, and to offen full copies of any material that the supervisor would like to read in more detail.

At the implementation level, you should be generating ideas about specific research questions to ask and specific research methods to investigate them. You should be doing this increasingly as the PhD progresses and you learn more. Your supervisor will probably advise against most of these ideas; what you need to do is to assess the reasons for this advice, rather than going into a corner and sulking. One thing which most students never consider is that a good supervisor will be generating ideas about their own research all the time, and discarding the vast majority of them on various grounds. If you expect to have a higher hit rate than your supervisor while you're still an apprentice, then you're being a bit silly.

What to ask for

There are various things that you should ask for, with appropriate courtesy, at various stages of your PhD.

From an early stage, you should ask for appropriate training, both in research methods relevant to your research and also in other areas which will help you – for instance, many students would benefit from assertiveness training and relaxation training, as well as time management and numerous other ancillary skills. You should ask specifically for skills advice if you need it (e.g. what is the form of a conference paper; how does one read a paper and make notes about it?) It's particularly helpful if the supervisor can work through an example with you, rather than just telling you how to do it. A lot of students are embarrassed to ask for this sort of advice on the grounds that they think they should already know it. That's a faulty assumption. The point of the PhD is that it's about learning these skills; if you had them already, there wouldn't be much point in doing the PhD.

When you are at a later stage and have some findings to discuss, you can ask your supervisor to recommend (or introduce you to) other experts who might help. This needs to be done with discretion. Your supervisor will probably not introduce you to someone who will steal and publish your ideas (a frequent source of generally unfounded nightmares for PhD students), but you do need to have enough knowledge of academic etiquette to handle such encounters properly.

What to tell your supervisor

You should keep your supervisor informed:

- about the state of your work;
- about what interests you and what concerns you;
- about outside opinion: report feedback from talks and papers accurately and promptly; be specific about both compliments and criticisms;
- about decisions and turning points (the supervisor can often provide helpful insight and forestall hasty misjudgements);
- about life circumstances: let your supervisor know about personal or practical matters that are affecting your work, preferably before they turn into a major issue.

Things you can do for yourself

There are also various things you can do for yourself. You should keep your supervisor briefed about all of these, in advance. This is partly common courtesy and partly practical self-interest (so that the supervisor can stop you if you're about to do something remarkably stupid on your own initiative).

Another thing worth doing is to assemble an informal 'committee' of people (both staff and students, both in the department and external) who are able and willing to help with your PhD. The key thing to remember is that this is to complement your supervisor, not as an alternative to your supervisor. The informal committee can be helpful for things ranging from low-level logistics (e.g. babysitting) and low-level practical skills (e.g. learning how to use your computer properly) up to general emotional support and specific academic advice on topics complementing your supervisor's advice (e.g. help translating foreign language articles about your area of research).

Another thing you can do is to give seminars and/or circulate draft papers. This both gives you experience and provides you with feedback.

In brief, there are a few cardinal rules about dealing with your supervisor which are subtly different from the three golden rules of public presentation described elsewhere in this book. When dealing with your supervisor, you should:

- be honest;
- be articulate (say what you mean and what you need);
- be informative (keep the supervisor informed);
- be respectful;
- be adult (i.e. responsible for yourself).

Source: Edited version of Chapter 4 'Supervision' of Rugg, G. and Petre, M. (2004) *The Unwritten Rules of PhD Research*. Buckingham: Open University Press.

3 Scoping Your Research

Jane Montague and Chris High
with contributions from Carina Paine,
Jackie Topp and John Smith

LEARNING OUTCOMES

After reading this chapter and working on its associated activities you should be able to:

- Demonstrate your willingness and ability to plan and focus your research.
- Set boundaries for your project and draw upon/use sources of support as appropriate.
- Demonstrate original, independent and critical thinking in the design of your project.
- Demonstrate flexibility and open-mindedness in planning and focusing your project.

3.1 Introduction

To get you going on planning and organizing your own research, we'll start with the experiences of three students.

First, Carina Paine – at the time of writing she had just completed her PhD as part of the Forensic Psychology Research Group at the Open University (OU). Carina's study was about ways to improve children's remembering of faces – important when they are potentially witnesses or victims of crimes. Carina told us about some of the practical problems she faced in carrying out her fieldwork, and some of the strategies she used to tackle them.

Box 3.1 Practicalities

Because of the applied nature of my research it was critical to the development of my PhD to understand police officers' current practice and experience with child witnesses. Therefore, during the early stages of my PhD I conducted a questionnaire survey of police officers in the UK to identify their current practice with, and experiences and opinions of, child witnesses. In addition, I met some police officers more informally and found this was really helpful, providing a practical perspective to my work.

The results of this survey (along with the existing research) informed a series of laboratory-based experimental studies with children aged 6–8 and 10 years.

I spent a lot of time thinking through data collection. As the experimental research of my PhD involved interviewing young children, I was required to conduct my data collection in a number of primary schools. Working in schools meant that I had to prepare thoroughly and anticipate a number of eventualities. I had to first gain Criminal Records Bureau clearance. Following this clearance I had to timetable my research around busy school diaries. I also needed to secure parental permission in order to interview each child. Even with permissions I still then had to anticipate children's possible absence from school, etc., and ensure I had a large enough pool of child participants to accommodate such occurrences. Although it was really satisfying to have overall responsibility for this and other experiments, it was very time-consuming and could be quite pressured.

At the end of each study I had vast amounts of data, much more than I required, and I did not include some data in my final thesis. This was disappointing as some of the findings I did not write up were interesting. However, I needed to appreciate the wider audience for the research and prioritize what should be included. My thesis provided new theoretical and practical approaches to the applied issue of interviewing of children in order to construct composites. The fact that my thesis had many practical implications, in addition to its theoretical contribution, was a great motivation. I hope my findings will lead to future research in the area and influence practice for police officers working with actual child witnesses.

Our second example is from Jackie Topp, a research student at the OU's Faculty of Health and Social Care. Jackie's research examines the experiences of disabled mothers and here she talks about some of the important issues that directed the course of her study – ethics and recruitment. Ethics are discussed in more detail later in Chapter 9 of this book, but the example is included here to demonstrate how different issues can crop up at any time during your research and direct its progression.

Box 3.2 Ethics and Recruitment

Fundamentally I wanted my research to make a difference to the lives of disabled women. With this in mind I knew that I would have to work with the statutory and voluntary agencies so that my findings could potentially be used for policy changes. I had decided to work in just one county in order to make it easier for working with different agencies and I contacted all the local health care, social care and voluntary agencies.

Working with health care personnel and vulnerable adults has ethical implications that I needed to address. I knew I would have to have my proposal supported by the Local Medical Research and Ethics Committee and duly completed the long, very medically orientated form. I was pleased that the Committee soon accepted my proposal and I was in a position to approach the personnel who would be most likely to have contact with the women who met my research criteria.

Unfortunately for me, the ethical implications for my study continued to become quite a long-drawn-out affair. Although I had my MREC approval, the NHS introduced clinical governance at the beginning of 2004. This proved to be quite a difficult situation as now each Primary Care Trust that I worked with needed to give approval for my study. Although I was working in only one county, this was covered by three PCTs. As clinical governance was such a new procedure the post of co-ordinator was not filled immediately and was, I found, only a secondment. This meant that I had to deal with a change in co-ordinators and a lot of confusion as to who I needed to seek permission from within each PCT. This process held back my study for some months as far as accessing participants through the health care route went. Fortunately, as I had my MREC approval I was able to continue to contact voluntary and social care organizations.

I wrote to, spoke with, and visited a vast number of organizations trying to find support for my study and gain access to potential participants. I came across many problems during this procedure as the social basis of understanding for my study was not always recognized by people who did not understand the politics of disability. I also found that agencies, quite rightly, were protective about their clients who were, after all, vulnerable adults. They did not want any additional stress put on their clients and in many cases would not even introduce my study to them. I felt this denied potential participants the opportunity to decide whether they wanted to take part. Also, I found that when these 'gatekeepers' realized that I was a disabled person they also became protective of my welfare. After all, I was a vulnerable person going to strangers' homes and I could have been at some risk in certain circumstances, particularly where the woman had a history of mental

(Continued)

Box 3.2   (Continued)

health issues and drug abuse. I found this situation quite frustrating as the 'researcher' in me was extremely keen to talk to such women. However, the decision rested with the 'gatekeeper' and access for me was again denied.

Slowly, however, I began to recruit participants. I succeeded in interesting women with various types of impairment and found that these were often 'hidden'. Although my study was fundamentally based on disability as socially caused through discrimination against people with a physical, mental health or learning difficulty, the type of impairment that each woman had dictated how I could approach my exploration of their experiences. I decided that using narrative analysis would be the way forward for me to achieve the purpose I aimed for. This shows that the process of the PhD is never static and that the researcher always needs to keep an open mind about the methods and practices employed in the research.

Our final example is a more reflexive account from John Smith. His PhD was based in the Knowledge Media Institute at the Open University.

Box 3.3   Reflexivity

When, at the age of 18, the moment came to decide what I wanted to study, I remember thinking 'What? Computer science? Sitting in front of a computer monitor for hours! Not for me!' and I decided to study civil engineering instead. Twelve years later, I find myself doing exactly what I was trying then to avoid, and I love it.

It has been a long and chaotic academic journey. I graduated as a civil engineer in 1997, and I was good at it. I was accepted for a PhD at the same university, and without realizing it I found myself doing research in Knowledge Management (KM). It was my supervisor's idea, but I lacked the skills to progress and had limited financial and scientific support. To acquire the skills and background knowledge that I needed, in 1999 I moved from home to Brighton and started an MSc in Intelligent Systems at the University of Sussex. During my MSc, not only did I discover the fascinating domain of Artificial Intelligence and Biologically Inspired Computing, but also realized that moving back to my home to continue the PhD I had left behind was not the right career move. Instead, I grasped the opportunity for a PhD at the Knowledge Media Institute (KMi) of the Open University. I was aware of KMi's excellent reputation from my research in KM, but had no personal contacts with any of the researchers at the institute. Nevertheless, KMi's subject areas appeared relevant to my interests, and so in 2000 I began to investigate the

---

Box 3.3   (Continued)

application of Soft Computing (namely Genetic Algorithms and Neural Networks) to the domain of KM, and was really excited about it. KMi's working environment was inspiring.

At the end of the first year of the PhD process I encountered a clash of ideas between my supervisors and myself. What I envisioned doing was not exactly what they had in mind. I guess argumentation is inherent in science, but given their experience I decided in the beginning of the second year to compromise and so I started working towards the research direction that they pinpointed. Five months later, however, I felt that little progress has been made. I was frustrated and disappointed, and so despite a senior colleague's calming words – 'Don't worry! It is part of the process. In the first year of the PhD you just don't know what you are doing. In the second you are doing it wrong. And only during the third you produce the deliverables' – I decided to take action.

A change of supervision team allowed me to resume along my initial direction. I don't know if it proves that I was right in the first place, or that I just tried hard to prove I was, but eventually things got back on track. The isolated islands of knowledge that were formulated during the first year started to aggregate into mountains, my ideas and argumentation solidified and were soon translated into a series of experiments. Of course the experimental process was cumbersome and it lasted all the way until the end of my PhD. It was a process of trial and error that took time to stabilize and to start producing results. Nevertheless, it provided great insights and allowed vague ideas to reach their final form – getting your hands dirty with experimentation makes you realize what research is all about. It was finally all worthwhile – it was exciting when the thesis started taking shape. After approximately six months it was so satisfying to have the first draft ready. However, to my surprise it took another four months before I finally submitted after a long iterative process of feedback and revisions.

Activity 3.1

Write some notes on what you have learned from reading these three accounts. Your task is then to draw insight from this, and make a start at determining some principles to guide you in scoping your own research. We suggest you do your best to think of three.

You may well find it helpful to discuss your reactions with a couple of other people – maybe other students studying with you, or perhaps a friend or partner. You can do this in conversation or through email. Pool your insights to arrive at some really crisp and helpful principles to follow.

As you read through the chapter, see whether the sections we have used link with the principles you have chosen.

Comment

The three principles we identified were:

- **You've got to plan your work carefully, as you've got an awful lot to do in a pretty limited time.**

- **You must set very clear boundaries, and focus your efforts on what can reasonably be done in the time.**

- **At the same time, you need to monitor constantly how the plan is going, and be flexible and able to modify it as unexpected problems arise.**

In this chapter we will look at some of the strategies you can use to make plans, set boundaries and build in flexibility, using illustrations from the three recently completed research projects you just read about, plus some others. Once you have worked through the chapter, you should have a much clearer idea of what your research is going to be about, and how to continue to focus and develop your thinking.

That is not to say that you are trying to freeze your ideas in place, and that your view of what your research is about will not have changed by the time you complete it. Life (and research) doesn't usually work like that. But experience shows that putting some effort into developing your thinking about the purpose of your research at the outset will help you to engage with your work more quickly, and form a basis for being able to see whether you are making progress. The more thinking you do and the more feedback you get as you go along, the better the final piece of research is likely to be. To help you with this, the exercises in this chapter are designed to provide you with the basis of a presentation to your supervisor, outlining your current work plans for your project.

3.2 You've Got to Have a Plan

While undoubtedly you noted the need to be flexible, it's also vital that something as big as a PhD thesis really does need a lot of planning.

Again, we'll start with an illustration. Box 3.4 shows how an OU PhD student, Kat Stothard, planned the early stages of her PhD project – a study of how people's experience of diabetes affects their self-care behaviours. This is structured similarly to Activity 2.8 in the last chapter and you may wish to compare Kat's planning of key tasks and how she did them to your own notes on Activity 2.8.

Box 3.4 Example Task List

Key tasks	How I did them
1 Generate research questions concerning research topic (for example, research on diabetes and on self-care behaviours).	Brainstorming, making notes and trying them out on supervisors.
2 Begin literature survey, by deciding preliminary sub-themes, then searching and thinking about each sub-theme, one by one.	I started with some preliminary sub-themes: (a) diabetes; (b) self-care behaviours; and (c) personal experiences of team working. But I soon realized that the sub-themes were too large, so I focused on: (a) type 1 and type 2 diabetes; (b) self-regulation; (c) coping strategies; and (d) self-efficacy.
3 Make a plan by January for the project, e.g. ethics, questionnaires to be used, possible participants.	I started by making a list of major tasks I needed to do to fulfil these, e.g. what does the ethics committee require?; what questionnaires are available – will I have to design my own?; finding means of accessing diabetic people.
4 Make notes on appropriate methods and tools.	I thought about what has been done before. Then I made a list of potential methods and discussed these with my supervisor.
5 Think about how to obtain access to participants.	Approach hospital department dealing with diabetes – talk to doctor in charge.
… And so on	… And so on

There are several ways, such as the task list above, in which you can make headway with your research. It is simply a tool for thinking about what you're doing in an effective manner and then putting your ideas into practice. However, though we say 'simply', these ways of thinking are by no means easy and require considerable effort on your part. For example, you may begin your research with a precise purpose where your whole research programme is mapped out from the start. Alternatively – and much more likely – you will start with an area of interest and refine and focus it on the journey through your research. In chapter 6 of Cryer (2000, p. 61), 'Towards recognizing quality in research', Pat Cryer outlines the process of focusing, your research through an examination of the roles that you may perform as a research student. Four distinct categories she includes are:

- **Explorer – to discover a gap (or gaps) in knowledge around which to form a research problem.**

- **Detective and/or inventor – to find solutions(s) to the research problem that defines the gap(s).**

- **Visionary – to develop an original twist or perspective on the work and a fall-back strategy in case the work doesn't go according to plan, and (where necessary) to find a way of ring-fencing nebulous or discrete investigations into a self-contained piece of research appropriate for the award being sought.**

- **Barrister – to make a case in the thesis for solution(s) to the research problem.**

Though these are presented in the rough chronological order in which they arise during a research project, the boundaries between these roles are by no means completely clear-cut – there may well be movement to and fro between them throughout much of the process of the project. In Box 3.5 Carina Paine discusses the careful planning that went into decisions she made about her research.

Box 3.5   Planning and Reviewing the Research Area

Following the development of my initial proposal and draft research aims I conducted an extensive literature review. There were several areas of literature that were relevant and it was important to separate the issues I wanted to use to direct my research from other issues which, although of interest, did not require any further development.

From this initial review I developed some research aims, which looking back were somewhat vague and far too broad.

A lot of planning and reviewing of the research area was required in order to tighten my research aims. These became more focused and I developed some more detailed research hypotheses as I did more reading. By tightening my research aims I was able to make a realistic and achievable research plan for my three years of funding. Fortunately I realized early on that my PhD was only a

> **Box 3.5   (Continued)**
>
> 'snapshot' of the research area I was interested in. This helped me to focus and prioritize my work to meet the objective of producing a piece of work worthy of a PhD within my time scale.
>
> In developing my research plan I thought about a variety of experiments that could be interesting. Thinking about each experiment included the consideration of a number of factors (e.g. approval by the university's ethics board, the ease of access to participants, an appropriate time scale, the resources required, the amount of planning involved) in order to generate a number of best possible directions for my PhD to take. However, it was essential that the long-term plan for my PhD was flexible and could be continually revised as my research progressed.

Much of the time research ideas are just that – ideas. They are a good starting point for a research project but need refining to turn them into something that can be effectively researched. This refining begins as soon as you start trying to do something with your ideas. You may try to put them into some sort of order, for instance, or begin to look at how you might investigate them. Once you start to organize your ideas like this a whole series of sub-issues may emerge that were not initially considered. These may fog the research topic and make it very hard to grasp. So, though a good idea can come at any time, not all ideas are amenable to research.

Carina's account demonstrates clearly the iterative process of research. By building on her initial proposal for her research with a trawl of the relevant fields of literature, she was able to focus in on specific aims for the research. This in turn led to her deciding on a project that was both manageable and interesting. This account links back to the ideas presented in the learning outcomes outlined at the beginning of the chapter. Because she was willing and able to learn, Carina managed to focus her research ideas into a set of workable hypotheses. She understood the necessity to be creative and critical in designing her set of experiments and was able to recognize that she was only required to produce a 'snapshot' of her particular research area.

This readiness to accept the limitations of what can be achieved in three years is a feature of research that it is important to consider from the outset. As noted in Chapter 2, you are not required to revolutionize your topic area – though that may be an exciting idea – but merely to add in a novel, original way to the already existing body of knowledge. Some of these issues are addressed in further sections of this chapter, which focuses on bounding and being flexible in your research. Others feature in Chapter 5, which looks more closely at fine-tuning your project and finding a suitable framework in which to base your research. First, however, we present in Box 3.6 the account of student Jackie Topp, describing her initial decision-making process for her PhD.

Box 3.6   Developing an Idea

To develop my proposal, the broad outline presented at my interview needed much more focusing and refining in order for me to complete in three years. When I started on the PhD journey there were so many ideas and avenues that I could follow that the decision as to which way to go was very difficult to make at an early stage. However, I realized that whichever direction I took would be the right one for me. Slowly, I outlined my ideas, discussed them with my supervisors, and began to undertake a broad literature search covering the politics of disability and the topic of becoming a mother. I found there was very little written about disabled women becoming mothers and I knew that this mainly unexplored area would be my niche.

Jackie identifies a relatively unexplored area and designs a research project to fill this gap. However, she had to do much reading and planning to reach this point.

Using information taken from these examples, the rest of this section outlines some of the practical ways in which you can begin to focus your own ideas, and keep track of your progress.

Keeping a research journal

As was mentioned in Chapter 2, an important resource you create for your project is some kind of continuing record of its progression – ideas, and thoughts about how to research them, rough notes, task lists and so on. This will help meet the requirements for the sort of ongoing record that is now part of your PhD research progress as detailed below (and in more detail on the website).

Box 3.7   Progress Files and Personal Development Planning

For those of you working in the UK there is now a requirement by the Quality Assurance Agency (QAA) for all HE institutions to follow a similar procedure for recording the progress of their students. These records are briefly outlined here, but a fuller description is available on this book's website. Progress files and personal development planning also features in Chapter 12.

Box 3.7 (Continued)

Progress file

A progress file contains several different elements. First, a record, provided by the institution, of an individual's learning and achievement. Second, an individual's own personal records of learning and achievement, which can provide a resource from which personal statements, etc., can be derived. Third, a set of structured and supported processes aiming to help individuals to reflect on their own learning and to plan for their own educational career and development. This process is commonly known as:

Personal development planning

This is a structured and supported process by which an individual can reflect upon their own learning, performance and/or achievement and can plan their personal, educational and academic development. The aim is to enable students to understand more clearly what and how they are learning and to review, plan and take responsibility for it.

The full guidelines are available at the QAA website (there is a link to this on our book website).

In addition to these more structured requirements, it is also important that you keep your own – possibly slightly less formal – record of your PhD progression. The student task list in Box 3.4 included several that involved keeping a written record of different aspects of research. The most obvious way to do this is to keep some form of logbook or diary – what have become popularly known as research journals. You can use a research journal to record anything and everything to do with your research, as Carina Paine did (see Box 3.8).

Box 3.8 Carina's Research Journal

Throughout my PhD I kept a research journal in the form of a hardback A4 book (and had quite a few books in the end!). I used the journal to keep notes on meetings with my supervisors, notes on my data collection, information about the development and design of experiments, any ideas or questions I came up with, to write 'to do' lists and anything else I wanted to write down! It was really useful to keep a journal, mainly because all my notes were in one place and not lost on separate bits of paper.

Even though my own PhD was very different from this – I (Jane) adopted a qualitative methodology to explore the ways in which older women talked about their relationships – my own research record took a similar approach. I included supervision feedback, conference and workshop notes, comments from friends, abstracts that I submitted, minutes from meetings and so on. I also included my own reflective comments about various things that happened during the development of my research. Consequently it was a valuable means of accessing information that may not have seemed particularly significant at the time but whose usefulness often became more readily recognized in later stages of my research.

Keeping a written record is by no means the only method of recording your research process. For instance, in contrast to these examples, Jackie Topp stored her own PhD research record electronically. She had been recommended to keep a research journal by her supervisors but found keeping handwritten notes to be troublesome. However, acknowledging the usefulness of keeping at least some kind of record, she found a different method that she felt was more suitable for her. She typed quick notes on a range of aspects of her PhD and kept them in a diary folder on her computer. This enabled her to keep track of her ideas, and by maintaining a hard copy of them alongside her supervision notes and feedback she was able to easily access and refer back to them whenever necessary. These examples demonstrate that there are no hard and fast rules about how or where to keep your records. Whether you feel a hard copy or an electronic copy is most useful is a matter of personal preference. The point is to get into the habit of noting down things as they happen to you. There is more on keeping a research journal in Chapter 6 on 'Academic writing' and how this links into the writing process.

Activity 3.2

If you have not already done so, begin your own research journal – either electronic or handwritten (if electronic don't forget to keep a back-up!). Think about what you will find useful to record in it. One way you could begin is by recording your task list as outlined earlier in this section. You could then follow on with the activities from this book as you complete them.

Critical friends

The discipline of writing in a journal or constructing your ideas more formally, for example in essay form, helps you focus, because writing helps you to make judgements about the value of what you have come up with. The skill of academic writing is developed in more depth in Chapter 6, but for now we will look at one student's experience of writing in his PhD. In Box 3.9 John Smith, whose research explored features of knowledge management, highlights the importance writing had for him.

Box 3.9   Writing

At the beginning of my PhD I worked really hard on my literature research, reading every paper that was even remotely relevant to my research interests. I remember feeling lost among the amplitude of knowledge, research domains and their overlaps. What I was learning seemed like isolated islands in a vast ocean of knowledge and it was so difficult to make sense out of it. However, then someone advised me, 'Don't burn yourself out. The PhD is a marathon, not a sprint, you have to manage your resources'. And he was right, so I changed my attitude.
I started organizing my time, setting milestones, maintaining a rhythm, keeping track of my progress. The key was writing, writing and more writing. Summaries, ideas, progress reports, paper drafts, plans, etc., they all contributed significantly. It is only through writing that one reflects upon what she/he has read so far, discovers hidden connections and applies her/his own perspective and understanding. These texts are also logs, keeping track of what has already been done and function as drafts to work on and receive feedback from your supervisors. They are also work that is 'value for money' – they can be revised to become papers, or even chapters of the thesis itself.

However you record your ideas, getting feedback on them is a good idea from the earliest stages of your PhD. This is a staple of supervision sessions, and you may be asked to produce particular pieces of writing by your supervisors or you may have produced something that you want them to comment on. It is just as useful to share your ideas with your peers – perhaps other research students or academics familiar with your general area of research. Harry Wolcott (1990) points out that it is important to choose reviewers of your work with care and you should be particularly precise in telling them exactly what kind of criticism you feel will be the most helpful to you at each stage.

Be aware that in any piece of writing it is much easier to identify problems such as awkward sentences and grammatical errors than it is to say something constructive. However, by asking friends for feedback you have the opportunity to request a balanced view rather than getting comments focusing disproportionately on weaknesses or (equally unhelpfully) observations focusing solely on strengths. Constructive criticism is a key factor here.

Finding a good reviewer is about developing a relationship of trust. Inviting friends and/or fellow authors to be constructively critical about your writing – and perhaps returning the favour for them – is an accessible way of getting a balanced review of your work. As Wolcott suggests, it is fair to assume (rightly or wrongly) that friends and colleagues will do their best to enable you to say what you are trying to say rather than focusing on any yet-to-be-demonstrated literary competence. You may decide, for example, to ask a friend who is at the same stage of research as you, or someone you know who has a proven record of successful research writing in the academic field you are working in.

My own preference was to ask knowledgeable friends and peers to review my writing. Colleagues who belonged to the same study or research groups as myself proved particularly useful, even if they came from different academic fields; the fact that we all belonged to the same group meant we had some interests in common. For part-time students it may be more difficult to find a peer reviewer. You could ask your supervisor to suggest another research student or colleague. A dilemma that should be attended to here, in thinking about possible reviewers, is that no two people will agree completely on what you have written. Whether they are friends, research supervisors or even peer reviewers for something you are attempting to get published, they will all have their own perspective on what you have (or should have) written. There is no easy solution to these contradictions, but you should always keep in mind that this is your research and you know better than anyone what it is that you are trying to achieve. What your reviewers say may be useful, but it is up to you yourself to implement or ignore the comments that you are given.

3.3   Setting Your Boundaries

As should be clear by now, your research is a designed learning process, and an important part of the design is outlining a framework within which to work. In our experience, there are many reasons for wanting to be clear about what you want to do and how you can go about doing it when undertaking research. Clarity about this allows better judgements about the allocation of time and resources, and hence contributes to better quality research. Developing a research idea is a process of negotiation – with your research supervisors, with any other research stakeholders, and above all with yourself. Being very clear about what it is that you hope to do helps you to negotiate with others, because then it's a lot easier for them to understand.

Many students often have difficulties in the early stages of their research as readings and ideas can send them off in several different directions. As you start to explore a topic, it can suddenly seem overwhelming with too much and overly vague literature, unclear methods, and a bewildering mixture of theoretical perspectives. Sometimes the idea is just too big, and is impossible to study with any degree of certainty.

One of the simplest strategies you can use to begin to focus on what it is that you are doing is to set some boundaries – in other words decide what it is that you are not doing. By reviewing what you can eliminate in terms of methods, theory, empirical focus and so on, you make the job of focusing on something that you can complete within the scope of a research degree that much easier. Rather than being overly restrictive, boundary setting can be helpful in taking a creative approach to your research, because through having set safe limits to what you're focusing on you can have fun exploring what is left. And if you find that your boundaries no longer apply, then you can review them, but at least you're aware of the decision to change focus, and can weigh up the costs in doing so.

Working with boundaries

A boundary is nothing more than a conceptual line that distinguishes one thing from another. Making sense of our experiences in terms of boundaries is nothing particularly special, it seems central to the way humans think, and happens every time we name something to ourselves. So they arise everywhere in our experience, because they allow us to distinguish something from its background. When you think about your research in terms of boundaries, you are simply pointing to those things that you think are relevant to your research in contrast to everything else.

It is important to note that setting boundaries like this is an aid to focusing rather than a final end-point. An important part of working with boundaries is to revisit them regularly to assess whether they need to change. Vickers calls this the practice of 'grouping and regrouping of objects of our attention, without forgetting that the boundaries that we temporarily draw around them do not define the only ways in which they can properly be viewed' (Vickers, 1980, p. 5). The reward for the awareness of boundaries and a commitment to iteratively reassessing and renegotiating them is that you are much less likely to get stuck in inappropriate ways of thinking about and doing your research.

In order to give you an idea of how this might work in practice, have a look at the following example, which is based on my own PhD project (High, 2002) at the Open University. The project involved an investigation into whether a particular set of methodological and theoretical tools were appropriate to facilitating learning processes within sustainable development. The starting point for this was making sense of the research title 'learning systems for sustainable development', a process which took a year to really get to grips with. The table in Box 3.10 gives examples of boundaries to the research that were identified early on, and some discussion of the consequences of those boundaries for how the research was carried out.

Box 3.10   Research Boundaries and Their Entailments

Boundary	Explanation and comments	Practical consequences of recognizing this boundary
Sustainable development	I wanted to research the application of systems ideas in areas relevant to sustainable development, rather than in any other fields	When selecting case studies I needed to ensure that they were related to sustainable development, and therefore needed a good working definition for sustainable development
Systems theory	I was based in the systems department at the Open University, and needed to draw on the theoretical basis of my discipline.	This took a long time to get to grips with, because there is no coherent discipline to draw on. Instead I needed to become familiar with a number of strands of systems theory in order to be able to make an informed decision about which tradition to work with
Research into methodology	I sought to understand learning processes in sustainable development in order to contribute towards an approach which might help people improve them, rather than undertaking purely theoretical research or indeed purely action-oriented research	Braiding theory and practice means working with both in parallel. The empirical work therefore needed to be oriented towards action research *with* people, but without letting go of my own conceptual framework
Social research	I wanted to do research that involved people and took their activities as a focus	I chose research methods that were appropriate for social research.One consequence of this was that I needed to con-sider research ethics
Ethical research	I wanted to do research that was ethical, and considered the interests of the people I worked with	I needed to establish and maintain a set of ethical standards based upon my understanding of the conse-quences of social research, and established norms within my field

Activity 3.3

A simple activity in which you can begin to establish focus through boundaries is to spend some time constructing a table like the one in Box 3.10. Name boundaries for your project, and then think through some of the consequences that may occur. Notice how some of the boundaries named in the example above flowed out of the one before.

Setting milestones

Alongside conceptual boundaries, another important technique for staying on track with your research is thinking about milestones – intended boundaries in time. Setting milestones means making a list of critical review and target dates (for example, due dates for assignments to supervisor, workshop presentations or formal reviews). The basic principle is that planned work should take precedence over unplanned work, which is a way of getting around the problem of always saying, 'I must finish this by the end of the week', but then finding things have slipped. If you need to review your plans, that is fine, but it should be part of your regular planning to track how well you are doing.

If you have not made a promise to deliver, or been told to deliver, the chances of it happening on time are not that great. You may have some milestones set institutionally – key deadlines by which you are committed to finishing particular stages of your research and which are likely to be included in your progress file (discussed in Box 3.7) – and your supervisor(s) will, doubtless, ask you to deliver pieces of work at specific times. But you are the key person in formulating sensible milestones. They can be daily, weekly, monthly, or longer, but as a general rule they form a natural point in the research where you can assess your progress (Sharp et al., 2002, pp. 68–9). Your research journal is the obvious place to set yourself deadlines, but it is also worth making them public to help you stay on track, or at least to make you think through an explanation of why they are not met. One student's girlfriend set the deadline that she would only marry him once his thesis was submitted; it must have worked, because they did get married when planned!

We recommend a weekly and monthly stocktaking of your research deadlines, which need take no longer than an hour. However, there are also bigger milestones in the first year of a two- or three-year project. These might include:

1 **getting an analysis or software package up and running or gaining access to participants;**

2 presenting your thesis ideas and plan to your supervisor(s) and peers;

3 drafting a literature review.

Each major task actually constitutes a serious milestone that can be written up, and can then often be used as an early draft of part of your thesis. Treating the writing up as the milestone will help you get into the habit of writing early and often. Not only will it help you organize your thinking as you work and help you complete on time, but it will also bring home one of the basic realities of academic life: with few exceptions, research doesn't exist until it is written down.

Most PhD research students have two important early milestones (which are both core requirements for successful transfer on to a PhD from a postgraduate course). One is to produce a literature review for their project. This is the subject of Chapter 7, and will be dealt with in more detail there. The second is to produce a detailed work plan, which we take up in Chapter 5. If your research project is for one year, you will do this in the first few months, but for a two- or three-year project the detailed work plan will usually be produced at the six- to nine-month point. Mark these milestones on your schedule, and whenever you review your progress, make a point of considering whether you have made any progress towards them, and whether you are on schedule or not.

3.4 You've Got to Be Flexible

One of the main reasons for setting clear boundaries in your research is that it creates a safe platform from which you can then begin to look for the surprising elements of your ideas. By setting boundaries you can then 'go wild' inside them. They enable you to create the best conditions for creativity, while knowing that you will never drift too far away from the point of the project. The key to achieving this is to be flexible in your thinking about your research; many things may change throughout the process and an ability to assimilate new information and consequently to accommodate it somehow into the research is an absolute necessity for a successful outcome. A key point to keep in mind when doing research is that, in practice, it is seldom as easy or straightforward as the sequential pattern implied by, for example, Kat Stothard's task list in Box 3.4 or the discussion of setting milestones in the previous section. It is quite usual to have to go through similar procedures several times, and your work may overlap across its different phases so that at the same time as writing up one case study, for example, you may be completing the field research for another. There are several things that you can do to actively ensure the (relatively) smooth progression of your research. Some of these we've touched on already – such as careful planning – and others will follow in more depth in later chapters. However, the final section of this chapter is intended to draw your attention to some of the things that you can do quite easily yourself when things are not going according to plan.

Revising your plans

As we mentioned in the previous section, one of the easiest ways of keeping track of your research and monitoring your progress is to revise your plans regularly. By keeping on top of your own scheduling, and by being flexible in what you can do at any one time, you will be in a much better position to keep up with the demands of your research. Inevitably things will not always go according to plan, and this is where a flexible outlook will stand you in good stead. As we saw in the earlier examples in the chapter from Carina, Jackie and John, many things can hold you up in a research project: you may have to wait for ethics boards to meet; you may have supervisory problems; you may have to re-administer a questionnaire because you have suddenly discovered a major fault in one of the questions. Whatever the problem, you need to have contingency plans in place for when things go wrong. The important thing to remember is that being in charge of a research project such as a PhD or a Master's dissertation is very different from the structured programme generally involved in, for example, an undergraduate degree. There will often be a constant process of negotiation and renegotiation within the research project that requires movement between tasks. Being able to undertake different tasks in parallel is extremely important to the success of a research programme, and moving from one task to another and perhaps to yet another is a skill that develops as you go along. This is where it is useful to have an alternative timetable in which some tasks can be substituted for others. There are likely to be many parallel activities in your research project and your planning needs to allow for this.

A simplistic example is shown in Figure 3.1. Here you can see that Task C is one that can run in parallel with Tasks A and B. However, Task A must be completed before Task B can begin and similarly both Tasks B and C must be completed before you can begin Task D. In my own case (Jane), I worked for much of the time alongside my PhD research, so my own timetable included both PhD tasks and tasks to do with work as well as other, more personal, things that I had to fit into my schedule.

If, for example, an interview gets cancelled or a piece of equipment is suddenly unavailable, there is no reason that the whole day should be wasted. There are always other tasks that can replace those initially planned. One student, for example, who had planned an interview in Norway found that the person he wanted to talk to was on holiday for four weeks(!). He therefore brought forward another interview with a person

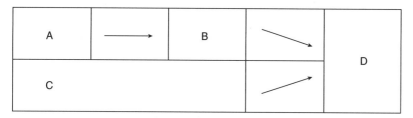

Figure 3.1   Networking tasks

in the UK. Ideally the interviews should have been the other way around, but that was not worth the delay. Apart from the normal day-to-day activities that accompany PhD life – shopping, childminding and so on – without exception every research project involves an inordinate amount of administrative work. This might be answering emails, filing research articles or visiting the library to track down that ever-elusive book. Even if there is no possibility of you substituting a major research task for whatever has had to be cancelled, any of these (often unappealing!) minor tasks can be used to fill in the time. We will end the chapter with a final activity.

Activity 3.4

To end this chapter, and to help you to begin actively thinking about flexibility, go back through the examples that we have presented in the chapter and identify places where you think flexibility has been a part of the process. Using these ideas as a base, design a schedule outlining how your own research tasks may overlap – either with one another or with other items that need including in your timetable. This is especially useful in enabling you to balance other demands such as work, family, social life and so on.

References

Cryer, P. (2000) *The Research Students's Guide to Success* (2nd edn). Buckingham: Open University Press.

High, C. (2002) 'Opening spaces for learning: a systems approach to sustainable development', PhD thesis, Centre for Complexity and Change, Milton Keynes, The Open University.

Sharp, J.A., Peters, J. and Howard, K. (2002) *The Management of a Student Research Project.* Aldershot: Gower Publishing Company.

Vickers, G. (1980) 'Education in systems thinking', *Journal of Applied Systems Analysis*, vol. 7, pp. 3–10.

Wolcott, H. (1990) *Writing Up Qualitative Research.* London: Sage.

4 Logics of Enquiry

Wendy Stainton-Rogers

LEARNING OUTCOMES

After reading this chapter and working on its associated activities you should be able to:

- Define positivist and constructivist approaches to research, list the ways in which they are similar to or different from each other, and locate your planned research in one or other approach.
- Explain what is meant by a 'logic of enquiry', describe three – induction, deduction and abduction – and explicate the differences between them, and say how explicating is different from explaining.
- Identify an example of two of the three logics of enquiry in your own field of research, and compare their benefits and drawbacks.
- Reflect upon your plans for the approaches and methods you will use in your research, drawing upon the insight you have gained by working on this chapter.

4.1 Introduction

What sorts of students raise alarm bells for supervisors? I reckon it's the ones who, right from the start, are convinced they've already got all the answers. All they need to do, they say, is 'get a bit of data' to back up their brilliant ideas, and the rest will be easy. Scary too are the students who arrive already doubting everything they wrote in their proposal and in a complete spin about what to do.

Thankfully, most students fall much more comfortably in between these two extremes – and with any luck that includes you. You've got a real sense of purpose and still feel excited by your topic while, at the same time, you're keeping an open mind and expect your ideas to change as you gain knowledge in your subject and expertise as a researcher.

This chapter is intended to kick-start this process. It encourages you to explore the different 'logics of enquiry' that underpin different kinds of research, and to consider which one (or maybe ones) best suit your project. To clarify this exploration, I have borrowed the term 'logics of enquiry' from Norman Blaikie (2000), who uses it to define the different ways that researchers can generate and test theories and thereby 'make a significant contribution to knowledge'.

So what is knowledge, anyway?

At first sight this may seem a very strange question – everyone knows what knowledge is, surely? It's what we know, as opposed to what we believe or surmise or assume (which are all rather subjective and could very well be wrong). Actually it's not at all that simple, as Activity 4.1 should persuade you.

Activity 4.1 Miss Lovely Legs

Miss Lovely Legs, Boksburg, 1974. (Photo: David Goldblatt.)

(from Terre Blanche and Durrheim, 1999)

What do you make of this photograph? Write a couple of paragraphs about what it tells you. What knowledge can you gain from it?

When you have done this, read the three different commentaries on the picture. Which one comes closest to the knowledge you gained?

Last night Charmaine du Preez was crowned Miss Lovely Legs Boksburg for 1974. Charmaine is a 2nd year student at Sukses Secretarial College and says her hobbies are reading, watching films and gym. Charmaine said that she was thrilled that the judges chose her out of so many deserving competitors and would try her utmost to live up to everything expected of her during her reign.

(Staff reporter, *Boksburg Times*)

Although one does not want to further denigrate the participants in such contests, nor ascribe personally malign motives to those who consume these images, the political implications of such 'cattle parades' are inescapable: women are turned into objects in a male-dominated world. Such practices are the visible manifestations of an all-pervasive patriarchal culture.

(Patsy Smith-Collins, *International Journal of Feminist Studies*)

In this photograph Goldblatt again explores the semiotic (and now perhaps even nostalgic?) possibilities of 1970s suburbia, so fetchingly oblivious of the larger political forces playing themselves out in the context of apartheid South Africa. The careful juxtaposition of the foregrounded white contestants and the predominantly black audience plays with the irony of white culture as an object of black consumption.

(Mandla Nkosi, *Art World*)

One picture, three very different 'ways of knowing'! This illustration comes from a recent research methods textbook written and published in South Africa. It makes the point, extremely powerfully, I think, that pictures like this convey multiple meanings, according to how they are 'read'. The newspaper staff reporter's version of what is going on comes across as highly 'factual', based upon an interview with the winner of the competition. Yet the feminist scholar's reading is entirely different. It focuses on highlighting quite other 'facts' about gender, as does the media studies commentator about race. Each reading tells us something – contributes to our knowledge. But whose knowledge is best – and how could we judge? The answer has to be, it depends on what question you are asking, and it depends upon the standpoint from which you are asking it.

Looking at the 'big picture'

So, where does this leave you? Keen, I hope, to 'stand back' and take a hard look at where you are going and how you will go about the research you will do for your thesis. In most fields this research will be empirical, and hence involve questions about which methods you will use, what kinds of data you will collect and how you will analyse them. But even in areas which are more interpretative, you still need to think carefully about the assumptions that lie 'behind' the choices you make about your research questions and the forms of interpretation you will use. Whatever you do, you need to start with a close scrutiny of the logic of your planned enquiry, and the ideological and philosophical assumptions upon which this logic is based.

Before you embark upon the major research project that will be at the core of your doctoral studies, it is crucial that you have some idea of what you are doing and why – the assumptions and judgements you are making. Otherwise you run the risk of what Curt (1994) calls the 'got-a-brand-new-hammer, what-can-I-bang-in?' approach to research, where the studies you do and how you do them depend more on your (or your supervisors') methodological comfort zone than clear-headed choices about the best way to go about them. Apart from anything, you will be expected to defend your choices in your thesis and your viva, so you may as well get them clear from the start. But much more importantly, it's far better to sort this out now than find, well into the project, that you are on the wrong track because you didn't fully understand the implications and hence didn't make purposive choices.

4.2   The Science Question

Life was a lot simpler fifty years ago. To study for a PhD, it was generally a simple choice between Arts or Science, and they were totally different. Scientists did empirical research, gathered data and tested hypotheses – and social scientists did much the same, albeit with sometimes rather different methods. By contrast, Arts students took an interpretational approach. Their aim was to gain a better-informed appreciation of some aspect of the topic they studied.

However, whichever approach was taken, pretty well everybody – from anthropologists to art historians, penologists to zoologists – assumed there were 'right answers' on which agreement could be reached and that true scholarship could uncover. So, for example, both a classicist and a physicist would agree that a PhD was a quest for the truth, whether that 'truth' was about what happened in ancient battles or what happens when metals get hot.

These days it's a lot more complicated, not least because of the impact of constructionist theories which radically challenge any and every claim to have an absolute benchmark for establishing facts – scientific or of any other kind. Added to this is an explosion in new disciplines (such as media and cultural studies), expansion of doctoral study into professional and applied fields (such as marketing and social work), and a rapid and growing breakdown of disciplinary boundaries. Taken together, these add up to a much more complex intellectual landscape where, research-wise, there are few simple paths to follow. Rather there are an almost infinite number of routes that could be taken. The question is, which one to choose?

Natural science – the one true route to knowledge?

In the arts, humanities and disciplines like cultural and media studies it is usually assumed that research is not based on science at all, but on interpretative methods of various kinds.

In terms of the rest, for a long time now the question has been asked: is there just one 'philosophy of science' – a single set of principles that underpin worthwhile and well-respected empirical research? Or are there different principles that apply to different kinds of research? For example, should research in the human (sometimes called social) sciences (such as anthropology and sociology) be pursued in different ways from natural sciences (like physics and chemistry)?

Karl Marx was certainly on the side of singularity: 'Natural science will in time subsume the science of man [*sic*] just as the science of man will subsume natural science: there will be one science' (Marx, 1975, p. 355). As a young man Sigmund Freud too declared his goal was to 'furnish a psychology that shall be a natural science' (Freud, 1950, p. 295) and for most of his career at least saw this as an ideal to be pursued. However, in later life he became convinced that 'mental events seem to be immeasurable and probably always will be so' (cf. Jones, 1955, p. 470).

Today there remains a strong contingent of researchers who regard the natural science model as the 'gold standard' for all research, irrespective of the field of interest. This viewpoint remains prevalent, for example, in psychology. A good illustration is this 'mission statement' from a popular introductory text:

> Social psychology employs the scientific method to study social behaviour ... science is a method for studying nature, and it is the *method*, not the people who use it, the things they study, the facts they discover or the explanations they propose, that distinguishes science from other approaches to knowledge. ... The alternative to science is dogma, or rationalism where understanding is based upon authority: something is true ultimately because authorities (e.g. the ancient philosophers, the religious scriptures, charismatic leaders) say it is so.

> (Hogg and Vaughan, 1998, pp. 6–7)

Human science

More than 50 years ago the phenomenologist, Alfred Schutz, argued for a distinct and separate science for studying the social, because:

> [T]he world of nature as explored by the natural scientist does not 'mean' anything to molecules, atoms and electrons. But the observational field of the social scientist – social reality – has a specific meaning and relevance structure for the beings living, acting and thinking within it.
>
> (Schutz, 1962, p. 59)

Human science, according to his argument, cannot be pursued as if humans had no stake in what is being investigated. People – what they think and do and how they see the world – are both the objects of research and they are the researchers.

There are a number of ways to describe this stance, but possibly the most common is *social constructionism*. A good illustration is the argument made by Donna Haraway in a chapter called 'Primatology is politics by other means'. In it she claimed that while the science of primatology (the study of social systems and culture in apes) is presented as objective and rational in its methods and analytics, it is not. Rather it is a storytelling craft:

> [L]ife and social sciences in general, and primatology in particular, are story-laden; these sciences are composed through complex, historically specific storytelling practices. Facts are theory-laden; theories are value-laden; values are story-laden. Therefore facts are meaningful within stories.
>
> (Haraway, 1984, p. 79)

Haraway was a primatologist herself at the time (these days she's more into cyborgs). She observed that in primatology's early days, only men did research. Women, if around at all, merely assisted them. At that time, as a consequence, she claimed, primatology's research and theorization concentrated on macho subjects like dominance, hierarchy, territory and competition among apes. However, when women got to take charge, they studied different, more girlie topics like co-operation and nurturing. What matters, she said, is not who does the best science, but who can tell the best stories – the most convincing accounts of what is going on and why.

Activity 4.2   Storytelling

This activity is best done with others – with other students, researchers or academics working in your field, or one or more of your supervisors. It's good fun, but also quite insightful.

> ## Activity 4.2   (Continued)
>
> Think of your own subject or field, and contemplate the implications of viewing it as a 'storytelling craft'. Who gets to tell the best stories these days? Are they the 'founding fathers', or have they been superseded by more convincing storytellers? How and why did the shift occur?
>
> You might also like to try turning one or more of its theories into a parable, folk story or Chaucerian tale. For example, Freud's theory of development can be recast as a *Jack the Dragon Slayer* tale, where growing up is all about facing – and overcoming – a sequence of challenges. Piaget's theory, by contrast, is the story of the *Ugly Duckling*, where growing up is more a matter of complete transformation.

4.3   Ontology and Epistemology

Let's now begin to get to grips with the philosophy. This entails considering two main aspects of enquiry – ontology and epistemology.

Ontology

Ontology addresses questions about what things are and their being-in-the-world. Ontology is about the nature of the world – what it consists of, what entities operate within it and how they interrelate to each other. Different ontologies make different assumptions.

Positivist ontology regards the world as objectively 'out there', real and completely separate from human meaning-making. It sees the world – whether the physical or the social world – as an ordered system, made of discrete and observable events that have objective reality and operate in a systematic and lawful manner. Viewing the world like this makes it perfectly feasible to study 'what it's like' and 'how it works', quite independently from any consideration of humans' role in making sense of it.

By contrast, *constructionist ontology* regards the world as we know it as, literally, just that – the world as we (humans) *know it*. Based on a constructionist epistemology, it asserts that the *only* world we can study is a semiotic world of meanings, represented in the signs and symbols that people use to think and communicate, language being the prime example.

Epistemology

Epistemology is the study of the *nature of knowledge* – what counts as valid knowledge, and how it can be gained. Basic questions asked about knowledge are: What can we know? How can we know it? Why do we know some things but not others? How do we acquire knowledge? Can knowledge be certain?

Positivist epistemology

Positivist epistemology regards knowledge as only gainable through gathering facts about the world through observing it in a systematic and objective manner. This is usually pursued through experimental method – the testing of hypotheses to gradually build and refine universal 'laws of nature'. In order for this to be possible, positivism holds that there is a straightforward one-to-one relationship between things and events in the outside world and people's knowledge of them. As Willig puts it: 'positivists believe that it is possible to describe what is "out there" and get it right' (Willig, 2001, p. 3).

Today few scientists claim that this is ever entirely possible, since human perception and understanding are fallible – people will always be somewhat selective and biased by their preconceptions (Chalmers, 1999). However, most natural scientists believe that they can progressively pin down 'the facts' and get close enough to reality to, at least, solve practical problems like curing diseases and finding new sources of energy that we can use when fossil fuels run out.

Constructionist epistemology

Constructionist epistemology views knowledge very differently. There are three key tenets:

1   **that knowledge is constructed rather than discovered;**

2   **it is multiple rather than singular;**

3   **it is a means by which power is exercised.**

Knowledge is constructed, not simply discovered. Constructionists do not deny the existence of a real, material world – a world of 'death and furniture' (Edwards et al., 1993). But they do deny that this real world can ever be simply '*dis*-covered' – as if all that needs to be done is to gradually strip off the veils of human ignorance to reveal the facts about the-world-as-it-really-is. Moreover, they stress that the knowledge obtained by natural science is – like all other knowledge – a *representation* of the 'real world', influenced by what scientists chose to observe, how they interpret what they find, and, crucially, the stories they tell about what they have observed and found.

There is not just one true knowledge. Consequently, constructionists believe there is no way to get *direct* knowledge about the real world. Therefore constructionist epistemology holds that there will never be one single reality (i.e. one true knowledge). Rather, people construct a variety of different knowledges, and each of these knowledges is made – and made real – by human meaning-making. A good example is the knowledge constructed by medical science. This knowledge is technologically pretty good at telling us, say, that avoiding 'risky' sex can reduce the likelihood of becoming infected with HIV. But it's not nearly as good at telling us why some people do engage in risky sex, even though they know it is dangerous. And it's no good at all at telling us whether risk-takers should be refused expensive drug treatment if they do become infected.

Knowledge and power. Constructionism draws on postmodern theory, which offers an extensive and elaborate body of theorization about the relationship between knowledge and power. It holds that those who create knowledge thereby gain power. Friedson (1986), for example, has described doctors as the 'architects of medical knowledge' who thereby gain control over what is defined as an illness and what is not. This gives doctors power over what happens to others – whether they can be free or locked up, or even, in some cases, whether they live or die. Constructionists thus not only challenge the claim that natural science is the only way to discover 'the facts', they also tell us to be wary of the power this gives to science to tell us what is and what is not true, especially when dealing with social actions and phenomena. Since scientists are human, they always have a stake in the stories they tell about human interests and concerns, as Haraway argued so persuasively.

Comparing positivism and constructionism
To bring out the contrast, it is helpful to compare the two:

Positivism	Contructionism
Regards the world as *objectively* 'out there', real and completely separate from human meaning-making.	Claims that the *only* world we can study is a world of meanings, represented in the signs and symbols that people use to think and communicate.
Asserts there is only one true, objective knowledge that transcends time and cultural location.	Accepts that there are multiple knowledges, and that knowledge is highly contingent on time and cultural location.
Views knowledge as based on facts that are 'out-there-in-the-world' waiting to be discovered.	Views knowledge as constructed through people's meaning-making.
Asks of knowledge 'is it true?'	Asks of knowledge 'what does it do?', 'how can it be used – by whom, and to what ends?', 'whose interest does it serve?', 'what does it make possible?'

Activity 4.3

Here you need to be able to compare two different studies. They should come from as different fields as you can possibly find, but one must be positivist and the other constructionist. Perhaps ask your supervisor or one of your research student colleagues to suggest two such papers. If possible, get hold of the original paper describing the study. Read them carefully, thinking of these questions:

In what ways are the two studies different? This should be easy, but try to come up with at least one difference you have not thought of before.

In what ways are they similar? This is probably going to be harder, but think laterally and be prepared to include what may seem like trivial similarities.

When you have done this, make a list of the things that surprised you. See what insight you can gain by seeking either to explain or to explicate these surprises. We'll come back to this later.

4.4   Logics of Enquiry

Norman Blaikie (2000), in a fascinating book about designing social research, adopted a term which I think is extremely helpful – logics of enquiry. I don't always agree with him, but his systematic examination of the logics *behind* different research designs brings considerable clarity to what is often a rather muddled area. Blaikie identifies four logics of enquiry, but here I will concentrate on just three: induction, deduction and abduction.

Induction

Induction is a process of drawing inferences from observations in order to make generalizations. Early advocates like Francis Bacon saw it as the use of meticulous observation and measurement, conducted with a mind cleared of all prejudices, in order to gain access to the objective facts of nature. Ideally, it consists of four main stages:

Observation	Observe and record all facts without being selective or having any preconceptions about their significance.
Analysis	Analyse, compare and classify these facts to identify regularities, without reference to any hypothesis.
Inference	From this analysis of regularity, infer generalizations about the relations between the facts, i.e. the 'laws of nature'.
Confirmation	Test these 'laws of nature' through further observation of facts.

Within the inductive strategy, knowledge is gained by gathering objective data in order to establish regularities, applying inductive logic and thus producing general laws of cause and effect. The plausibility of a general law increases as more and more instances are observed.

Another important feature of induction is that it *derives* theory from the observations made. Bacon saw it as reading 'the book of nature' – a kind of uncovering (or discovering) facts-of-nature through stripping away preconceptions.

Deduction

The deductive logic of enquiry is in marked contrast. Whereas induction collects and analyses data without preconceptions, deduction (often called hypothetico-deduction) is explicitly based on preconceptions of a kind – that is, hypotheses drawn from theories. Deduction is theory-driven.

While its roots go back to Euclid and Aristotle, contemporary hypothetico-deductivism is based on Popper's attempt to overcome the limitations of induction (Popper, 1959). He argued that just because repeated observations may 'confirm' a general law, this does not – and cannot ever – prove that it is true. However many observations you make, and however convincing the evidence seems, there is always, logically, a small but nonetheless real possibility that the pattern of regularity you have observed is a matter of chance or your imagination.

Popper argued that induction can generate hypotheses but it cannot test them. To test a hypothesis it is necessary to use a deductive approach. Deduction thus involves putting a rule or a theory's predictions to the test, but crucially, in ways that allow for it to be *disproved*. This may seem to you an odd thing to do. Was Popper really arguing that researchers should set out to deliberately prove that their theories are wrong? Not at all; rather he was saying that studies must be designed in such a way that the hypothesis *can* be falsified.

Popper's argument can be summarized as follows:

1 **The world operates in a lawful manner, and the aim is to discover these laws.**

2 **This is done by generating theories and testing hypotheses about cause and effect, in order to be able to explain the how and why of the world.**

3 **However, it is not possible to unequivocally establish these laws. All that can be done is to eliminate false theories, thereby moving gradually closer to the truth.**

4 **But we have no way of knowing for certain when we have arrived at a true theory, so even those theories that have survived testing must be regarded as provisional.**

Explanatory research

So far I have concentrated on the differences between induction and deduction. However, induction and deduction share in common the positivist assumptions about epistemology and ontology (as described earlier). Crucially they also share two inter-linked features: a common goal – to *explain* the world; and a common approach to dealing with complexity – *reductionism*.

Explanation is at the core of the positivist quest for knowledge. The word 'explain' comes from the Latin *explanare*, and means, literally, 'to level out' as in rolling out pastry. The primary purpose of explanation is to produce a lawful account of cause and effect – that is, one expressed as a simple, general law.

As such positivism is highly *reductionist* – it smoothes out complexity. As the theories get fine-tuned, the generality usually gets reduced somewhat in order to reduce complexity. But even when research is conducted at a very fine-tuned, detailed level, there is always a strong reductionism going on, given the vast number of potential factors that will be involved in any situation. In other words, to deal with the immense complexity of the world, positivism seeks to exclude it.

Explanation thus involves getting rid of extraneous detail to get to the 'simple truth' of lawful cause and effect. The philosopher Hempel describes explanation as a process of seeking to fit 'the phenomenon to be explained into a pattern of uniformities' that 'shows that its occurrence was to be expected, given the specified laws and the pertinent particular circumstances' (Hempel, 1968, p. 50). To search for explanation is to seek for the 'gold' of underlying lawfulness by getting rid of all extraneous 'dross' of massive amounts of detail.

Induction does this by looking for regularity. Deduction does it by developing hypotheses that can be tested by selecting just a small number of variables to study and seeking to exclude all others. Data is gathered and then analysed through another purification process – statistical analysis. The product is an explanation – an abstract and pure statement of cause and effect.

Explicatory research

Now let us turn to constructionist research, which, as we have seen, assumes that the world is a product of the ways people construct, manage and interpret meaning, and gaining new knowledge is always a process of interpretation. Another way of putting this is to see it as having a different goal from positivist research – not explanation but explication.

Together with Joan Pujol, I have argued that explication is a different way to deal with the problem of complexity, which avoids some of the problems of seeking an *explanation*.

> Explaining amounts to a process of concealment – concealment of complexity. It strives to cover up all the irritating little bits and bats that cannot be neatly accommodated within pre-existing theoretical frameworks. But complexity is stubborn stuff. No sooner has explanation tied it down in one place, it pops out in another. Thus, inevitably, explanation continually spawns a 'residue of the unexplained'. This outpouring of this residue requires the constant creation of new theory machines to process it. But as no theory machine can ever completely dispatch of the irritatingly persistent 'residue of the unexplained', there is a constant proliferation of theories.
>
> (Pujol and Stainton Rogers, 1996)

The argument we are using here is that when positivist method is used to study the highly complex (such as things going on around human meaning-making), it can all too easily become a 'theory machine' that has gone out of control. Like the sorcerer's apprentice, it can begin to drown in a proliferation of theories it generates, where each generality is successively made more and more detailed and specific. But to no avail: grind the theory machine as it may, it always leaves behind a 'residue of the unexplained' and always will. Hence, in situations of high complexity, explicatory rather than explanatory research should be pursued.

The word 'explicate' comes from the Latin *explicatus*, and means, literally, 'to unfold'. Explication does not try to get round complexity by aspiring to fit phenomena into an existing theoretical framework. It deals with complexity in a different way – through abduction. It uses anomalies and inconsistencies to home in on just those elements of a complex situation that do not 'fit the facts'. Explicatory research treats the 'residue of the unexplained' as the focus of enquiry rather than an irritating 'blip' to be ironed out or ignored. It involves deliberately looking for 'the irritating little bits and bats that cannot be neatly accommodated within pre-existing theoretical frameworks' and scrutinizing them carefully, for they may well be the most valuable clues to solving the puzzle of what is going on.

Abduction

Abduction is a much less familiar term than either deduction or induction. It is most associated with the writings of the philosopher Charles Sanders Peirce (see, for example, Peirce, 1940/1955), who was involved in the development of semiotics. Peirce defines abduction as 'the process of forming an explanatory hypothesis' (Peirce, 1955, p. 67).

The abductive logic of enquiry involves *constructing* new theory rather than testing it, by a process of identifying naturally occurring surprises or deliberately creating them. To understand how this works, it helps to start from Peirce's formal statement of the logic behind abduction (such a statement is called a syllogism):

Result – The surprising fact, C, is observed.

Rule – But if A were true, C would be a matter of course (i.e. not in the least surprising).

Case – Hence, there is reason to suspect that A is true.

This is easier to make sense of by way of an example. I have used one suggested by a psychologist, Gary Shank, who has written the most accessible account of abduction I have found so far (well worth reading if you have the time: Shank, 1998).

Box 4.1 An illustration of abduction

An example can make abduction easier to understand. Think of a band of skilful hunters who get their prey through having extensive knowledge about how to track and find them. The hunters need to be able to identify different hoof marks and droppings and to recognize different smells and different patterns of broken twigs. What happens when they notice something surprising, such as a smell they have not come across before? They have to try to work out what kind of animal this smell comes from. They do this by drawing on the knowledge they already have.

Let us assume that this band of hunters have hunted in this terrain for many years, and they have not encountered any new animals in all that time. So it is unlikely that some new beast has suddenly moved in (this is possible but unlikely). What do they make of the new smell? Their best hunch might be that the smell must come from a familiar animal that they already know about. Something therefore must have happened to bring about this smell.

Now the hunters have to consider what that could be. To do this they need to draw upon their existing knowledge again, and this may include the observation that the only circumstances where they have noticed animals giving off different smells before has been during their mating season. Although this is something that they have not come across with all the animals they are familiar with, they have observed it before in some cases. So, they will conclude, the most likely explanation is that this is the mating-season smell of an animal they know, but have not observed during the mating season before. This cuts their work considerably. All they now need to do is work out which are the animals for which

---

Box 4.1 (Continued)

they do not already know about their mating-season smell. Then they know that the smell must come from one of these.

Shank (1998) re-expresses the syllogism like this:

Result – This is an unusual smell.
Rule – It is reasonable to suppose that animals give off unusual smells during their mating season.
Case – This quite possibly is the smell of a familiar animal during the mating season.

Another way of understanding what abduction means is to accept the argument that it was *abduction*, not deduction, which enabled Sherlock Holmes to solve crimes (Sebeock and Umiker-Sebeock, 1979). Holmes had the knack of being able to pinpoint the clues that mattered – discrepancies that did not fit. It was by finding a solution for these puzzles that Holmes so impressively revealed 'who-dun-it?'.

Shank argues that we should give up on proliferating ever more detailed models and theories and, instead, concentrate on developing the craft tools to pursue research into meaning. And abduction, he says, is the way to go. Just as Sherlock Holmes would always reach a point of identifying the crucial clue – such as 'the dog that did not bark' – abductory research deliberately looks for the 'residue of the unexplained': anomalies, inconsistencies and incongruities in what has been examined. And just like Sherlock Holmes, the researcher then has to puzzle out what can possibly account for the anomaly. This then provides not an explanation (i.e. an explanatory statement of cause and effect) but an explication: an unfolding and uncovering of what is likely to be going on. Researchers, Shank says, do not need to wait to be surprised – though they should treasure serendipitous surprises when they come across them. Surprises can be made to happen.

Go back now and look at your notes from Activity 4.3. Your task was based on one of the methods Shank has suggested for doing abductory research – juxtaposition. Looking for surprising similarities between things that are very different, he suggests (or surprising differences between very similar things), offers a means to gain insight we would not otherwise find.

Paradigm shifts

Whether by induction or deduction, positivist researchers generally seek to gain knowledge of the world by systematically refining their theories. The aim is to build ever more accurate and sophisticated models of social processes and phenomena. However, another philosopher of science, Thomas Kuhn (1970), argued specifically that this kind of incremental fine-tuning of knowledge is not the only form of progress. Indeed, he claimed, this is not how innovative progress is made:

> Normal science ... is a highly cumulative enterprise, eminently successful in its aim, the steady extension of the scope and precision of scientific knowledge. ... Yet one standard product of the scientific enterprise is missing. Normal science does not aim for novelties of fact or theory and, when successful, finds none. New and unsuspected phenomena are, however, repeatedly uncovered by scientific research, and radical new theories have again and again been invented by scientists. History even suggests that the scientific enterprise has developed a uniquely powerful technique for producing surprises of this sort.
>
> (Kuhn, 1970, pp. 52–3)

I contend that what Kuhn is going on about here is *abduction*. The scientific discoveries that really capture our attention, where a real breakthrough is made, are not through induction or deduction but abduction. Alexander Fleming's discovery of penicillin was just such a discovery. The story goes that he was preparing culture dishes of bacteria in order to be able to study the effects of various chemicals. One day he came into the lab and noticed that one of them had gone mouldy. He was about to throw it away as it contained 'contaminated material' when he noticed something odd. Around the mould was a clear area. Strange, he thought, what is going on? He looked for an explanation of this surprising observation. The best explanation he could come up with was that the mould seemed to be killing off the bacteria. The next stage was to test his explanation using the hypothetico-deductive method and, well, the rest, as they say, is history!

Activity 4.4   Abductory Research

Your task here is to identify a piece of research that uses an abductory logic of enquiry in your own field of interest. You are looking for a method that works by looking for inconsistencies, contradictions, anomalies.

(Hint: Look back at the commentaries on 'Miss Lovely Legs'). Alternatively, consider discoveries like that of penicillin.)

Write notes explaining why your example is abductory.

4.5   Review and Conclusions

My interpretation of the main similarities and differences between the three logics of enquiry is set out in Table 4.1.

Table 4.1 Logics of enquiry

Logic of enquiry	Paradigm	Epistemology	Ontology	Research aim	Data are gathered	Method
Inductive	Positivism	Knowledge is objective and can be tested against a benchmark of 'truth'	The world exists 'out there', separate from human meaning-making. It consists of discrete and observable social events and phenomena that are lawfully related.	To explain the world in terms of 'laws of nature'	... to develop theories	Observe the world, identify systematic regularities, induce universal laws and increase confidence in them by further observation
Deductive					... to test theories	Develop theories, derive and test hypotheses in ways that allow them to be falsified
Abductive	Constructionism	Knowledge is constructed, multiple and a means to exercise and/or resist power	The world as we 'know' it is constructed through human meaning-making. It is a world of representations, signs and symbols.	To explicate the social world – to gain insight and understanding of how it operates	... to develop hypotheses	Observe or create anomalies or surprises – examine 'the residue of the unexplained'

Before you say it, I will acknowledge that it is highly reductionist! It vastly oversimplifies, but I hope you also find it helpful to clarify what you are contemplating in terms of your research.

Activity 4.5 Reflection

Your final task is to reflect upon your planned research, having completed this chapter. Some aspects you may want to consider include:

1 What is the logic of enquiry I am planning to follow?
2 How am I going to manage complexity?
3 Am I looking for explanations or explication?
4 How convinced am I that these are the right choices?
5 Should I consider other alternatives?
6 If so, what do I need to do next?

It would be useful to discuss the result of this activity with your supervisor.

References

Blaikie, N. (2000) *Designing Social Research: The Logic of Anticipation*. Cambridge: Polity Press.

Chalmers, A.F. (1999) *What Is This Thing Called Science?* (3rd edn). Buckingham: Open University Press.

Curt, B. (1994) *Textuality and Tectonics: Troubling Social and Psychological Science*. Buckingham: Open University Press.

Edwards, D., Ashmore, M. and Potter, J. (1993) 'Death and furniture: the rhetoric, theology and politics and theory of bottom line arguments against relativism', mimeograph, Discourse and Rhetoric Group, Loughborough University.

Freud, S. (1950) 'Project for a scientific psychology', in the *Standard Edition of the Complete Psychological Works of Sigmund Freud*, vol. 1. London: Hogarth Press.

Friedson, E. (1986) *Professional Powers: A Study of the Institutionalization of Formal Knowledge*. Chicago: University of Chicago Press.

Haraway, D. (1984) 'Primatology is politics by other means', in R. Bleir (ed.), *Feminist Approaches to Science*. London: Pergamon.

Hempel, C. (1968) *Philosophy of Natural Science*. Hemel Hempstead: Prentice-Hall Europe.

Hogg, M.A. and Vaughan, G.M. (1998) *Social Psychology* (2nd edn). Hemel Hempstead: Prentice-Hall Europe.

Jones, E. (1955) *Sigmund Freud: Life and Work*, vol. 2. London: Hogarth Press.

Kuhn, T.S. (1970) *The Structure of Scientific Revolutions* (2nd edn) Chicago: University of Chicago Press.

Marx, K. (1975) *Early Writings*. Harmondsworth: Penguin Books.

Peirce, J.S. (1940) 'Abduction and induction' in J. Buchler (ed.), *The Philosophy of Pierce: Selected Writings*. London: Routledge & Kegan Paul (republished as *Philosophical Writings of Pierce*, New York: Dover, 1955).

Popper, K.R. (1959) *The Logic of Scientific Discovery*. New York: Basic Books.

Pujol, J. and Stainton Rogers, W. (1996) 'Explication', *Manifold*, vol. 6, 17–19.

Schutz, A. (1962) *Collected Papers I: The Problem of Social Reality*. The Hague: Martinus Nijhof.

Sebeok, T.A. and Umiker-Sebeok, J. (1979) '"You know my method": a juxtaposition of Sherlock Holmes and C.S. Pierce,' *Semiotica*, vol. 26 (3/4), pp. 203–50.

Shank, G. (1998) 'The extraordinary ordinary powers of abductive reasoning', *Theory and Psychology*, vol. 8 (6), pp. 841–60.

Terre Blanche, M. and Durrheim, K. (1999) 'Histories of the present: social science research in context', in Durrheim, K. and Terre Blanche, M. (eds), *Research in Practice: Applied Methods for the Social Sciences*, Cape Town: Cape Town University Press.

Willig, C. (2001) *Introducing Qualitative Research in Psychology: Adventures in Theory and Method*. Buckingham: Open University Press.

Further readings on this subject are on this book's website.

5 Planning and Organizing your Research

Chris High and Jane Montague

LEARNING OUTCOMES

After reading this chapter and working on its associated activities you should be in a position to:

- Show initiative, develop your ability to work independently and be self-reliant.
- Assign yourself key tasks and schedule your time.
- Set your first milestone.
- Draw up a work plan for the project development phase of your research and an outline plan to completion.
- Identifying funding needs and sources, and make a case for receiving resources.
- Identify training needs to fulfil your work plan.
- Develop and maintain co-operative networks and working relationships with supervisors, colleagues and peers, within the institution and the wider research community.
- Demonstrate self-discipline, motivation, and thoroughness.

5.1 Introduction

A research degree contains an important tension right at its heart. On one hand you will receive guidance and training that will help you learn the skills a professional researcher needs to plan, develop and carry out research projects. On the other, you will have significant autonomy. You may have previous experience of contract research or of planning and organizing projects. Alternatively, you may be part of a larger research team, working on a joint project. Nevertheless, your own research will be yours in a way that may not be familiar. The tension is significant because it will not always be clear what it is that you need to know in order to complete a successful project and become a better researcher, but you will sometimes need to move forward anyway.

While your research supervisors and your institution have a duty to provide you with guidance and training, their stake in what you do is different from yours. Realistically, your project is not going to take up very much of a supervisor's time and attention, but it will occupy a large part of your own. They want you to complete a project, but as was discussed in Chapter 3, it is your responsibility to narrow down which project you can and want to do, and it is your task rather than theirs to carry it out. Part of moving towards the goal of being an independent researcher is learning how to move from an idea of what to research to an idea of how to research it. One of the most practicable ways for you to learn this is to take responsibility for the planning process yourself. Rather than expecting your supervisors to tell you what to do, it is much more productive to rely on them for critical feedback on your ideas. Being proactive and presenting a plan to them that they can help you improve will lead to much more useful feedback. You are far more likely to be able to understand their advice if you have first invested in your work yourself.

The aim of this chapter is to help you to get to the point where you have enough material on your proposed research to present to your supervisors an outline of what you want to do and how you want to do it. Building on the exercises in Chapter 3, this chapter will lead you through some of the planning and organizing tasks you will need to undertake. This chapter also gives you an opportunity to think about some of the generic competencies that you will be able to use in the future (see the discussion in Chapter 12, particularly Section 12.4). Clearly, if you want to go into a research career, nearly everything you do within your PhD research is an opportunity to develop skills that you will need in the future. Even if you choose not to continue along this path, the expertise developed through project planning for postgraduate research will serve you well in many different fields. As was discussed in Chapter 1, and is picked up in Chapter 12, there is an increasing emphasis on transferable skills in the way that postgraduate training is constructed, and both the input from your supervisors, as well as that from any institutional training programmes you are expected to take part in, should benefit you. Your task here is to pay attention to the connections between what you are doing during your degree and what you might do afterwards, though you need to strike a balance between looking to the future and your most important link to it – finishing your degree.

5.2 Getting Organized

It is sometimes said that there are three key reasons why students experience difficulty in research projects. The first is trouble selecting a 'suitable' topic – one where it is possible to find out enough for it to be interesting and worth doing, without trying to do too much. The second reason is selecting an appropriate analytical framework – a means by which understanding can be enhanced. These two issues have been quite prominent in the last two chapters, through themes such as bounding and focusing, and the logics of enquiry. The third issue, dealing with your resources, forms the basis of this chapter. By resources, we mean all factors that support your research and over which you have some influence: time, money, relationships and, of course, your own skills and talents. The degree of control you have over these resources and their relative importance will vary according to the particular details of your project and the institutional setting in which you are working. The one that is most often critical is the way that you use your time, and we shall therefore pay a lot of attention to it in the following sections.

Planning the whole of your research period is key to its success, and the early stages are of the utmost importance. It is possible, if enough attention is given to it at this time, to make a reasonable plan for the whole project. Obviously, it is harder to see how things will happen during the later stages, and they will not be as clearly focused as the earlier ones, but nevertheless it is important to develop a plan for the whole period. This will give you some idea of what you need to do, when you need to do it, and what you need to have done already in order to start each activity. As a starting point for thinking about the planning of your research project, take a look at the three stages of a research project that Buchanan (1980) identifies: deciding what to do, doing it, and communicating what has been done (see Table 5.1).

Table 5.1   Stages of the research process

A Deciding what to do	1	Decide topic
	2	Define objectives
	3	Choose methodology
	4	Obtain information sources
B Doing it	5	Collect data
	6	Analyse data
C Communicating what has been done	7	Develop conclusions
	8	Develop recommendations
	9	Notify organization, or source of information, with findings

Source: Buchanan, 1980, pp. 45–8.

Buchanan's stages of research refer to generic processes that take place in many different kinds of research projects, and not just postgraduate research. In your case, stage 9 is likely to focus on writing a thesis, though you might also consider reporting to the people and organizations directly involved in your research as well as to a wider academic audience through conferences or in published articles.

Now take a look at the plan in Table 5.2, which is a schema that includes some of the possible steps in the research process for a PhD. Compare the early stages of this

Table 5.2   Important tasks for a PhD

Project development

Research proposal and mission statement
Literature review
Choosing a bibliographical system/package
Setting up a meeting system and schedule
Keeping records/research journal
Plan the whole research period and process
Investigate similar research theses done by others
Attend relevant courses and take training
Develop research questions/hypotheses
Plan for access to research sites, archives and/or equipment
Begin developing methods
First-year report and/or developed project proposal
Feedback and adjust research plan

Carrying out research

Develop method
Negotiate access to equipment, archives, field sites or interviewees
Design and conduct experiments/fieldwork
Begin analysis
Continue ideas log book and work research journal
Start drafting chapters
Extend and deepen reading
Keep record of readings
Adapt meeting style
Review plan
Annual research report
Seek feedback
Respond to feedback

Reporting your research
Update reading
Complete experiments
Complete analysis
Interpret results
Develop recommendations
Complete chapter drafts
Seek feedback
Respond to feedback

Source: Adapted from Murray, 1996, p. 5.

schema with the task list you developed in Chapter 2 (Activity 2.8) for the first few months of your project. They may well differ from this list in some respects, for example the time scale – for a Master's dissertation this will be much shorter. However, many of the tasks will be the same, and can be used as the basis for your own project plan.

Take especial notice of the tasks in italics, which indicate where writing is required. We emphasize the need to write all the way through the research process, because it is an important aspect of planning, and is often put off when actually it is required right from the beginning. It is very easy to let things slip and to fail to address important issues unless you confront yourself with them in print. But even more importantly, the time you need to set aside for writing is a major constraint. Because almost all research tasks have a writing component, it cannot be left until later in the research process. The reporting is when you should be pulling everything together based on draft material you already have, rather than starting from scratch. Advice on strategies with which you can approach the writing task is the subject of Chapter 6, 'Academic writing'.

Getting organized is important, because research always involves an element of risk and uncertainty and you can never be sure that all the information will be available at the time you need it. Some projects may have to be revised or even discarded because of inadequate information. Careful selection of your topic may have mitigated some of the risk and uncertainty inherent in a project, but there is still the problem of managing available resources, especially your time. Thus, although uncertainty means that your plan is likely to change as you go along and hence should be revisited periodically, it does not mean that you should not put effort into developing a research plan. Sharp et al. (2002, p. 51) outline the major components of this planning, covering aspects such as clarifying your aims and objectives, defining activities necessary for you to achieve these, identifying 'milestones' in your research and measuring your progress in relation to them (this aspect is discussed in more depth later in the chapter). Along with helping you to maintain a realistic focus on your research, making it a more manageable project overall, Sharp et al. point to several other advantages of planning, saying that it:

1 reduces the risk of overlooking something important;

2 helps you to realize when you have run into difficulties;

3 shows the interrelationship between your activities;

4 orders your activities so that everything does not happen all at once;

5 helps you keep track of the resources you have control over and identify what you rely on others for – money, access to people and facilities and so on – so that you can make suitable arrangements in good time;

6 indicates whether your objectives are feasible with the resources available – if not, something needs to change;

7 if you identify that you need to undertake particular training or that you need additional funding, your planning framework will give you some idea of the overall scale of your need;

8   provides discipline and motivation by indicating targets or milestones, and so is good for morale as you pass each milestone. It shows you are getting somewhere! Experience suggests that the best way to successful completion of the project as a whole is the successful completion of intermediate stages.

Activity 5.1

Using Table 5.2 as a starting point, make a preliminary list of the tasks that you think will be necessary in the project development phase of your research. Go on to sketch out the activities for the whole project (i.e. the 'Carrying out research' and 'Reporting your research' phases). Adapt this framework as necessary, particularly if you are undertaking a Master's dissertation or MPhil project.

5.3   The Problem of Time

Depending on what sort of research degree you are pursuing, and whether you are a part-time or a full-time student, you could be committed to anything from three months to six years of research. For a PhD, it is common to feel that there is so much time – how can the work expand to fill it? So why do students not finish on time? How can you finish on time? When asked at a viva voce how quickly they could have done their research, a typical reply is in about half the time – even allowing time for coffee, beer and email! In this section we offer some suggestions for preparing a time budget and time schedule.

We all tend to underestimate the time required for completing a research project, hence a formal, detailed, estimating approach is likely to yield a better calculation than an overall estimate that does not draw on any type of breakdown. However, even this detailed approach needs to incorporate a degree of flexibility – it is impossible to predict exactly what is going to happen over the course of the research process. The key therefore is to make a plan, and then review it regularly to check whether your assumptions still make sense.

Some typical activities for a questionnaire-based quantitative social science PhD are listed in Table 5.3, where Sharp et al. (2002) estimate durations in weeks. For PhDs based on a different methodology or in the humanities, some of the activities will be different or given a different weighting, but the main thing to see here is that the total is a little over three years! Even so, it allows only nine weeks for drafts of the three early chapters, which are likely to include a significant literature review. Note that Sharp et al.'s list is more detailed than the generic list in Table 5.2, although it does not include

Table 5.3 List of activities for a quantitative student research project in the social sciences

Activity number	Activity description	Estimated duration (weeks)
1	Written statement of concepts and theories	3
2	First draft of questionnaire for pilot study	6
3	Finalize questionnaire for pilot study	1
4	Decide likely method of analysing response to survey	4
5	Select participants for pilot study	4
6	Acquire statistical skills	8
7	Attend course on use of standard computer package	6
8	Write drafts of early thesis chapters (three say)	9
9	Carry out pilot study	4
10	Review pilot study	3
11	Prepare questionnaire for survey	4
12	Decide target population and sampling details	4
13	Carry out survey	12
14	Process data for computer	6
15	Interpret computer output	6
16	Evaluate nature and extent of response to survey	4
17	Write paper for presentation at conference	4
18	Relate findings to concepts/theories/hypotheses	6
19	Decide and carry out any further analysis or research	12
20	Complete writing of draft chapters (five say)	15
21	Review and edit thesis	10
22	Correct thesis and obtain bound copies	4
23	Prepare for oral examination	2
24	Allowance for holidays, job interviews, illness and general contingencies	24

Source: Sharp et al., 2002, p. 55.

the need to take relevant courses. It is used here as a guide to help you think about your work plan, though of course the research tradition you are working within may quite radically change the assumptions embodied in a similar list for your own research plan.

The estimated *duration time* referred to by Sharp et al. is the *elapsed time*, that is, the time taken to complete an activity. In practice, for example, four weeks of writing conference papers will be spread over several months, with other tasks undertaken alongside. Similarly, the 15 weeks allocated for writing draft chapters will be spread over much of the whole project.

Time estimates are difficult to make but will become more realistic with practice and experience. Your supervisor will advise and you can also take the initiative to discuss your plans with others who have already completed similar projects. Remember that it is necessary to make allowances for activities and occurrences that will not further your project work (for example, holidays or illness). Some activities will be carried out intermittently while some may continuously occupy your time, again presenting problems of estimation. It is common to underestimate the weeks and months needed to document the research, often by several times. The key to successful planning is to go back and rework the time estimates whenever necessary. In fact, it is important to make estimates in the early stages of a research project, even when the middle and later stages cannot be tightly defined.

The next activity is designed to help you produce your own plan or schedule, and is an important one to attempt. The schedules are geared to a relatively tightly bounded project and you should adapt them to suit your own needs. For example, you may find in schedule 2 that you use no government documents but instead need to consult a wide variety of journals that may need separating into different sections, or that you need to include newspapers and other media that warrant their own section. The main thing to keep in mind is that this is merely a guideline for your own adaptation. Remember that the time allowances are elapsed time – the actual time you are doing these tasks. In practice this may be spread over a longer period, particularly if you are a part-time student with other varied commitments. For a PhD, you will find it much easier to think about the first year of the project, but it is a good idea to make estimates for the whole project and revise them as you go along.

Activity 5.2

Complete Schedules 1–6 based on your own project.

Schedule 1   Revising and refining your proposal

	Your estimate of duration (days)
Preparation of revised proposal	_____
Detailed outline of the final project report/thesis	_____
Other	_____
Total	

Schedule 2   Search of the literature

Sources to be searched	Estimated number to be searched	Standard estimate	Your estimate	Duration (days)
Journal articles	_____	1	_____	_____
Books	_____	10	_____	_____

Hours for each (spanning Standard estimate / Your estimate)

Activity 5.2 (Continued)

Dissertations	_____	5	_____	_____
Government documents		3		
Other	_____		_____	_____
			Total	

Schedule 3   Research activities

	Estimated duration (days)
Review of literature	_____
Preparing instrument for collecting data (questionnaire, simulation, experiment, etc.)	_____
Testing instrument for collecting data	_____
Collecting data (running experiment, doing questionnaires, etc.)	_____
Data analysis	_____
Applying concepts and theories	_____
Analysis of results	_____
Other	_____
	Total

Schedule 4   Writing, editing, rewriting

Section/ Chapter	Provisional title	Estimated pages	Hours per page Standard estimate	Your estimate	Total duration (days/ hours)
_____	_____	_____	4	_____	_____
_____	_____	_____	4	_____	_____
_____	_____	_____	4	_____	_____
_____	_____	_____	4	_____	_____
_____	_____	_____	4	_____	_____
_____	_____	_____	4	_____	_____

Activity 5.2   (Continued)

Summary/conclusions/ recommendations	_____	8	_____ _____
Bibliography	_____	6	_____ _____
Appendices	_____		_____ _____
			Total

Schedule 5   Total estimated days

1	Revising and refining proposal	_____
2	Literature search	_____
3	Research activities	_____
4	Writing, editing, rewriting	_____
		Total duration

Schedule 6   Estimated completion date

	Day	Month

Starting date for
  completion
  estimate
	_____	_____

Working time _____ in days		

Estimated
  completion time
  (no delays)
	_____	_____

Delays expected:	Days
Data collection delays	_____
Data analysis delays	_____
Chapter reading delays	_____
Final reading delays	_____
Typing and printing delays	_____
Other delays	_____

Estimated final
  completion date
  (ready for assessment)
	_____	_____

(A downloadable copy of this schedule is available on this books websites)

The important idea behind these schedules is sensible planning and this depends on realistic time estimates. The best schedules are usually made by breaking activities down into smaller tasks and combining the resulting estimates. Even if you have an activity that seems impossible to put a time on, you should still try to make an estimate. What you might do is to estimate the other activities and then include a pessimistic, an optimistic, and a best duration for the difficult-to-estimate activity. It is better to have a weak estimate than none at all. Other important issues to consider at this point are, for example, what the appropriate quality standard for a task might be, or your own personal method of dealing with a specific task. For instance, is the task something integral to your research that warrants a lot of your time, or is it something peripheral that can be done well or adequately rather than perfectly? If you are making notes about your source material, do you go into great detail or can you summarize succinctly in a comparatively short time? Or, if you are writing a draft chapter, do you write, rewrite and rewrite again or do you spend a lot of time thinking before you actually get anything down on paper? All of these issues must be considered in scheduling your tasks – only you know exactly how you work best.

5.4   Scheduling Your Time

After preparing your gross time budget, the activities need to be sequenced through to work out which have priority. You have already worked on this in Chapter 3, when you looked at milestones and being flexible about your plans. Once you have a time budget, there are a number of tools available which can help think through which have priority. There are some useful project management software programs that help you to plan tasks.

You could also consider some kind of network analysis, examining the dependencies between particular tasks, which could look like an extended version of Table 5.3. Sharp et al. (2002, pp. 63–71) cover the topic in great detail, but the basic point we want you to consider here is that you need to assess which tasks must be completed before which other ones can start, and which tasks can run in parallel with which other ones. There are all sorts of project management tools that will enable you to consider the relationships between your tasks and visualize them as dependency diagrams or Gantt charts.

For example, Figure 5.1 shows a scheduling chart from Suretrack Project Manager, with the tasks labelled on the left, months at the top and the bars showing the time period over which each of the tasks are underway. Arrows between sub-tasks show where the outputs from one task need to feed into the next (and hence the deadlines for each to be completed).

Specialist project management software can be expensive and many professional project managers cope perfectly well using standard inexpensive software such as

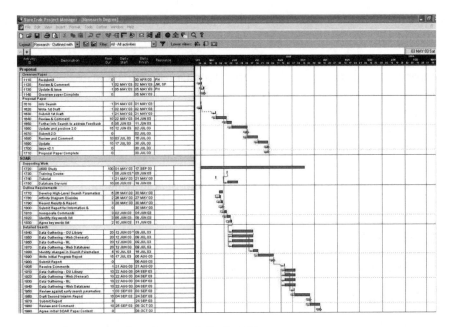

Figure 5.1   Screen shot from Suretrack Project Manager

Microsoft Word, Excel and Outlook, or their equivalents. However, it could be worthwhile finding out if your university supports any project management software. For part-time students it is also possible that your employer may have project management software that you could use for your research project.

The amount of detail that goes into planning is partly a matter of individual preference and temperament. Over-elaborate planning may be discouraging or time-wasting – planning charts in six colours, and so on – which can become procrastination to avoid starting the research. You do need some minimum amount of planning, but do not frighten yourself or get bogged down by making it over-elaborate (Bell, 1993, pp. 15–23; Sharp et al., 2002, pp. 57–68).

The management task is to put enough structure into the planning process so that it assumes priority over other less important activities. Some people find it helpful to begin each week's project work with a planning hour that establishes specific tasks for the week and estimates times for each of the tasks. Initially this could be a useful activity to undertake with your supervisor's guidance. More tasks than can actually be completed might be outlined, putting priority on their execution. Those outlined that have a lower priority provide alternative tasks that can be started if the high priority tasks cannot be completed for some reason. Finally, as tasks are completed, the actual time taken could be recorded. Thus, at the planning session at the beginning of the next work-week, the actual times can be compared with the estimated times and decisions can be made about the effectiveness of work and the amount of time that may need to be allocated for activities in the coming week.

Note that a schedule is a target. If you are not on target, your alternatives are:

1 **go faster;**

2 **allocate more time at the expense of something else;**

3 **scale down your objectives, hence the amount of activity needed.**

Discussion

A few issues regularly crop up as important in discussions with research students towards the end of their projects, when they reflect back on their research. Students often bring up these issues after a preliminary phrase like 'If only I had done this in the first few months' or 'If only I had stopped doing so much on that sooner'. The following is not a comprehensive list of tips, just a guide to a few of the more typical ones.

1 **It is very easy to take too long over one task and try to do everything. For example, it is not possible to do a comprehensive literature review that includes every single reference you have read. The purpose of such a review is to build confidence that your project is relevant and that a 'gap' exists that your research will fill, not to gather every appropriate reference.**

2 **The planning involved in deciding a medium- to long-term project, although absolutely key to success within the time available, cannot possibly visualize everything that will be needed. It is essential to be flexible and to be prepared to add and subtract tasks from time to time, after discussion with supervisors. One way of dealing with the unpredictability of research is to ask yourself, during your planning, 'What can go wrong?' This question in turn highlights some of the tactics you could employ in these instances, so that if, say, there is a delay in negotiating access, you will have allowed for this and will have an alternative plan in which you can substitute another task in the meantime.**

3 **Do be prepared to add tasks that no one has suggested. Remember, you are a good judge of tasks key to your research. For example, one of us had excellent supervision for their PhD but no one ever suggested the importance of meeting key researchers near the start of a research project. Students are often surprised that senior researchers welcome being given the opportunity to talk about their**

research to people who are just beginning. **They can turn out to be extremely supportive, useful contacts at conferences and formal events.**

4   **Last, but not least, something will go wrong in every research project. When it does, the first instinct is usually to panic or freeze. It is important at that moment to remind yourself, however anxious you are, that such events happen to everyone. Complaining that you are stuck is not enough; you should write down the problem as carefully as you can, since writing something down can often help sort out more clearly what the issues are that need to be resolved. It is at times like these that supervisors, or your critical friends, can demonstrate their importance. The issues usually need to be discussed as soon as possible so that alternatives can be found, or ways round the problem navigated. The longer you leave a crisis, the worse it gets.**

5.5   Managing Your Resources

Having developed a plan for how you will spend your time, you need to check whether the resource implications of what you think you need to do are reasonable. These considerations will be very different if you are doing your PhD part-time than if you are a full-time student. For example, part-time students may have much less access to university resources, so this must be carefully considered in the context of each individual project. It may be that there is little to think about, or that it is not considered your responsibility to think about resources at all. However, whether full-time or part-time, an assessment of what you need in order to carry out your project in terms of funding, skills and access to resources such as equipment will identify whether you need to do anything about garnering additional resources, or at least whether you need to find out more about what is available.

We assume that you have started your degree and that your basic studentship funding arrangements are already in place (here we include those who are self-funded), therefore you should not be in the position of having to write substantial proposals. Nevertheless, even if you have a generous budget and someone else is managing it, there are likely to be a number of things that you will have the responsibility for making decisions about. Furthermore, you may identify items that have no monetary cost implications, but where you nevertheless have to make a case for use of or access to them. This section deals with the issues of funding, training and access together, because the things you will need to think about to get them are similar: what do you need, what is already available, and what do you need to do about any shortfall, in terms of making a case to someone to make up the difference?

The details will depend on the activities you mean to carry out for your research, but items you might consider in your research plan could include:

1 **Purchase, loan or hire for minor equipment (e.g. a tape recorder).**

2 **Funding for travel and accommodation.**

3 **Workshop and conference fees.**

4 **Specialist software.**

5 **Internal and external training opportunities.**

6 **Access to individuals and organizations.**

7 **Use of equipment and facilities (e.g. an archive).**

Whether you are applying for a small amount of travel money, claiming expenses against a departmental budget or making a case to your supervisors for spending research funds in a particular way, the basic skills for constructing and keeping track of a budget are the same. An awareness of the issues involved in making these decisions is good practice for the future, because the ability to secure and manage funding and resources for research becomes increasingly important as your academic career progresses (Feibelman, 1993, pp. 83–93). This is a skill that you can note in your progress file and can be part of your career portfolio as discussed in Chapter 12. Even if you leave academia, the ability to put together a well-crafted budget will stand you in good stead, whether it is for constructing a business plan, project management in a commercial, civil service or community setting, or pitching for your Hollywood blockbuster! Attempting to spend more money than you have is a bad idea in any field, and the ability to keep track of past and future income and expenditure will always be useful.

The first step in constructing your budget is to develop a basis for making decisions about resources. There are two approaches to budgeting – detailed estimation and top-down budgeting – and both apply here. Detailed estimation requires you to work out approximately how much everything you need to do under your project plan will cost you. Starting from the list of tasks that you have developed earlier in the chapter, what are the resource implications of each? For example, if you need to travel anywhere, how much will it cost? If you need a particular software package, is it already provided by your university? If not, is there an alternative that is provided? If you need to buy it, how much will it cost to purchase? Will you need training in how to use it, and is this already provided by the university? If not, how much will it cost and when will it be available? Though it is important, don't get too bogged down in this. It is best to concentrate on the essentials, and use rough figures plus a safety margin.

Top-down budgeting starts with a total pot of resources, and decides how they are to be allocated. It is not unusual to be unclear about what your entitlements are, and the details will vary between departments, types of research and funding arrangements. The best place to start is with your supervisors, but you might also speak to other students who have been in the same department for a while, or have carried out similar research. Other ports of call include any centralized support services that your university or institution has to offer. Make a list of the total discretionary funds available to you, and any opportunities such as optional training that you have an automatic right of access to.

If the estimated budget is lower than the total pot of resources, then as long as you keep track of what is being spent you will be fine. You'll have space to make adjustments – a valuable commodity in its own right. There are bound to be opportunities that crop up later in the process (conferences you don't yet know about spring to mind) that it will be useful to take advantage of without having to scurry around too much. If, on the other hand, you need more resources that you don't yet have access to, you have three choices. You can do without, substitute something else, or go out and get it. If the latter, you need to think carefully about from where you might get it. At the Open University, for example, there are often pots of funds and other resources available within departments or research groups, at faculty level and from the university as a whole. There are also external funders to consider and here the permutations are endless. Each source will have specific conditions attached, therefore the best place to go will not necessarily be clear. Again, it is best to take advice from your supervisors and others around you, and there are often members of staff at a university or research institute whose job it is to know where to get funding for different purposes. Another tack is to track down individuals who have successfully applied to particular sources of funding, or who are visibly spending money on the sorts of things you would like to. How did they do it? How long did it take? How unusual is it to be successful with that particular funder? (Some links covering possible funding bodies are on this book's website).

This brings us neatly back to the question of time. Winning funding through applications is not guaranteed to work, and will often take up valuable time you could be spending on something else (writing for example). There is also the question of 'lead in' time: if it takes four months to get a decision and receive funding, you need to apply four months in advance of when you need the money. Of course this is assuming (a) you're successful and don't need to apply elsewhere and (b) the funding body keeps to their schedule. If you're considering making any applications, then you need to build time into your schedule for preparing and submitting a case, and you need to consider carefully the costs and the benefits concerned.

Activity 5.3

From your project plan, develop a resource budget for the tasks you have identified. Then make a survey of your entitlements, as detailed above. You are unlikely to have all the details you need straight away, so spend some time deciding what questions you need to ask and tracking down people who are likely to know the answers.

Now revisit your project schedule to take into account any activities you need to undertake to increase your access to resources. Is the time you will need justifiable and doable? And is it doable in that time?

Finally, having constructed a budget, you have a good basis to monitor how you are doing as you go along. Even if you take on board nothing else from this section, it is worth getting into the habit of keeping track of what you're spending and keeping evidence of it in the form of receipts, invoices and application forms. You don't need anything more complicated than a cardboard folder or box file, and a paper notebook or spreadsheet. Keeping track of spending will facilitate making expense claims where these apply, and will also provide you with a picture of how deeply you delved into your available resources if you total up your spending every now and then. It is also a habit well worth developing, as it will serve you well in almost any line of work. As with time management, the trick is to set aside regular time to consider your position. This means that crises related to insufficient attention to these issues – such as having a paper accepted for a conference but not having the funds to pay for it – can be avoided.

5.6 Making a Case

In this section we discuss some of the issues that need thinking about if you are going to make a case to secure funding, whether internally or externally. Similarly, if you need access to particular people or organizations, or permission to use equipment or facilities, you will often at some point need to make a written case for it (even if this is just a letter explaining what you want). These issues share many features with the requirements of a funding proposal, and there is also a plethora of advice available in texts such as Bell (1993, pp. 52–9).

To illustrate the importance of thinking through the management of making a case, consider the following example from Reis and Leukefeld (1995, p. 11):

A university-based new investigator has a great research idea, a straightforward design for testing the hypotheses, and a collaborator to cover one of the critical areas of expertise. This looks like the birth of a competitive proposal. However, during the process of completing the application, other responsibilities sidetrack the aspiring investigators. They take short cuts to get the application materials together and barely meet the deadline even after delegating the responsibility for finishing the application to the newest unit secretary.

This example highlights many of the difficulties of applying for funding if you have not spent enough time planning your application. To address some of these issues, we therefore suggest some tips that will help you. These are:

1   Concentrate on the essentials that you need. This gives your potential funder important information about your application and, more importantly, about you yourself. If you can outline your proposal succinctly and clearly, then they immediately realize that you have thought through your proposal carefully.

2   Make your case in terms that make sense to those you are applying to. Not only must the project be of interest to you, but it should also be presented to your potential funder or gatekeeper in a way that will attract a positive response. This means that you should use accessible language, locate it in a suitable framework and so on; for example, it is pointless to present a qualitative, social scientific project to a funding body you know only supports biological research. Similarly, a group of research participants (potential interviewees, say) will want to know what is being asked of them instead of or at least before wading through a theoretically based justification. This is where talking to others who know about the people you're applying to will help. Get as much feedback on your case as you can before you apply.

3   Demonstrate that what you want is reasonable. Again, the detail you include in the application should be enough to provide sufficient information for the potential funder to make a decision. So if you want to apply for funding for an international conference, for example, you could include suggestions of reasonably priced hotels, examples of airfares and so on. You should not select the most expensive place to stay or first-class travel – these would not be considered reasonable and are more likely to be met with a negative response. If you are negotiating for lab or equipment time, then part of your case is showing that the amount of access you are asking for is reasonable.

4   The most important consideration for your case, and one that relates to the body of this chapter, is that you spend sufficient time planning it. If you allocate enough time for planning at the early stages – and don't become side-tracked as did the investigator in the example above – you are more likely to be rewarded positively when your application comes to be considered.

5.7   Thinking About Intangibles

Along with these tangible resources you need to manage for your project, it will almost certainly pay you to spend some time thinking about your capacity to stimulate the interest and involvement of others – in other words, your 'social capital' is a resource as much as any of the others. Unless you are working in total isolation, it is likely that you will depend on the choices and preferences of other people to achieve what you set out to do. As an indirect set of resources, the relationships you already have and the ones you could build during the course of your research are easy to discount or take for granted, but dealing skilfully with other people can make a huge difference to almost all the stages of your research.

There are essentially two types of links you might like to consider between your research and your relationships. The first are your (actual and potential) connections to numerous people out there who could facilitate your research: for example, social or organizational research often means dependence on the goodwill of gatekeepers or key informants to gain access to particular research contexts. Some of these you will know already, but others you will not have yet met. Building and maintaining an appropriate network of contacts is an important and sometimes essential skill. Such networking is considered in some detail in Section 7.4. Examples of ways that networking could benefit your research include:

1   gaining access to expertise;

2   providing sounding boards and critical feedback;

3   practice in explaining/using language;

4   access to 'grey' material;

5   access to field sites;

6   enhancing your job prospects.

Activity   5.4

Write up a list of the people you will need to speak to during the early stages of your research.

Who do you need to talk to about your research and why?

What are you going to say?

For those whom you haven't met yet, what are the practicalities of getting in touch?

The second important set of relationships is with the people you depend on or who depend on you. Postgraduate research takes up a lot of time and effort, and will affect many of your most important relationships. In turn, the support you have from friends and family will have an effect on how you are able to carry out your research. A postgraduate degree is a professional training course, part of which is that you are learning how to be something. Consequently your identity changes as you proceed with the research. This may not impinge on your private life at all, but be aware that it often does. Preparing the ground and paying attention to maintaining important relationships can help you and others around you to make any changes constructive. Doing advanced research can be very isolating, and investing time in maintaining your social ties can be just as crucial to completing your research as many of the other activities you undertake. As with managing time and resources, managing relationships is a trade-off between spending enough time thinking about what's important and not letting planning and analysis become procrastination that gets between you and your research. Luckily, in this area, the skills you need are natural human ones, and it is easier here to build on your experiences as a social being than it is with some of the more arcane reaches of academic practice.

Whether you're introverted or extraverted, you will already have your own style of dealing with people and it makes sense to build on that rather than assume you have to be social in a way that you're not. Nevertheless, making the connection between your personal social skills and the management of your research project might at first be difficult, and a sensible question is how can you improve the linkage between them? There are numerous practice-orientated books you could turn to (e.g. Goleman, 1996), but perhaps the best advice is to spend some time watching how more experienced researchers (especially those you admire) handle these matters, and then try the same yourself. Above all, remember that not everyone is going to like you, or even be willing to co-operate with you. Spending some time reflecting on what happens to you and your relationships, perhaps in your journal alongside other aspects of your research, will almost certainly help you to improve as you go along.

5.8 Pushing Out the Boat

This chapter has focused your attention on how you manage the various resources that you need in order to carry out your research – particularly the sort of planning you need to undertake at this stage of your research. The activities in this chapter, together with those in the previous chapter, mean you are now in a strong position to say what you want to research, how you will do it and which research tradition your work fits in with.

Activity 5.5

Activity 5.5 draws together material from the previous activities in this chapter, as well as Chapters 3 and 4, to help you prepare a short presentation (20 minutes) that would be suitable for your supervisor(s) as part of your first-year evaluation process. Don't worry too much about the aesthetics of the presentation – there is plenty of advice on presentation skills in Chapter 10. This is primarily an opportunity to get feedback on your plans, and you should therefore concentrate on the content, rather than the context.

You want to keep the presentation short, so you will have to think hard about the key points you want to make in order to give your supervisor(s) a clear idea of your progress and future plans. You might decide to include the following, but this is just a guide: your research question(s) or hypotheses; a plan of how you will do the research in the first year; the resources you need to carry out the work, and any issues that need addressing with your supervisor(s).

Make notes on a structure for your presentation using the materials you already have on:

1 your research idea;
2 your research questions/hypotheses/objectives;
3 why the research is important;
4 what are the key research tasks in the first year;
5 how you might set about these tasks;
6 making a research plan for the first year, and sketching a plan for the whole project, with time scales;
7 what might be the key issues on which you want advice from your supervisor(s)?

Discussion

Ask your supervisor(s) to give you feedback on Activity 5.5. Your work on this activity will probably fit the bill for at least a part of your initial progress report if you are doing a PhD, and will prove invaluable as baseline for making decisions as your work progresses.

References

Bell, J. (1993) *Doing Your Research Project: A Guide for First-Time Researchers.* Buckingham: Open University Press.

Buchanan, D. (1980) 'Gaining management skills through academic research work', *Personnel Management*, April.

Feibelman, P.J. (1993) *A PhD Is Not Enough! A Guide to Survival in Science.* Cambridge, MA: Perseus Publishing.

Goleman, D. (1996) *Emotional Intelligence: Why it Can Matter More Than IQ.* London: Bloomsbury Publishing.

Murray, R. (1996) *Thesis Writing.* Glasgow: University of Strathclyde, Centre for Academic Practice.

Reis, J.B. and Leukefeld, C.G. (1995) *Applying for Research Funding.* Thousand Oaks, CA: Sage.

Sharp, J.A., Peters, J. and Howard, K. (2002) *The Management of a Student Research Project.* Aldershot: Gower Publishing Company.

6 Academic Writing

Theresa Lillis and Sarah North

LEARNING OUTCOMES

After reading this chapter and working on its associated activities you should be able to:

- Understand the role of writing as part of the research process.
- Adapt writing style according to purpose and audience.
- Know how to revise drafts of a thesis and sharpen their focus and coherence.
- Elicit and respond effectively to feedback on writing.
- Structure a thesis coherently.
- Understand the way in which abstracts and articles are typically structured, and be able to write in the same format.
- Develop an awareness of the typical features of writing in your own discipline by reading from a range of academic texts.

6.1   Introduction

As a postgraduate student working towards a Master's or doctoral degree, your ultimate goal is to write a thesis. However, you will do a range of writing at different times and for different purposes in your journey towards this goal: some of this writing will be just for you, such as research diary entries or notes on reading, and some will be more public, such as draft chapters for your supervisor, seminar or conference papers, and articles for journals. Most of this writing will be useful both in its own right and as part of the process of producing a thesis.

In this chapter we explore some of the different kinds of written texts that you may produce throughout your studies, including the final thesis itself. We focus in particular on the drafting of texts and key aspects of organization, argument and coherence.

Writing effective academic texts takes time and practice; you need to be immersed for considerable time in your reading and research activity in order to learn what counts as good academic writing in your particular discipline and specialist field. Although there is no substitute for this period of apprenticeship, the advice in this chapter can help by pointing to some of the specific features that contribute to making a piece of writing recognizable as, for example, a 'good article' or a 'good thesis'.

6.2   Writing and Research

We want to stress three key points about the importance of writing for your research.

Writing is an integral part of your research activity

This means that you shouldn't think of your thesis as 'writing up' or as something you do only at the end of your research. Writing is part of developing your ideas, and it's a good idea to begin writing about your research as soon as you have anything to say, however tentative and provisional. For example, after reading the literature on a particular topic, try to write a summary of the main points, or as you firm up thinking on your methodology, write an outline of the methods you plan to use and your rationale.

Writing is a recursive process

Good writing isn't a one-off task, but a process in which you'll find yourself cycling again and again through various drafts (see Figure 6.1). Some of these may end up as parts of your thesis, some will be used for other purposes, such as a progress report or conference paper, and some will represent only passing stages. But drafting, reflecting, reviewing and revising all feed into the way you think about your research, and contribute to the final shape of your thesis. In the following sections we will use samples of student writing to demonstrate the work that goes into turning rough drafts into a finished product.

Writing is for reading

Remember that the reason for writing academic texts is so that they can be read by others. When you write, you need to focus not only on expressing ideas but on helping the reader to understand and follow these ideas. In order to do this, you will need to consider which specific readers you are writing for (a particular examiner?; a specific editorial board?) and also to approach your own texts as a reader as well as a writer. When you read academic texts, try to do so both as a reader (focusing on the ideas) and as a writer (focusing on how a convincing text was written).

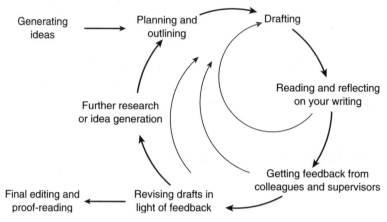

Figure 6.1   Writing is a recursive process

6.3   Keeping a Research Journal

Chapter 3 of this book looked at the use of a research journal to keep a record of your progress. A research journal is important. While you're engrossed in a particular phase of work, you tend to think it's all firmly stamped on your memory. But over many months of research, it's surprising how easily you can forget the details. So keeping a record of your thoughts and decisions in a research diary is very important. This is the place for all sorts of writing, ranging from brief reminders about appointments to records of supervision meetings, reflections on what you've been reading or thinking about, and grumbles about what's going wrong. As noted in Chapter 3, how you write your research diary is up to you, as long as you will be able to understand it later. Research diaries are normally private documents, but some people have started keeping them in the form of a blog; if you want to see some examples, try a web search using *blog* and '*research diary*' or '*research journal*' as search terms. The notes in your research diary may or may not feed directly into later writing, but if they do, they probably undergo considerable change.

Activity 6.1

Sarah Li published extracts from her research diary in her department's research newsletter (Li, 2002). Although she made these public, it's clear that she originally wrote them for her own personal use. Compare these extracts (shown below on the left) with an extract from a journal article that she published in 2004. What differences do you notice in the way the personal and the public documents are written?

Extract 1: Research Diary (Li, 2002)

5.2.99 Friday

Went to H2 setting to tape-record nurses' hand-over. L (nurse) said not to use the tape-recorder as she said: 'it is confidential'. Felt totally downhearted. Only spent an hour there. Felt being ostracised by staff there. R (nurse) was nice. Sensed there was conflict of some sort amongst the staff there. The tension in the main office was evident where Dr. ( ) was there! I felt utterly rejected. No cups of tea. I was on my own wandering just outside the office. K (nurse) ignored me till I forced myself to say 'hello' to her. L then said: 'you have to accept what you see here' when I asked her if it was alright for me to sit in the office. What did she mean by that? I don't want to come back to this hospice to collect anymore data. Must talk to Clive and my friend AA about this. I'd better latch onto D as he seemed nice also. [...]

24.11.99 Wednesday

Quite distressing hearing nurses talk about patients' deteriorating conditions. I wished I could go nearer the patients. Somehow I felt I did not have the liberty. The nurses all disappeared from the bedrooms. I took a quick peep but that was all. I am not getting anywhere. I think I might have to re-negotiate with D for more 'freedom'.

Extract 2: Journal Article (Li, 2004)

The subjects

Palliative care nurses were my primary focus. Patients, relatives and other professionals were 'incidental' although they may engage in talk with nurses or enter nurses' discussion. A total of 28 palliative care nurses from all three settings were observed. [...]

Consent

Permission was formally obtained from the Ethical Research Committee in three settings. Verbal consent was obtained from a series of introductory meetings with participants over a period of 10 months. Information sheets for both palliative care nurses and patients were provided. These were displayed on patient's notice boards in the wards. Written consent was also obtained. The ethical guidelines of each setting were followed throughout the research. [...]

Data analysis

I transcribed and imported each episode of my observation into the QSR NUD*IST program. [...] A systematic and rigorous content analysis on recorded field-note data was carried out. I then identified data which showed nurses talking about patients whom they wanted to help feel better, and moments where nurses gave physical care or talked about patients' psychological, social, spiritual conditions ...

Comment

Although they cover some of the same issues, these texts are written quite differently because they have a different purpose and a different readership. Obvious differences include the way the chronological narrative of the diary has been reorganized into conventional sections in the article, and the personal emotions have been suppressed. While the diary deals with the messy reality of research, the article presents it as a more coherent and unproblematic process. These differences in content are paralleled by a switch from informal to formal style:

Informal features in the diary	Formal features in the article
incomplete sentences: *No cups of tea* contractions: *don't* affective meanings: *downhearted,* *wished* colloquial expressions: *latch onto,* *quick peep*	longer sentences longer noun phrases: *a systematic and rigorous* *content analysis on recorded field-note data* technical terminology: *palliative care nurses,* *content analysis.* passive forms: *Verbal consent was obtained*

Although passive forms are frequently used in academic writing as a way of objectifying information, notice that Sarah Li still appears in the article as 'I'. It is sometimes suggested that the personal pronouns 'I' and 'we' should not be used at all in academic writing, but in reality this varies between disciplines, with higher frequencies found in humanities and social sciences than in sciences. Nowadays 'we' is rarely used unless referring to multiple researchers/authors (the way we have used it in this chapter). Whether or not to use 'I' is influenced by the type of act that the writer is referring to. For example, Sarah Li sometimes used 'I' when talking about her research acts, which is acceptable in social sciences but unusual in hard sciences. Using 'I' for writer acts, however, is more widely accepted.

Research acts: what you did, e.g.	I transcribed … each episode of my observation
Mental acts: what you think, e.g.	I would expect this to vary in line with …
Writer acts: what you write, e.g.	In this chapter I argue that …

Activity 6.2

Have a look at three theses in your own discipline. If you have an electronic copy, try searching for 'I' or 'my'. If not, scan through the first and last chapters. How often do writers refer to themselves using personal pronouns? Do they tend to use these pronouns to talk about research acts, mental acts or writer acts? How do you envisage referring to yourself (or not) in your writing?

6.4   The Process of Drafting

Many of the most daunting aspects of writing can be put into perspective if you see it as something that develops out of many rough drafts, each of manageable length. The important thing is to get going, without expecting to produce perfect results at the first attempt.

Here are some of the ways to get going with a section of writing. Which do you use? Do they usually work well for you? If not, you might like to consider trying one of the other approaches.

1 **Use mind-mapping to generate ideas and indicate relationships between them (i.e. write down ideas in any order and then sort out the links between them).**

2 **Write key points on file cards. Spread them out so that related points are grouped close together. Move the cards round till you find the best arrangement.**

3 **Enter main headings in a word-processing document. Start expanding ideas under each heading. Move things round as you go.**

4 **Write an outline of headings and sub-headings.**

Other ideas for providing a structure you can work with are on this book's website. However you begin, bear in mind that you will probably work through several drafts, gradually improving and refining the writing. You therefore need to be strategic in what to concentrate on at any given point. There's no point, for example, agonizing over punctuation if you still haven't decided whether the content of the paragraph is right. It's usually most effective to concentrate initially on the overall content (what to include and how to organize it), then later to focus in on more detailed matters (see Figure 6.2)

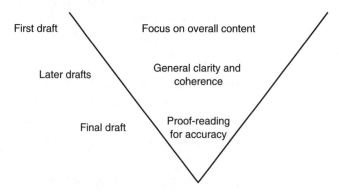

First draft   Focus on overall content

Later drafts   General clarity and coherence

Final draft   Proof-reading for accuracy

Figure 6.2   Refining your focus

Often, as you read more and gradually refine your focus, earlier writing no longer reflects your current views, and needs to be substantially rewritten. This means that it's OK to write these provisional drafts quite loosely, making sure you get your points down on paper without worrying too much about details of organization or style. Later on, rough drafts can be worked up to form submitted papers or parts of your final thesis, but there's no point polishing them until they need to go to supervisors or outside readers.

This section will concentrate on ways in which drafts can be improved by exploiting advice from supervisors, and by trying to anticipate how your writing will appear to a reader. First, we consider some general points about feedback from supervisors, before illustrating the drafting process in more detail with a sample of student writing. We focus here on changes made to overall content, clarity and coherence. The final stages of editing and proof-reading will be dealt with in Section 6.8.

Writer's block

Everyone suffers from writer's block sometimes, but here are some tips to keep it to a minimum:

The work seems overwhelming.	Don't set out to write a whole thesis, or even a whole chapter. Tell yourself you're just going to write the section on topic X, and it will seem much more achievable.
You're not up to it.	Setting your standards too high can make things seem impossibly difficult. Tell yourself it doesn't have to be perfect, it doesn't even have to be good. All you need is to write something rough that you can improve on later.
You've lost the plot.	Sometimes you can get bogged down in details and need to step back and rethink what you're doing. What's the big story? Try to diagram it, summarize it in a few sentences, or explain it to a friend. Come back to the writing once you've regained your sense of direction.
You're feeling stale.	Writing a thesis takes a long time, and at times you're bound to flag. A change of activity may break the block; for example, you could catch up with reading, or do some routine analysis. If this doesn't work, don't be afraid to take a break to recharge your batteries.

Some further tips on overcoming writer's block are on this book's website.

Feedback from supervisors

For many research students, the process of receiving and responding to critique is the most important influence on their development. Your supervisors will naturally be the most important source of feedback, both in face-to-face discussions and through written comments on your drafts.

To obtain helpful feedback, you do of course need to provide your supervisors with readable material – continuous prose, written in an appropriate academic style, rather than the rough notes and informal style of your research diary. However, there may still be places in a draft where you haven't yet decided exactly what to include, or haven't fully fleshed it out. Supervisors are usually willing to comment on incomplete material of this sort, though it's best to distinguish it from more finished text (e.g. by using a different font).

To develop a productive relationship with your supervisor, you may need to let them know what sort of feedback suits you best. For example, if they only seem to give negative comments, this may be because they're focusing on what needs revision; ask them to indicate which aspects are shaping up satisfactorily. On the other hand, if the only feedback is that everything's OK, let them know any specific issues on which you need feedback. Your priorities will change over time, and it's helpful to indicate particular concerns. Here's an example of a student seeking specific comment from her supervisor by writing a note at the top of the draft:

> I'm still not convinced that I've explained or justified my choice of methodology clearly enough yet. I'm particularly concerned that I may not have explained why I'm not using grounded theory. I'd appreciate your thoughts on this.

You can also ask questions to your supervisor within the text (e.g. by using marginal comments or footnotes).

When you respond to feedback, try to resist the urge to be over-defensive. Supervisors are not always right, but they are trying to help, so it's worth considering their comments carefully even if you disagree. For example, if you think they've got hold of the wrong end of the stick, consider whether your writing might have misled them – perhaps you can rewrite it so they will be persuaded to agree with you. Try to understand their point of view, and ask for clarification if you don't. Bear in mind, though, that you are responsible for your own thesis, and ultimately it's your job to weigh up the advice and come to a decision.

From start to finish

This section considers the changes made to a piece of writing from its genesis as part of a first-year pilot study, to its final appearance within a thesis chapter. It illustrates the way the student, Susan Moron-Garcia, responds to supervisor comments, gradually shifting her focus from general content to more specific issues of clarity and coherence.

Activity 6.3

The extract below is an early draft, with marginal comments from the supervisors. What do they seem to be focusing on? If you were the author, how would you respond?

Extract 3: Draft 1

The aim of the research is to examine whether or not the Web and internet-based technology currently used in Higher Education facilitates student-centred learning. It is claimed that Web and internet-based technology facilitates student-centred learning or leads to the use of more student-centred approaches to teaching and learning (Collis, 1996, Wegner 1999, Westera, 1999). It has also been <u>shown</u> that it benefits students in their learning and in acquiring transferable skills (Gibbs, 1999, Harrison, 1994, Laurillard, 1993, Martin and Fayter, 1997).

or claimed?

I think this is very controversial – there is only one person who has shown transfer in any learning

It was not clear, following a review of the literature referring to the use of Web and Internet-based technology in Higher Education, how widespread the use of this technology was and whether any of the usage included Virtual Learning Environments. Some of the new universities (post-1992) <u>appear to have made</u> a commitment to the use of commercially-available Virtual Learning Environments (Coventry, Middlesex and Sheffield Hallam, for example) and a number of them have developed their own systems (Huddersfield, Staffordshire and Wolverhampton), but <u>use at the older Universities was less evident</u>. It was <u>therefore</u> necessary to investigate what Web and Internet-based technology was being used and whether Virtual Learning Environments were part of this use. Four institutions (two pre-1992 and two post-1992 universities) were approached in order to obtain benchmark data.

are moving

not a helpful comparison

This sentence doesn't hold up with respect to the previous on

Comment

In this early draft, the supervisors' main concern is the content. The first comments suggest that some claims are not sufficiently justified. There are two ways that the writer might respond: by providing stronger evidence, or by hedging the claim (making it more cautious). The final comments suggest that the supervisors find it difficult to see the significance of what she is saying: what's the point of comparing older and newer universities, and why does this make it necessary to investigate what technology was being used? These comments suggest that the writer needs to indicate more clearly the steps in her argument.

Hedging your claims

Academic language needs to be carefully chosen to avoid making unjustified claims. Here are some examples of hedging claims to make them more tentative:

Unhedged	Hedged
It has been shown that …	It is claimed that …
This proves that …	It is possible that …
It is clear that …	This suggests that
VLEs facilitate …	VLEs may facilitate …
The results are convincing	The results appear convincing

After further discussion with her supervisors, Susan Moron-Garcia produced the draft below for her first-year report; notice the changes that have been made, and the points that still need clarification. On the right we have added our own comments on some of the changes that we noted.

Extract 4: Draft 2   **Comments**

The aim of this research is to examine whether the Web and Internet-based technology currently used in Higher Education, in particular Virtual Learning Environments (VLEs), facilitates student-centred learning. It is claimed that Web and Internet-based technology facilitates student-centred learning or leads to the use of more student-centred approaches to teaching and learning (Collis, 1996, Wegner et al 1999 and Westera, 1999). It is also claimed that it benefits students in their learning and in acquiring transferable skills such as IT literacy (Gibbs, 1999, Harrison, 1994, Laurillard, 1993, Martin and Fayter, 1997).

> The claims are now expressed more tentatively, though there's still some repetition that obscures the main focus.

There is no universal definition of either a learning environment or a VLE. However, it is possible to construct a broad definition based on the literature (Britain and Liber, 1999; Firdyilwek, 1999; Pimentel, 1999; Stiles, 2000). A VLE is a learning environment where the necessary interaction and collaboration takes place in the virtual world of Web and Internet-based applications. The tools provided aid the lecturer (teacher or instructor) in controlling and tailoring the virtual environment for use by their students, who are able to interact with, contribute to and move through the content. […]

> A new paragraph is added defining VLEs, and making it clearer that the focus is VLEs, rather than Web and Internet-based technology. Perhaps the first paragraph should be revised to match.

It was not clear from a review of the literature how widespread the use of Web and Internet-based technology actually was and whether the usage included VLEs. The evidence there deals with individual case studies describing personal motivation and experience (for example, Gibbs, 1999; Lee and Thompson, 1999). There are few examples of sustained and widespread use (Goodyear, 1998), unless we look to distance education. With regard to VLEs, some of the new or post-1992 universities appear to have made a commitment to the use of commercially-available VLEs (Coventry, Middlesex and Sheffield Hallam, for example) and a number of them have developed their own systems (Huddersfield, Staffordshire and Wolverhampton). However, the use of institutionally supported VLEs at the older Universities was less evident. A recent survey (UCISA, 2001) suggests that this may be due to more centralised structures in the post-1992 Universities.

> The claims about the use of technology are now specified step by step, and supported by references.

A pilot study was carried out in order to explore what Web and Internet-based technology was being used in institutions of Higher Education and whether VLEs were part of this use. The aim was to inform the design of a main study on the use of VLEs in Higher Education. Four institutions (two pre-1992 and two post-1992 universities) were approached in order to obtain benchmark data.

> The organization has been improved by creating a separate paragraph on data collection. Notice, though, that the aims stated here don't quite match those given at the beginning.

In this draft, Susan Moron-Garcia responded to supervisors' comments by changing what she included and how she organized it, and by strengthening the argument. The main ideas are now in place, and in later drafts the supervisors' comments focused less on content and more on clarity and coherence. Susan's focus thus shifted from general to more specific issues. In addition, later drafts showed that rather than just responding to the supervisors' comments, she began to take more responsibility for her own writing. This sort of development is normal in thesis writing, and you may find that you need less support from your supervisor as you become more confident about your own writing, and develop a clearer idea about the shape that your thesis will take.

To conclude this section, let's return to the extract above, and see how it was incorporated within a thesis chapter discussing the research methodology. As Susan Moron-Garcia's research developed, she was able to get a better picture of the way her pilot study related to the overall research. Fitting these ideas into her final thesis (Moron-Garcia, 2004) required substantial changes to content and organization; here we will focus only on two extracts. The first one sums up the aim of the pilot study:

> The overall aim of the research was to understand the use of VLEs, as a particular example of Web and internet-based technology, in face-to-face higher education.

Compared with earlier versions, the writer has tightened the focus of the research and expressed it more precisely. Notice also how the construction 'understand the use of X' allows her to give details of X at the end of the sentence, rather than in the middle. As a general principle, detailed information tends to be easier to read if it comes at the end of a sentence. This improves the clarity of the writing, making it easier for a reader to follow.

The next extract sets the background to the pilot study by reviewing the extent of VLE use:

> A review of literature about the use of Information and Communications Technology (ICT) to support teaching and learning in higher education did not indicate how widespread the use of Web and internet-based technology really was in universities in the UK; there were few published cases of VLE use. The available evidence dealt with individual case studies describing personal motivation and experience, for instance, Gibbs (1999) and Lee and Thompson (1999), or with the experience in individual institutions, Deepwell and Syson (1999). There were few examples of sustained and widespread use except in the case of distance education. The results from a UCISA survey published after this pilot study was carried out support this observation. Jenkins et al. state that: 'VLEs are a new development for many institutions and, with a few exceptions, the level of staff and student engagement is correspondingly limited' (2001, p. 3).

The focus of the paragraph has been tightened, with information about published studies now covered separately from information about different institutions, and the topic restricted to 'the use of ICT to support teaching and learning in UK universities'. This makes the paragraph more coherent, as it focuses on just one main issue. The writer also states explicitly that 'there were few published cases of VLE use' and the UCISA survey 'supports this observation'. By spelling out these steps in her argument, the writer makes it easier for a reader to understand what she is saying, and how it all fits together to build her case.

In this section, we have stressed the need to see your revisions as part of a cyclical process, first in broad brushstrokes, then gradually focusing in on fine detail. We will return to detailed editing and proof-reading later, but before you can put the finishing touches to any piece of writing, you will need to pay attention to the clarity and coherence of your argument, and this is the theme of Section 6.5.

Word processing with long documents

It can be difficult to work with long electronic documents, particularly if they include tables and graphics. A good precaution is to work on only one chapter at a time, and to save them as separate documents. You can then combine chapters into your full design as part of a final edit. Most work-processing software offers features that help you manage a long document. You will probably save a lot of time if you learn how to use the following:

Template	Allows you to control the appearance of a document. It's a good idea to set up a special template which follows your institution's regulations on thesis presentation, and use this for all your thesis-related documents.
Styles	Allow you to specify exactly how different types of paragraph look, e.g. headings, quotations, examples. Styles can be set within the template.
Numbering	Inserts automatic numbering. If you apply outline numbering to heading styles, all sections and sub-sections will be numbered correctly however much you move things around.
Captions	Add headings and automatic numbering to tables and graphics.
Cross-references	Automatically updates references to another part of the document (e.g. 'see Figure 9') when the numbering changes.
Outline view	Allows you to view an outline of your headings and sub-headings, and change the order of sections and sub-sections.
Table of contents	Automatically creates a table of contents (provided that you have used heading styles in your document).

There should be word-processing training available to you covering these aspects.

Make sure you have a good system of storing drafts so that you don't lose valuable material. Name files in a clear and consistent way, including date or version number. Keep old drafts somewhere safe – you may decide to go back to an earlier version. It's also wise to keep copies of all your work in a separate place, to guard against disasters like a house fire or computer crash.

6.5   Crafting an Argument

Argument is central to much academic writing but is a tricky notion and word because it is used to refer to many different things. In this section, we briefly consider some different ways of thinking about argument in your writing, at both global and more local levels.

Claims, evidence and warrants

One way of approaching argument is to think of it in terms of several elements, two key ones being claims and the evidence or reasons used to support such claims. A third key element, sometimes forgotten, is what Toulmin (1958) calls 'warrants'. Warrants are the underlying assumptions that the claims you are making and that the evidence or reasons used to support such claims are plausible or valid. An example of a simple chain of claim, reason/evidence and warrants is as follows:

Claim: Arsenic is poisonous.

Reason/evidence: Evidence from a range of sources indicates that swallowing arsenic has fatal consequences.

Warrants: That arsenic is an identifiable substance; that 'poisonous' is a meaningful term; that the methods used to collect the evidence were valid.

In a large piece of writing, such as a thesis, you will often find the three elements of claim, reason/evidence and warrants in distinct sections, as indicated below:

Claim: Computers are a useful resource for active learning in school classrooms [Conclusion].

Reason/evidence: The study I have carried out demonstrates that children were actively learning [Data sections].

Warrants: That 'useful resource' and 'active learning' are meaningful notions [Introduction, Literature review]; that the methodology used is valid [Methodology]; that the methods of data collection and analysis are valid [Data sections].

(For an overview of the different elements in a thesis, see Section 6.7.)

You may also find it useful to think of claim, reason/evidence and warrants at a more local level, for example at the level of a paragraph or a sentence. Consider the following examples:

Claim: VLEs are in limited use in new universities. *Evidence*: The survey carried out and discussed in detail in Chapter 3 showed that only 5 of 50 new universities were actively developing and using VLEs

Claim: VLEs are in limited use in new universities *Evidence*: (Goodyear, 1998).

Two common types of academic evidence are used in the extracts above: empirical data and a citation. We return to the importance of citations in the following section.

You will notice that the warrants (for example, the assumption that VLE and 'limited use' are meaningful or precise notions) are not stated. This could be for one of two reasons: (1) the writer has already explained such warrants in another part of the text; (2) the writer assumes that this warrant does not need to be stated because it is self-evident to a reader from the same disciplinary community. This last point is important because it indicates that it may not be necessary or even desirable to state all warrants at every step of your writing. (Consider the claim made about arsenic above. In most contexts it is unnecessary to state the warrants because both the claim and the warrants are part of common knowledge.) In general, the only way in which you will know which warrants can be assumed and which need to be stated is through your ongoing participation in a particular academic disciplinary community and through discussions with your supervisors and other researchers.

The use of citations in crafting your argument

Whatever the nature of the claims you make and evidence you use, the position you adopt or advance in your thesis must be carved out of your response to existing studies and theories, through the use and 'orchestration' of citations. The way you use authorities in the field, through your use of relevant citations and quotations, is important for two reasons: first, through citations you demonstrate your knowledge and familiarity with your particular field of enquiry, but second, and as importantly, you use such authorities to develop your own argument.

Here we will focus on how one writer uses citations in drafting one particular kind of argument – or 'sub-argument': an argument of definition. As you know, in academic study, few, if any, meanings of terms can be taken for granted and terms which are core to your particular study will certainly need careful explanation and justification.

Activity 6.4

Read the draft of a section of Anne Hewling's thesis chapter where she is trying to deal with a concept central to her research, 'culture'. Her principal aim in the chapter overall is to argue that her particular use of the term is valid. The extract here is a draft section of the beginning of a chapter outlining the theoretical framework of the thesis. As you read, consider the following questions:

1 What is her main argument about the term 'culture' here? How does she use citations?
2 What authorities/authoritative texts does she refer to?
3 Where and how does she orchestrate these authorities to craft her argument?
4 How successful do you think this draft is in developing an argument of definition?

Extract 5: Drafting a sub-argument of definition

Ways of looking: 'scoping the problem'

'Culture is one of the two or three most complicated words in the English language' (Williams, 1983) and, 'there is really very little agreement on what people mean by the idea of culture in the first place. The word "culture" often brings up more problems than it solves' (Scollon & Wong-Scollon, 2001 p. 138). Despite this the concept is understood and used by all. Barker notes,

... there is no 'correct' or definitive meaning attached to it ... Culture is not 'out there' waiting to be correctly described by theorists who keep getting it wrong. Rather, the concept of culture is a tool which is of more or less usefulness to us as a life form. ... (2000, p. 35).

But, until such a time as the concept is '... given usable content ... the term culture is empty, ... completely circular as an explanatory tool.' (Bond et al., 2000).

A number of options for 'usable content' for the concept of culture can be found in any dictionary, for example:

- the customary beliefs, social forms, and material traits of a racial, religious, or social group (Merriam-Webster Online Dictionary)

- the way of life, especially the general customs and beliefs, of a particular group of people at a particular time (Cambridge Advanced Learner's Dictionary)

Whilst offering broadly similar ideas, these two definitions differ considerably in their focus and specificity. It is clear that culture seems to involve a collection of people who form a distinct group. In common in both definitions are ideas and beliefs and the notion that these should be shared by the people involved. There is consensus neither on exactly how to determine who should be included in any one grouping, nor what might be fundamental criteria for membership (or creation), of that group, beyond the notion of shared ideas and beliefs. Neither definition makes it clear the exact nature or substance of the shared beliefs and customs. More fundamentally, one definition suggests that the ideas and beliefs involved may be fixed whilst the other makes clear that the definition of them pertains to a certain (unspecified) period in time. However, interestingly, the first definition – which does not mention time – is offered in parallel with a further definition of culture:

the act of developing the intellectual and moral faculties especially by education (op.cit.)

By using concept of 'developing', i.e. not fixed or stationary but evolving, the ideas of time and process are added. However, none of the definitions offer any ideas of place or space in relation to the groups they refer to. One final definition of culture, more narrow in scope but perhaps more frequent in popular usage, is noted by the dictionary: the idea of culture as the product of art, music, and literature etc. – 'high' culture. Here culture is the result of intellectual creativity and endeavour within a specific group (culture) but over and beyond the realm of routine or mundane daily activity. This definition is not distinct however, from those discussed above:

> ... there is some practical convergence between (i) the anthropological and sociological senses of culture as a distinct 'whole way of life', within which, now, a distinctive 'signifying system' is seen not only as essential but as essentially involved in *all* forms of social activity, and (ii) the more specialized if also more common sense of culture as 'artistic and intellectual activities', though these, because of the emphasis on a more general signifying system, are now much more broadly defined, to include not only the traditional arts and forms of intellectual production but also all of the 'signifying practices' – from language through the arts and philosophy to journalism, fashion and advertising – which now constitute this complex and necessarily extended field. (Williams, 1981, p. 13)

Such definitions are useful in providing an overall understanding of culture for a general readership and everyday use but they fall short of substance for the purposes of this study. The roots of these general definitions lie in a number of fields, most notably anthropology. These fields of knowledge and the potential they offer for examination of how culture is implicated in the remote access online classroom are explored further in the remainder of this Chapter.

Comment

The general argument being made here seems quite clear and can be summarized in terms of a series of key steps or 'moves': (Move 1) Culture is a difficult term to define and, (Move 2) whilst there have been attempts at such a definition, (Move 3) there is little agreement over this term. (Move 4) There have been some useful attempts to develop a definition, (Move 5) but there is a need to pay some attention to this term for the purposes of this study.

In making these moves, the writer orchestrates the voices of authorities in order to set up the problem of defining culture, and the need to find a workable definition. Here are some of the ways in which we think she is attempting to do this:

She opens with a quotation from a key thinker to indicate the complex notion of 'culture' (line 2). She thus both demonstrates immediately a familiarity with one authority in the field and in doing so, she sets up authoritative support for the claims she makes in her own voice later (lines 19–30, lines 33–41) about the difficulties surrounding the use of this term.

The writer not only sets up the definition of culture as a problem, but explicitly states that it is a problem through the voice of academic authorities, by citing Scollon and Wong-Scollon (lines 4–5). She uses the voice of these academics as an authoritative 'mouthpiece' for the overall argument she is making.

She introduces the phase 'usable content' (line 11) by quoting from an authority in the field, but explicitly links this notion to concrete examples of one important way in which the notion is made 'usable', that is, through dictionary definitions (lines 15–18).

The writer includes a further quotation from one scholar, Williams (lines 42–52), which she uses to explicitly link some of the definitions discussed within specific disciplinary fields and indicate a convergence between these and a more 'common' definition. The writer builds on this quotation to emphasize (and summarize) the point being made across the section – the range of definitions in existence. Note also that, by using two quotations by the same scholar – one at the beginning and one towards the end of this section – she is displaying allegiance not only to a particular scholar but to a particular approach within a field.

She concludes this section by making an important evaluative claim about the studies and scholars she has cited – 'they fall short of substance for the purposes of this study' (lines 54–55) – and about the need to delve further into specific fields, in particular anthropology, in order to develop a relevant conceptual framework. She has therefore orchestrated the voices of established scholars, not only to indicate what they offer but also their limitations.

It is interesting to note that she uses the sub-heading 'scoping the problem' to signal to the reader that a key strand of the argument is that culture is a complex notion which cannot be simply described or defined but rather has to be considered within specific parameters.

Remember that this is a text still in progress and you may have noted that some further crafting is needed. Two aspects which may need further consideration are: (1) the writer uses dictionaries as a source of definitions, rather than using only academic texts; (2) the writer makes extensive use of quotations, which may be unacceptable in some disciplinary areas or to some supervisors. In order to find out what kinds of texts are considered as appropriate sources and which conventions are acceptable in your particular field, it is important to look at theses in your discipline and to discuss this with your supervisors.

Activity 6.5

Listen on DVD audio programme to the comments by Anne Hewling for more about the drafting of Extract 5 and how it fits into her thesis overall.

Forging a clear argument

In discussing Extract 5, we emphasized the way the writer makes key moves as a way of advancing her argument on the difficulties surrounding the definition of culture.

Another way of thinking of these moves is to view them as together representing the author's 'main path' through her text. The language you use to refer to the work of other researchers plays an important part in forging this main path. Below are examples where the language used indicates that the work of others is being used to support the main argument that computers are a useful resource in education:

> As already indicated by Smith (2004), computers are a very useful resource …

> 'Computers are a powerful resource for learning in the classroom', Smith (2004:26).

> It is clear that computers are a useful resource (Smith 2004) …

> As shown by (Smith 2004) computers are a useful resource …

But it is important to note that in order to forge a main path, the writer doesn't simply introduce quotes and theorists that support her argument but she also introduces ideas and cites work that she does not find convincing: 'faulty paths'. Surprisingly perhaps, these faulty paths and detours help to strengthen the main argument or path. The purpose of faulty paths is 'to mark perceptual boundaries and increase the clarity of the main path' (Geisler and Kaufer, 1991, p. 11). An example of a faulty path in Extract 5 is the definitions the writer includes at lines 13–18:

> A number of options for 'usable content' for the concept of culture can be found in any dictionary, for example:
>
> • the customary beliefs, social forms, and material traits of a racial, religious, or social group (Merriam-Webster Online Dictionary)
>
> • the way of life, especially the general customs and beliefs, of a particular group of people at a particular time (Cambridge Advanced Learner's Dictionary)

The introduction of the faulty path here is signalled by 'A number of options', which allows the writer to simply list them without indicating any allegiance to them. Other ways in which faulty paths could be introduced are as follows:

> It has been suggested that there are a number of options for defining culture. For example Brown (1994) . . .
>
> • Brown (1994) claims to have offered a number of options for defining culture . . .
>
> • Brown (1994) and Singh (2001) argue that culture can theorize as follows: . . .

These lead the reader away from the main path but they can function as further justification for the main argument. By including definitions of culture, the writer shows that she is willing (and able) to consider all possibilities but, after due consideration, has decided to dismiss them. This dismissal is signalled to the reader by the language used in Extract 5, where the writer uses the contrastive link 'however' and makes a categorical criticism:

> However, none of the definitions offer any ideas of place or space in relation to the groups they refer to.

This serves as a 'return path', whereby the reader, having taken a detour to consider some possible definitions, is drawn back by the writer to the main path – back on track to the main argument. Other ways of signalling a return path are as follows:

> Although Smith (2004) argues that ..., this study indicates ...

> Smith (2004) suggests that ... However, findings from this study indicate. ...

> Whilst Smith (2004) indicates X ... it is unclear whether ...

Other modes of constructing and representing knowledge

Academic argument as illustrated in this chapter is construed as a predominantly rational activity, conventionally reflected in the step-by-step advancing of claims which are supported by evidence and explicitly stated reasons. Whilst most academic writing is expected to conform to this practice, in some disciplines and paradigms other forms of constructing and representing knowledge are being adopted. Some student writers, in addition to conventional argument, are including other forms of writing in their theses. Pauline Evans (2000), for example, decided to write not only in the conventional academic way using logical argument, but, in addition, to include less conventional forms which combine the 'scientific' with what she refers to as the 'dramatic self' in her thesis writing. Thus, she included brief extracts from her research diary and what she refers to as 'choruses', in an attempt to bring to life the voices of her participants. Examples of these less conventional ways of writing are given below:

Extract 6

> Why do I have to use a theory? These theories have been conjured up by those who have not been there (in my research). By virtue of the fact that these theorists (usually men) have spent a long time in the academic world, why should so much importance be attached to what they say?

Extract 7:   The Catsbury Chorus

Tell me, what do you think a nursery class is for?

Parent	Well the children learn
	so many different things.
Children	I think. I come
	Cos it's school.
	Cos mummy brings me in the car.
Parent	And they do the things
	They couldn't do at home.
Children	I come I think
	To make things.
	I come because it's school.
Headteacher	The main purpose has to be
	Socialisation … caring

Activity 6.6

To what extent are alternative modes of representation permissible in your context? Discuss with a colleague any ideas you have about including less conventional academic styles and formats. If you are uneasy or unsure about what your overall approach might be, discuss this with your supervisor.

6.6   Writing for Public Forums

In this section we turn our focus to professional writing, both because of its importance in your research career, and because understanding the way it is structured will also help you in structuring your thesis (which we will look at in Section 6.7). Increasingly, research students write for public dissemination and publication before completing their theses and in some departments and institutions this is seen as an essential part of postgraduate experience and training. You may therefore be writing conference abstracts and papers, and journal articles – either on your own or with a supervisor – at the same time as you are carrying out a specific piece of research towards your thesis or writing a particular section of your thesis. Whilst these 'public' texts may differ considerably, it is worth bearing in mind some general points.

CARS – creating a research space

You may have carried out an excellent piece of research, but unless you make it clear why and how your research is relevant to a specific research community – through its recognized conferences and journals – you will find it difficult to get conference proposals accepted or articles published. One useful way of making sure that your contribution is recognized is to think of your text as a series of important moves. We briefly mentioned 'moves' in Section 6.5 of this chapter, and it may prove helpful to think about them in more detail here. 'Move' refers to the function of different parts of your written text rather than the content; a move is about what a particular bit of text is doing, rather than what it is saying (as writers we are often much more concerned about the latter). Readers such as supervisors and conference and journal reviewers tend to implicitly recognize when a specific move is missing, so it can be helpful to think about the moves you are making in your writing.

The CARS (Create a Research Space) model was developed by John Swales based on analysis of substantial numbers of article introductions (1990, p. 141). It emphasizes the importance of showing how your research in some way fills a significant gap in the knowledge and understanding of a particular field.

Activity 6.7

Look at the original abstract on cross-cultural understanding in Extract 8 (taken from the website for the 2003 Conference of Psychologists for Social Responsibility). Can you identify any important 'moves' that the writer makes?

Extract 8: Amal Winter: Insights on Cross-Cultural Understanding: The Arab/Muslim World, a Case Study of Misunderstanding

(1) In a 1999 article, Ervin Staub identifies 'difficult life conditions' as giving rise to scapegoating and ideologies that identify enemies and lead a group to turn against another. (2) This concept is relevant to the escalating violence between America/Western world and the Arab/Muslim world but it is not sufficient. (3) This presentation will focus on the relationship between Arab/Muslims and the West from an Arab/Muslim point of view. (4) It will emphasise how the changes experienced by those who live in predominantly Muslim countries of the Middle East have given rise to religious fervour and a renewed belief that Islam

will improve their political and economic conditions either peacefully or with violence. (5) Drawing on Edward Said's work which illustrates the distortions caused by cultural hegemony and superior military/economic position and a recent Zogby International poll of Arabs reporting their own world-views to other Arabs, it will show how Western scholars and academics, including psychologists, have exaggerated the differences and diminished the similarities between 'East and West' and developed negative perceptions/misperceptions of the Arab/Muslim world to maintain neo-colonial positions. (6) It will challenge psychologists to examine their own presumptions and practices and suggest ways to encourage better cross-cultural understanding.

In Table 6.1 we have mapped out the key moves the writer makes, using Swales' framework.

Table 6.1   The CARS model

Key moves in Extract 8	Sentences where moves are evident
Move 1 Establishing a territory by introducing and reviewing items of previous research in the area	1
Move 2 Establishing a niche by indicating a gap in the previous research, raising a question about it or extending previous knowledge in some way	2
Move 3 Occupying the niche by outlining purposes or stating the nature of the present contribution	3–6

Activity 6.8

EITHER: Look at some more abstracts taken from a conference website related to your discipline. Can you identify the three moves shown above in each abstract? Are there any abstracts which appear to have a different structure? OR: If you are currently writing a conference abstract, check to see whether you have included the three moves.

The research article structure

An abstract that you write for a conference proposal may become a paper that you write for a conference or conference proceedings, or an academic journal article.

Getting a paper published in academic journals is a very competitive business so it is worthwhile spending a little time thinking about the key elements of a research article.

The most common structure for academic journal articles is often referred to as IMRD, and as we shall see in Section 6.7, this basic pattern is also found in theses:

- **Introduction**

- **Method**

- **Results**

- **Discussion**

Articles in different academic disciplines often use this IMRD structure even if they label sections in different ways. Such labelling may be procedural (focusing on the research procedures) or topical (focusing on what the article is about):

Procedural sectioning	Topical sectioning
Introduction	An international economy
Method	Spread of English
Results	Changes in the 21st century
Discussion	
Conclusion	

From Hasman, M.A. (2000) 'The role of English in the 21st century', *English Teaching Forum*, vol. 38(1), pp. 3–5.

Many research articles use a combination of both types of labelling as exemplified in Extract 9; here 'Methodology' is subsumed under 'Introduction', and the middle sections of the article are structured entirely with topically based headings. The core elements of a research article are similar to those of a thesis which are outlined in Section 6.7.

Extract 9:   IMRD with Topical Sectioning

Abstract

Introduction
   Methodology
Three Case Studies
The Learning Society and ILAs
ILAs in SMEs: a case of individual responsibility?
   Case 1: Peter, Sharp Tools, and HiTec Training
   Case 2: Norah, Church House and Communicating Care
How Many Cheers for ILAs
The ED Alternative
   Case 3: Fancy Goods
Conclusions

From 'The "Learning Society" and small and medium-sized enterprises: empowering the individual', by Rick Holden and John Hamblett (*Journal of Vocational Education and Training*, Vol. 53, No. 1, 2001, pp. 121–39).

Although academic articles may share similar patterns, there are many variations, which you have probably noticed in your academic reading. Such variations include the topics covered, the type of research paradigm represented and the journal style. It is therefore essential that, before you prepare an article for submission to a journal, you identify the journal you are planning to submit to. This will help you sharpen your focus for the article as well as decide on the most appropriate structure. One obvious way of identifying a journal that might be interested in your research is to list the journals whose articles you have been reading as part of your own research.

Activity 6.9

Identify a journal that you are planning to write an article for (either in the near or more distant future) and consider the following questions. What type of article structure and sectioning is common in your discipline and specialist sub-field? What do you notice about the kinds of sectioning in articles in your target journal? Do they follow the IMRD pattern/mixed procedural and topical sectioning? On the basis of the kind of pattern that you have identified, what kind of structure will you adopt for your article? Why?

Receiving and responding to feedback from reviewers

When you submit an article to a journal, if the editor considers it a potentially worthy paper for inclusion in the journal, he or she will forward it to one, two or possibly three reviewers. These are experts in your field who are typically asked to evaluate submitted articles using the following kinds of criteria:

- **relevance to the journal;**

- **originality;**

- **methodologically validity;**

- **clearly written and well presented.**

You may be able to find a journal's criteria on its website. The journal's reviewers will be asked to make a recommendation as to whether your paper be published as follows:

1 [ ]   publish as is

2 [ ]   publish with minor revisions

3 [✓]   publish with major revisions

4 [ ]   revise and resubmit

5 [ ]   reject

Most papers that eventually appear in a journal will have fallen into categories 2 to 3, so you can always expect to make some revisions. Many researchers are also asked to revise and resubmit. Whilst everyone's preferred response would be 1 or 2, you should treat 1–4 as a 'success' in that it means your research is of interest – you just have to do more work on your paper. Receiving 5 is very disheartening but, once you get over the initial disappointment, you should also try and view 5 positively because, along with the rejection, you should receive some comments on your work. Bear in mind that reviewing is not an exact science and that reviewers have very different approaches to offering feedback: some are extremely encouraging, whereas a few can be downright dismissive. Try not to take the comments personally. And always seek further feedback from people whose opinion you value if you are unhappy about any specific comments which you think are unjustified: you may not be able to persuade a particular reviewer or journal to accept your article, but you can seek advice about which aspects of your research are worth developing further.

Activity 6.10

Read one reviewer's feedback (in Extract 10) on a co-authored paper which received 'publish with minor revisions'. How might the authors respond to such comments? What decisions would they have to make?

Extract 10

This is a good paper which I recommend for publication subject to some revisions which I consider essential. My major concern – given the applied focus of the journal – is the lack of attention paid to the relevance of the study to practitioners. Given the competition for space in the journal, I feel convinced a section pointing up such relevance is crucial. In terms of the account of the study itself, I think more information about the project in general should be included – the data collection process, the type of data, number of participants – and there is a need to clarify connection between larger project and the focus of this paper. At a theoretical level, there is some confusion I think. The terms core/margins and inner/outer seem to be used with different meanings in mind yet there appears also to be a conflation. I suggest that only one of these sets of terms be used to avoid confusion.

When replying to the journal editor, the authors not only included their revised article but also a cover letter, detailing their responses to the reviewers. This is illustrated in their responses to the reviewer's comments above.

Comments made by reviewer 1	Writers' letter to the editor
1 The relevance of the study to practitioners needs to be made clear	We agree and have done as follows: added two paragraphs in the introduction; incorporated references to previous research in the conclusion; expanded the implications section, including examples of specific pedagogical strategies.
2 Use of terms core/margins, inner/outer. Suggest one of these sets of terms to avoid confusion.	We acknowledge the potential for confusion. At the same time we note that reviewer 2 seems to find the argument clear. In order to take account of reviewer 1's comments we have cut the reference to 'inner/outer' in the introduction and throughout reduced the references to core/margins. But we have kept both sets of terms in the article because we feel they are necessary for the argument.

As can be seen, whilst the authors state explicitly where they agree with reviewer 1, they are less direct in the expression of their disagreement on point 2. Note that they have in fact rejected this particular criticism and use the authority of the second reviewer to resist the pressure to cut what they see as relevant terms.

This section has highlighted two aspects of writing for public forums which relate closely to thesis writing. First, as you probably noticed, article authors need to consider carefully their responses to reviewers' comments, in a similar way to research students responding to supervisors' comments. In defending any aspect of your writing to external reviewers or your supervisors, it is important to show that you have taken account of their comments and that you can justify the decisions you finally make. Second, despite their differences, both academic articles and theses share some basic structural features which we now turn to in the following section.

6.7 Structuring the Thesis

Planning the final structure

The structure of your thesis is something that will develop over time, as you gradually refine your ideas. At the beginning your plans are likely to be fairly rough, with just a general indication of what might be included in each chapter. As you progress, you will fill out the detail of each chapter or section that you are currently working on. However, you are likely in the course of writing to become aware of unanticipated links and gaps that force you to modify the structure, so you should be prepared to let the thesis grow organically.

Although there are many different ways of structuring a thesis, some elements are common to all theses. The chapters may be labelled and organized in different ways, but almost always involve the core elements shown in Table 6.2, each associated with particular functions.

Table 6.2   Core elements of a research thesis

Core element	Main functions	Comment
Introduction	To establish the significance of the general research area To locate your research within the field To outline the aims and the nature of your research	This is usually written at the end when you have full drafts of all chapters and a clear idea of the main contribution of your research and its relationship to the field
Literature review	To provide an overview of relevant research To locate your research more specifically in relation to the literature To set boundaries around the 'field' of relevant research. Identifying a core question for investigation	You will probably write many versions of this as you progress. You will need to show how your own research emerges from and responds to issues in the field, and you will not know exactly how your contribution fits in until you have carried out your research

(Continued)

Table 6.2   *(Continued)*

Core element	Main functions	Comment
Methodology	To provide an overview of the methodology adopted To justify the choice of methodology in relation to epistemological traditions and research aims	First drafts of this are often written early on when you are exploring and deciding on a specific methodology to suit your research questions. It tends to be less liable to change than other chapters, unless your research centres on the methodology itself
Data analysis	To offer closely argued analysis of the data To present findings and discuss interpretations	Data analysis forms the core of a thesis; you should be prepared to begin writing this material early on, and to redraft it extensively
Conclusion	To summarize the research and main findings To locate the findings within the field as defined earlier in the thesis To offer a critique of the research and its limitations	This normally forms the final chapter. It tends to be written last, in tandem with the introduction, so that you can sharpen up the way your research questions, methodology, analysis and findings relate to each other

Activity 6.11

Look at the tables of contents in Extracts 11, 12 and 13, taken from theses in three different disciplines. You will notice examples of both procedural and topical sectioning, but can you identify which chapters seem to match the core elements of Introduction, Literature review, Methodology, Data analysis, and Conclusion? What variations do you notice?

Extract 11

Keith Waldron (2001) 'Performance indicators for public sector scientists'

1   Executive Summary

2   Introduction, Aims and Objectives

Extract 12

Susan Ormrod (2002) 'Sense-making and authorising in the organisation of mental health care'

Extract 13

Andy Morris (2002) 'Geographies of multiculturalism: Britishness, normalisation and the spaces of the Tate Gallery'

Comment

Keith Waldron's structure is closest to the model in Table 6.2, though you may have noticed that his introduction and methodology elements each span two chapters, and he also provides an 'executive summary', which is characteristic of business studies. In Susan Ormrod's thesis, the chapters have been grouped into five parts. The first part deals with introduction and methodology, but it is more difficult to see which parts provide literature review and data analysis. When a thesis is organized to deal with different aspects of a topic, it is possible to provide the literature review element not in a separate chapter, but at the beginning of each topic. In Susan Ormrod's thesis, the introduction to each part provides this type of literature review. Andy Morris's thesis stands out as different as it is not based on empirical research; the introduction and conclusion are present, but the remaining chapters are organized around key aspects of the theoretical discussions. As you can see, theses can vary enormously in their structure. Exactly how the chapters of your own thesis will be organized and labelled will depend ultimately on your specific aims, and the practices of the disciplinary area in which you are working.

One important challenge to the conventionally accepted model of thesis structure and representation comes from researchers working within post-positivist paradigms (see Chapter 4). You've already seen an example in Section 6.5, of Pauline Evans's inclusion of 'dramatic' material in her thesis (Evans, 1997), and experimentation of this sort is increasingly common in some disciplines. Despite this, it is important to bear in mind that theses are judged against the functions listed in Table 6.2, so although other elements may be included, your thesis must still meet these requirements.

Activity 6.12

This activity can be carried out using either an outline of your own thesis chapters, or using a completed thesis in your field. Draw two columns, and in the left-hand column list the chapter headings. In the right-hand column list the functions of each chapter. Check to see how closely the functions you identify relate to the functions shown in Table 6.2. If there are significant differences, can you explain the reasons for this?

Steering the reader

One of the most difficult aspects of writing a large document such as a thesis is ordering the information. The tangle of ideas in your head needs to be transformed into a linear piece of writing in such a way that it is clear to a reader. There are general principles that may help; for example, information may be ordered chronologically, in cause/effect sequence, in order of importance, or from general to specific. One of the most important principles is the move from given to new; that is, to start with what is familiar to your reader as a basis for what is new. This is why, for example, a thesis typically begins by reviewing the literature that already exists and will therefore be familiar to other scholars in the field, before moving on to discussing the writer's own research, which will be new to most readers. The same principle operates at all levels, and can help you decide the order of chapters, of sections, of sub-sections and of paragraphs. The next activity looks at the way the given/new principle operates at paragraph level.

Activity 6.13

The following extract comes from Rosamunde Codling's PhD thesis on 'Wilderness and aesthetic values in the Antarctic' (1998, p 19). We've printed the clauses separately on the left to make it easier to analyse the way they are linked together. Read through and notice how the words in italics relate back to earlier clauses. Our comments are on the right, but you may prefer to cover these while you to try the activity for yourself.

Extract 14:   Paragraph Coherence

Aesthetic values	Comments
(a) Discussion about *aesthetics* has taken place for centuries.	Relates back to the heading
(b) but in Britain, the *18th* and *19th centuries* saw increased interest in the application of aesthetic values to landscape.	Specifies two of the 'centuries' mentioned in (a)
(c) *More recently*, there has been a demand for the development of practical procedures that can form part of a wider planning process.	Contrasts with 'the 18th and 19th centuries'
(d) *This* has led to 'landscape assessment' in the United Kingdom and 'visual resource management' in the United States.	Refers to the 'demand for the development of practical procedures'
(e) *These methodologies* differ, so detailed appraisal is necessary.	Refers to 'landscape assessment' and 'visual resource management'
(f) *Any process to be used in the Antarctic* will also need to work in extreme climatic conditions, with all the logistical and safety difficulties imposed by the nature of the continent. [...]	Relates to the choice of methodology discussed in (c)–(e), indicating why 'detailed appraisal' is necessary
(g) *Recent British work* has also sought to include landscape perception within survey procedures.	Continues chronologically from the British work mentioned in (d)
(h) *Perception* may be expressed in a wide variety of forms, frequently not easy to map or tabulate, but none the less real.	Refers to 'landscape perception'
(i) *Sources such as technical studies, literary references, photographs, paintings and films* are seen as contributing to a greater understanding as to how the landscape is seen or appreciated.	Specifies the 'wide variety of forms'
(j) Even in the early days of exploration, *logs and diaries* contained descriptions of the Antarctic,	Gives more examples of the 'wide variety of forms'

(k) and *from the turn of the century* expeditions regularly took artists and later photographers with them.	Contrasts with 'the early days of exploration'
(l) *Such documents* are informative on both objective and subjective counts.	Sums up all the different sources mentioned in (i)–(k)

This piece of writing has been constructed so that ideas are linked together coherently, allowing the reader to move smoothly from familiar to new ideas. We are not suggesting that the writer consciously thought about given and new information in each clause; it's more likely that her attention was focused on how to guide the reader through her ideas. There are always different ways of organizing information, and part of the skill of good writing is being able to play with the organization until you find one that is coherent and clear to the reader.

The same issue arises with respect to the thesis as a whole. Having spent so long on it, you will be aware of the way that ideas are related: the key issue that unifies a section, the themes that run through several chapters, the points introduced in one place and picked up later. Someone approaching your thesis for the first time, however, will not necessarily appreciate these relationships unless you make them clear. Compare, for example, these two sentences:

Participants were aware of the video recorder.

Another significant factor is that participants were aware of the video recorder.

Although both sentences convey the same information, the second sentence also indicates how this information relates to the rest of the text, as a new item in a list of significant factors. Language that is used in this way is known as metadiscourse. One example of metadiscourse is the use of headings to indicate the structure of a thesis; notice how the heading 'aesthetic values' in Extract 14 helps the reader grasp the significance of the text. Metadiscourse also occurs within the text, for example:

It may therefore be concluded that …

Despite these criticisms, it can be argued that …

The next feature to be considered is …

The aim in this section is to …

As illustrated in Table 6 …

Metadiscourse frequently occurs at the beginning of chapters or sections, where the writer provides an overview of what is going to be covered, or at the end, where they sum up. Thesis writers often include a section consisting almost entirely of metadiscourse which provides an overview of the whole document. This typically occurs at the end of the first chapter. The next extract, however, comes from a thesis which is organized in four parts, with the main overview coming at the end of the first part.

Activity 6.14

Below you can see an extract from Susan Ormrod's thesis on 'Sense-making and authorising in the organization of mental health care' (2002, pp. 27–8). She has introduced the Care Programme Approach (CPA) in Part One of the thesis, and is now providing an overview of the remaining parts. How does she distinguish these parts in terms of (a) subject matter and (b) approach?

Extract 15:   Overview of the Thesis

Part Two is a scene-setting story, with chapter 4 telling the tale of the CPA as a national policy initiative. Here I draw on government documents and 'trade' literature. Chapter 5 tells the story of attempts to implement the CPA in the NHS Trust studied. Here I draw particularly on an account I wrote as a 'management consultant' to the Trust, together with other studies of CPA implementation. Both these stories are written with a managerial voice and the image of organization is one of structures and functions.

Part Three looks at teamwork as it was practised by the teams I observed. Here the topic is organising, rather than organisation. The approach is ethnographic, though informed by ethnomethodology and by various conceptual tools drawn from Goffman and others influenced by him. Since these are multidisciplinary teams, the literature on this topic is reviewed and the story is told as a contribution to debates about multidisciplinarity and interdisciplinary relations.

Part Four looks at the products of team deliberations described in Part Three. The products are the organisational personalities created for patients by teams as patients are transformed into objects of mental health work. Again the approach is ethnographic. This is a field of study where 'labelling theory' has occupied a central space. The relevant literature is reviewed and this part of the thesis is told as a contribution to the critique of labelling theory.

Comment

Susan Ormrod's thesis is organized according to different criteria. The three parts are distinguished by the different topics they address – the CPA, teamwork, and team outcomes (labelling) – but in addition they are distinguished according to the approach taken (managerial or ethnographic), and the data drawn on (documentary sources, observation, subject literatures). Although the structure is complex, she has made this clear to the reader through the metadiscourse of her overview.

6.8   From Writer to Reader

For much of your time you will approach your academic writing as a writer. However, it is important that you also make time to approach your texts as a reader in order to focus on two key aspects: (1) as a prospective reader of the ideas; (2) as a proof-reader looking out for any slips in word processing, grammar or referencing. It is always a good idea to leave some time between writing and reading as it can be hard to 'see' what you have actually written (rather than what you think you have written) when it is your own work. It can also be helpful to take frequent brief breaks in your reading to ensure that your concentration remains high. You may find it helpful to consider the following questions as you adopt these different ways of readings.

As a prospective reader
Think of your prospective readers and consider how they may read your text. Decide whether you are reading as a thesis examiner, a journal editor, a research student and what you may be looking for. We have suggested some key areas in this chapter.

Content. Check for clarity of main ideas, relevance and interest to readers, evidence of familiarity with specific discipline or specialist subfield.

Argument. Check that the main argument is clear, that moves are obvious, that alternative positions have been considered, that appropriate evidence is provided, that citations are used both to show knowledge of the field and to advance your argument.

Organization. Check that text sectioning, such as paragraphs, sections and chapters, helps convey ideas clearly, for example that all core elements are included, that there is a progression from familiar to new information, that different issues are dealt with in separate paragraphs and that links are made (you don't suddenly jump between topics).

Language. Check that the style is appropriate, that language adequately represents your intended meanings, that language is used to signal coherent links across sentences and paragraphs, that metadiscourse is used to steer readers through the text.

As a proof-reader
Most people find it much easier to read from a hard copy, but you can of course also make good use of your computer by checking for errors using its spell-check or search

functions, For example, you can search for 'realise' and 'realize' to make sure you have been consistent, or search for 'argueable' if you have a tendency to misspell 'arguable'.

Layout. Don't forget that word processing can help – seek advice on possible layouts.

Accuracy of language (spelling, punctuation, grammar). There are many resources available both on the web and in books – see 'Recommended reading'.

Referencing and bibliography. Advice on this is found in Chapter 7 and there are a number of websites on this subject.

6.9   Recommended Reading

Good overviews
Burton, S. and Steane, P. (2004) *Surviving Your Thesis*. London: Routledge.

Murray, R. (2002) *How to Write a Thesis*. Buckingham: Open University Press.

Wolcott, H.F. (2001) *Writing Up Qualitative Research*. Newbury Park, CA: Sage.

Useful guidance on academic language and text construction
(for users of English as a first or foreign language)
Swales, J. and Feak, C. (1994) *A Course for Non Native Speakers of English*. Ann Arbor: University of Michigan Press.

Swales, J. and Feak, C. (2004) *Academic Writing for Graduate Students: Essential Tasks and Skills*. Ann Arbor: University of Michigan Press.

References

Codling, R. (1998) 'Wilderness and aesthetic values in the Antarctic', unpublished PhD thesis, The Open University.

Evans, P. (1997) 'Talking about nursery education: perceptions in context', unpublished PhD thesis, University of Bristol.

Evans, P. (2000) 'Boundary oscillations: epistemological and genre transformation during the "method" of thesis writing', *Social Research Methodology*, vol. 3 (4), pp. 267–86.

Geisler, C. and Kaufer, D.S. (1991) 'A scheme for representing written argument', *Journal of Advanced Composition*, vol. 11 (1), pp. 199–222.

Li, S. (2002) 'My research diary', Current Research Newsletter, Department of Sociology, Goldsmiths College, no. 17.

Li, S. (2004) ' "Symbiotic niceness": constructing a therapeutic relationship in psychosocial palliative care', *Social Science and Medicine*, vol. 58 (12), pp. 2571–83.

Moron-Garcia, S. (2004) *'Understanding lecturer use of virtual learning environments in face-to-face teaching in UK higher education'*, unpublished PhD thesis, The Open University.

Ormrod, S. (2002) 'Sense-making and authorising in the organization of mental health care', unpublished PhD thesis, The Open University.

Swales, J. (1990) *Genre Analysis: English in Academic and Research Settings.* Cambridge: Cambridge University Press.

Toulmin, S. (1958) *The Uses of Argument.* Cambridge: Cambridge University Press.

7 Undertaking a Literature Review

Stephen Potter
with material provided by The Open
University Library for their Information Search
Guides and from Peter Taylor for The Open
University course STM895

LEARNING OUTCOMES

After reading this chapter and working on its associated activities you should be able to:

- Establish the purposes for which you are undertaking a literature review.
- Plan and organize your literature review.
- Identify sources of information and relevant research methodologies and techniques within your research field.
- Document your sources.
- Arrange information search research training.
- Demonstrate your willingness and ability to learn and acquire knowledge.
- (In conjunction with Chapter 6) Write up your literature review in a creative, innovative and original manner.
- Use the literature review process to listen, receive and give feedback and respond perceptively.
- Demonstrate initiative, your ability to work independently and be self-reliant through undertaking a literature review.

7.1 Introduction

This chapter begins by looking at planning your literature review and how your review links into the wider task of planning and undertaking your research project as a whole. Section 7.3 of this chapter then considers the practicalities of information searching, which you should undertake in conjunction with training organized via your own department or library. Section 7.4 looks at how information searching includes people and organizations, with Section 7.5 providing some advice on recording results and keeping your information search organized. Section 7.6 concludes this chapter by providing advice on writing your literature review. This last section in particular needs to be used together with material in Chapter 6, on academic writing.

A literature review is a major activity for any research degree or taught Master's dissertation. Depending on your previous experience in information searching, it will take at least 10 hours to complete this chapter, including undertaking some basic information-searching activities. In addition to this, you will certainly need to refer to this chapter again at several points in undertaking your research project.

7.2 The Purposes of a Literature Review

What is a literature review

A 'literature review' forms a crucial part of any research degree or dissertation. Increasingly, not only literature is involved, but also other forms of information. Electronic sources are now widely used, but information can come from people, not just written sources, and remember that statistical information and databases as well as articles and books may be involved. Basically, as part of your research project, you need to find out 'where things are at' in your topic area. A number of terms are used when reviewing 'where things are at', including 'literature review', 'topic review', 'subject review' or 'state-of-the-art review'. This chapter uses the traditional term 'literature review' even though a review will of necessity include sources other than just literature.

In beginning a literature review it is essential to think carefully about the purposes you are trying to achieve. There is no point in simply wading into the literature and other contacts thinking you can 'immerse' yourself in your subject. Particularly today, when electronic information systems are so powerful, there is an immense danger of simply being overwhelmed by the vast volume of information that is out there.

So, first, it is important to think through the purposes of reviewing literature. In your research you will need to draw upon what other people have done at several points, at differing depths and for different purposes. Although your thesis or dissertation is likely to have a chapter headed 'Literature Review' (or whatever you call it), this is not the only place where you will need to show an understanding of what others have done on your chosen topic area.

Activity 7.1

Note down what purposes will be fulfilled for your research project by reviewing the literature on your topic area. Note how you will use the literature and other information.

Make a list, plus any brief notes you think are necessary.

Discussion

A literature review is involved early in a research project where you are expected to evaluate your topic area. Although you need to show that you know how your topic area has developed and what the main discussion points are, a literature review is more than just a scene-setting exercise. From your review should emerge a second purpose – that of identifying your own research focus. The design of your own research project should emerge from the evaluation of issues and debates that you have reviewed. If your literature review does not identify your research project as being an issue that needs investigating, then you have not fulfilled this core purpose.

Your literature review should also inform the choice of research method, through an analysis of the methods used by others – or possibly from an analysis of the weaknesses of methods used by others. This need not necessarily be written up in the same review, and could be part of a separate methodology chapter in your thesis or dissertation.

Later, once you have your results, another purpose of a literature review is to relate your research to existing knowledge in order to show what your contribution has been. This is a crucial part of your research; through it you will show the relationship of your findings to that of colleagues in the field.

Conceptions of a literature review

To follow the above activity and initial observations, we shall use the work of an Australian education researcher, Christine Bruce (1994). She surveyed Master's and doctoral students in the early stages of their research projects and asked them to reflect on what they understood a 'literature review' to be. These students came from a wide variety of academic disciplines. From their responses, she developed a typology of six conceptions of a literature review. These conceptions were:

1   **The Literature Review as a List. A collection of discrete items on a particular subject, possibly with keywords or a short description.**

2   **The Literature Review as a Search. Identifying information that is useful for a research project.**

3   **The Literature Review as a Survey. Investigating writings and research to discover the knowledge base and the methods of investigation used.**

4   **The Literature Review as a Vehicle for Learning. Using the literature as a sounding board to check out the researcher's ideas and perceptions of a subject; seeking to gain understanding derived from reading the literature.**

5   **The Literature Review as a Research Facilitator. Helping develop a particular stage of the research process, for example, on a particular methodology, on refining the research question, when something unexpected has happened and the research needs to take a new direction.**

6   **The Literature Review as a Report. A written discussion of previous investigations.**

Your list of purposes in Activity 7.1 may or may not map on to this typology (you might have responded to the question in a different way), but see whether you can slot your list of 'purposes' for a literature review into Bruce's categories. Write the above 'conceptions' numbers next to the items on your list (you may end up with something in more than one category; and if there is a 'main' one, underline it).

The changing purposes of a literature review

A major conclusion from Bruce's article was that, in the early stages of research, postgraduate students tend to have a 'list', 'search' and 'survey' concept of the literature review, but Bruce notes that 'students' thinking needs to be challenged as early as possible in their research programme so that it is clear that the final product of the literature review is a coherent synthesis of past and present research. It is not a list or annotated bibliography on the area of interest, although these may represent early stages in progress towards the end product.' Your understanding of what others have done must inform your own research; eventually you will have to show where your research fits into the body of knowledge of which it is a part.

As was noted in the Discussion on Activity 7.1, your purposes of reviewing literature will change as you progress through your research. For example, you may be more interested in understanding the results of a piece of work in the early stages of your research, in the research method used once you start thinking about your own data gathering, and perhaps why there are differences between your results and those in the literature when your data are gathered in.

One postgraduate commented:

> I have learned how one's review of the topic changes and grows. I have probably tried three plus versions of it by now, and it is still changing. It will change, grow, expand and deepen over time. This movement is a good sign. Several writings may actually be part of the process of achieving the understandings wanted from the review.

The following list of purposes for a literature review is based on a variety of sources, including Bruce's 'conceptions' and research-training experience at a number of universities in Britain by the team that have put this book together. Nevertheless, you may have additions of your own.

1 **To gain knowledge on the subject area. This is a matter not only of finding out what are the major research issues and debates, but also of developing your ability to appraise critically what others have done. Who has done decent and interesting work? Why do you think their work is good?**

2 **To find out where the literature is thin, or where there are gaps in knowledge. It is important to note not only what research has been done, but also what has not been adequately researched.**

3 **To gain feedback information in order to rethink and focus a research topic. This concerns sorting out key issues, identifying 'hot' research topics and using your literature review to assist you in formulating or refining your core research question.**

4 **To find out whether there are related or parallel literatures which have developed in isolation. Information or method from one area could help another. For example, a research student, looking at the work conducted by private consultancies commissioned to help develop the EU Ecolabel, noticed they failed to take account of closely related energy studies and methodologies developed in government research labs in the USA. Two related literatures had developed in isolation from each other.**

5 **To discover how others have researched the chosen topic area. Look at literature and other sources to explore methods, research questions, data availability and analysis as well as results.**

6 **To justify how and why you have done the research in the way you have. For example, one OU student used a hybrid case study/modelling method in his transport research because he felt that models on their own were inadequate. Other researchers had reached a similar conclusion which supported this important decision.**

7 **To have a body of information to compare with your research findings. When reporting and discussing your results you need to compare them with what other researchers have found out.**

These purposes are relevant to all postgraduate degrees. However, the depth to which they are pursued will vary according to the criteria for a Master's dissertation and for each research degree (which were discussed in Chapter 2).

Broadly, at an appropriate level for each degree, an examiner will expect a student to have used their knowledge of the topic to show that:

1 **You know your subject area.**

2 **You have made a critical review of other work in the field – not just a list, but a demonstration of understanding. Think of it as providing a guided tour of a topic, pointing out important features (not every insignificant molehill).**

3 **You know the relationship of your work to the rest of the field.**

Activity 7.2

Read the offprint 'Reviewing the literature' from Judith Bell's book which you will find at the end of this chapter. This focuses in particular on the production of a critical review of existing work.

Read as far as the end of the Alan Woodley extract. This is a very short review for an article about educational research, but it is written so that anyone can comment on how good it is as a critical literature review.

Having, in Activity 7.1, considered the purposes of a literature review, note which of them is fulfilled by Woodley's review.

When you have done this, read Bell's last paragraph.

> ## Activity 7.2   (Continued)
>
> ### Discussion
>
> Alan Woodley's review is certainly a critical appraisal; he notes what other researchers have done and says that one line of investigation appears to be more satisfactory. The review also shows that he was using information to rethink and focus on a core research question and to explore how others have researched in this area. Method is a key component of this review, and the work Woodley has done specifically emerges from an approach in the literature that he considers to be most valid. In this introduction he does not report his findings, but clearly he has a body of information to compare with his own results.

Literature reviewing for method, focus and comparison

A critical assessment of the work of others should become the springboard for your own work. Your own programme of research needs to emerge out of your literature review (as it did in Alan Woodley's case) by showing that a particular aspect requires attention.

However, as noted previously in this chapter, you will need to draw upon your knowledge of your subject area throughout your research work, not just in order to set it up. This links to Bruce's 'higher' purposes of a review: as a 'vehicle for learning' and 'research facilitator'. Put simply, as you progress in your research project you will need to draw upon the work of other people to help you:

1   Identify the methods of investigation that could be used to undertake your project and to justify the appropriateness of the method and techniques you do use. This should form part of your methodology chapter.

2   Focus on the exact research problem or question you will address – you need to identify a core question for investigation. You may be able to find out how others have focused and will need to show that this question has not previously been addressed (or at least not to your satisfaction).

3   Sort out problems that emerge – for example, if you are unable to gather data in the form you want, is a close approximation available? Find out if others faced similar problems and how they sorted things out. This can help you save time by drawing upon the experience of others. In one case, a new surveying methodology emerged when traditional methods were ruled out due to privacy laws.

4   At the end of your thesis, to compare your results with those of others to show how and where your contribution has taken place. Relating your own work to what others have done is an important hallmark of a good research degree, yet often a literature review is seen only as a 'scene setter'. You should not only report your results but reflect on how your research adds to knowledge in your field. For example does your work:

   (i)   agree (or not) with what others have done?

   (ii)   extend the work of other researchers?

   (iii)   provide new meaning to what others have done?

   (iv)   break new ground?

   (v)   challenge the method of measurement or evaluation indicators used?

   (vi)   challenge a policy response?

   (vii)   challenge a theoretical approach to the subject?

7.3   Locating Sources of Information

Learning how to locate sources

Locating information for your literature review is a large subject, and one where changes in technology are occurring all the time. There are whole books on this subject alone (e.g. Hart, 2001). As such, this section can only provide overall general guidance and initial leads for information searching. Your supervisor or department should be able to book you on a training course; if not, it is worthwhile contacting the person responsible for knowledge retrieval/information searching at your library, who will be able to help you with training. Part-time students should also have access to their university's training facilities and library. In addition, most public libraries today have staff specializing in IT who can provide information-searching advice.

If you are otherwise unable to obtain training in the practicalities of information searching, a number of university websites have public access advice on information searching (e.g. via the OU Library's home page), and there is also some further advice on this book's website.

Your supervisors may also suggest information guides appropriate to your subject area. As noted above, there are specialist books on information searching. Surveys also appear from time to time in journals and publications of professional bodies (for example, the Institution of Mechanical Engineers produces *Sourcebooks* and *Information Packs*). Do ask your supervisors about key sources.

Searching the internet is now very easy, particularly through search engines such as *Yahoo, MSN, Google* or *Google Scholar*. However, there is a danger of thinking that an internet search is entirely comprehensive and capable of identifying all materials that you need to review. This is not the case, although internet coverage is constantly getting better.

In the first instance, many documents (particularly older ones) are simply not available on the internet, or may have restricted, password, access. Indeed, some sources are only available as hard copy. However, if something is important to your subject area, then, even if it is not available on the internet, it is likely to have been cited by others, so you might find out about it that way. However, the more specialist your research becomes, the more likely it is that there will be sources that have not been drawn upon by someone who has placed their work on a website. Hence it is important not to be over-reliant on the internet, to use it carefully and to ensure that you cross-check with other sources of information (which is why, in Section 7.4 of this chapter, emphasis is given to people and networks).

The other important point is that you search the internet properly. This particularly concerns the use of online databases. Bibliographical databases contain citation information (author, title, journal, subject keyword and frequently abstract) for all the articles they index, so that publications can be easily traced to the original source. As well as being able to search the literature by author or subject, some of the specialist databases allow users to search for information on specific questions of interest.

Databases of references and other sources of information are a crucial source for a research degree literature review. In the past these were largely on CD-ROM, but now most are available online. But you should be aware that general internet search engines may not get far into the *contents* of databases. This is an important point. A reference or source of information may be down at a deeper level than a general search engine penetrates (which may only look for key words in the database's title or description of contents). You therefore need to ensure that you identify databases and then undertake a search within them.

A further major point about internet searching concerns the quality, reliability and type of material you will discover. *Google* or *Yahoo* will search the whole web and throw up all manner of articles, some of which will be useful but the majority of which will not be particularly relevant or reliable. As you are probably aware, there is an awful lot of very dubious material placed on internet sites. You need to be discerning about what a search produces and learn how to customize your search to produce relevant results. For academic research it is particularly important to consider:

1 **Is the author (or their institution) known and respected in this field?**

2 **Is reference made to other work in this field, e.g. does it demonstrate current awareness?**

3   Is there a bias – political or personal – to this piece of information that affects the way that it is presented?

4   Does the information seem objective? Is there an underlying marketing or propaganda motive?

5   Is the information properly referenced, i.e. is it possible for you to verify the points made?

6   How current is the information? Is the information properly dated?

Although a general internet search is very useful, a key way to get only the more reliable sources is to use more bespoke databases, such as ISI Web of Science. Identifying appropriate databases for your subject field is therefore an important activity. Although a wider internet search is useful, it is crucial that you combine this with a search of such area-specific databases.

Activity 7.3

Ask your supervisor or your librarian for a list of the most appropriate databases in your field.

A list of useful databases is provided on this book's website, but should not be viewed as comprehensive.

Sources of information

Whether you identify sources of information on your subject by the internet, database searches or by manual methods, you need to ensure that you cover all the ways in which academic information is disseminated. These include:

Journals

Journal articles are the predominant channel of communication for academic research. There are many hundreds of journals published by academic departments, societies and commercial publishers around the world. As well as academic journals, there are also professional and trade journals, which can contain very useful information, so ensure that any search you undertake covers both (more academic-type databases may leave out professional journals).

Conference papers and proceedings

These are another major channel of communication for academic research. Some conference proceedings are formally published, and so appear on databases, but many are not. Some abstracts and indexes list conferences separately, and index the papers as for journal articles. Conference proceedings can be searched on the British Library's database and there are also specialized services through which you can find out whether the proceedings of a particular conference have been published, whether there have been recent conferences on particular topics, or whether papers on your subject have been given. It is also worthwhile contacting the organizers of the main conferences in your field to see if they have a list of papers presented in recent conferences.

Books

Books are also a key means of disseminating academic research, although the production of a book takes a while and so the contents are likely to be on research conducted at least two years ago. As well as books on research findings, there are also 'handbooks' or 'manuals' where facts and figures are collected together in a form convenient for quick retrieval. It is also useful to look at standard teaching texts which provide a review of a topic area (Open University correspondence units and set books can also be a good source of basic information).

Dictionaries

There are specialist dictionaries for a number of subject areas.

Newspapers

Newspapers can be useful for a number of reasons, particularly for more current topics where information has not filtered into journals, or for analysis of contemporary perspectives. Most are indexed and available via a website.

Other students' dissertations and theses

These can be important sources of information on both sources and research methods. University libraries and national libraries (such as the British Library) will have PhD theses indexed. The *Index to Theses with Abstracts Accepted for Higher Degrees by the Universities of Great Britain and Ireland* is available on the internet. In some cases, the permission of the author or university may be needed before a thesis can be seen.

MSc dissertations are unlikely to be placed in libraries, so you may need to make a direct enquiry to an individual university department asking about any dissertations relevant to your subject area.

Government documents

A whole range of reviews, statistics and information are available through government sources, both national and through intergovernmental agencies (e.g. the UN and CEC). There are specialist databases on these sources.

For the UK, the first places to look are the Stationery Office and the National Statistics websites. Many ministries also produce their own lists of reported data. Comprehensive coverage of British official publications is provided by *UKOP Online*. This database contains references to everything published since 1980, both by the Stationery Office and other government bodies.

Statistics and market data

There are a vast number of sources of statistical and market data, which are well documented on specialist databases.

TV/Radio

TV and radio are an often overlooked sources, where research may have been undertaken for a documentary, historic or 'in-depth' news feature. Documentary scripts are often available, or contact details for a programme's producer or researcher. Many 'serious' documentary programmes have a website (and scripts may be available on request).

Grey literature

There is also a so-called 'grey literature' that only partially gets on to databases. This includes a variety of semi-published sources, including:

Company reports. Many companies will send a copy of their latest report if you write to them. Some electronic databases such as the *ICC British Company Annual Reports* and the *UK Company Factfinder* contain the full texts. Many companies now place their annual reports on the internet.

Trade literature. Much can be accessed through the Business Information Service at the British Library. Some may be on company or trade association websites.

Unpublished research documents. Often it is project working papers and unpublished interim reports that contain important information on methods and details. When you identify projects and results through formal sources, it is worthwhile asking authors about any associated unpublished papers.

Exhibitions and performances. Exhibitions are an important means of dissemination in arts subjects and also a source of information across all subject areas. Catalogues may be available and indexed. For the performing arts, programmes (particular for first performances) can be a source of information.

In many cases, such grey literature may be available from the originating body, from larger libraries or from the British Library Document Supply Centre. There is also *SIGLE* (the System for Information on Grey Literature in Europe), which is useful for difficult-to-trace papers, pamphlets, theses and translations from government, local government, universities and learned societies.

Searching databases

Clearly there is a large amount of information available, which, because it is ordered in a logical fashion, can be searched. However, the sheer volume of information means that it can only be efficiently searched using electronic search engines. Given the nature of search engines, it is probably best to use more than one search engine to ensure that your search is comprehensive.

Selecting your keywords

The first step to carrying out a search is to define what it is exactly you are looking for, so you start by writing out your query. For example, a search on a health and social welfare project might be examining the question:

'I want to know what causes malaria and how it can be prevented'.

One way of answering this question is to type one or more keywords into a search engine. Choosing the keywords is often the most difficult task and so keyword searches may be 'causes' and 'malaria', and 'prevention' and 'malaria'. Clearly there are not too many other words we could use instead of malaria, but 'causes' could be replaced by 'routes' or 'sources', and 'prevention' could be replaced by 'avoiding', so we need to think carefully about the words we use to make sure the search returns the most focused set of sources.

Ways of searching

Whether you are searching a library catalogue, a specialist database or the whole internet, you will notice that there are many similar features (e.g. a box to type in your search terms or a clickable help button), so many of the same principles apply in searching any of the bibliographical and full text databases that you may need to use.

Single keyword searching. Most databases will provide a search box or boxes on the opening screen. If you type a single keyword in the search box and click on 'Search', you should see the number of hits (this is the number of resources which match your search terms), the title of the resource (which is a link to the website), plus a description of what the resource is about, and its URL (the location on the World Wide Web).

Phrase searching. Most databases will allow you to search for a phrase, but they will vary as to how your phrase has to appear in the search box. For example, to make sure a string of words is only found if they appear as a phrase, you may need to type the phrase in inverted commas, for instance 'malarial vectors'.

Combining search terms. You can combine search terms to broaden or narrow your search. If you type 'malaria' into a search box and make a note of the number of results you have found, then do a new search for 'preventing' and again note the number of hits, and finally type 'malaria AND preventing', the number of hits is drastically reduced. Only the records that contain both of these words, in any order and in any position in the record, are retrieved.

AND is one of a series of 'Boolean operators' which can be used to broaden or narrow your search. Figure 7.1 shows what is meant by a Boolean operator, the AND operator. Think of the 'malaria' oval as containing a set of keywords, and the 'preventing' oval as containing a set of keywords. In the overlap area are references that contain one of the malaria words AND one of the preventing words. If you use the OR operator you will get all the records that fall in both ovals, including the overlap area.

Most searching systems allow you just to type 'and', 'or', and the other operators. Others use symbols. When looking at a database or using a search engine, be clear about the conventions it uses. All databases should have a help function and it is worth checking when you first use a database to see how search terms should be entered.

The other Boolean operator is NOT. Typing 'molecular NOT chemistry' will find records which contain the word 'malaria' but that do not contain the word 'preventing'; that is, just the non-overlapping part of the left-hand oval in Figure 7.1.

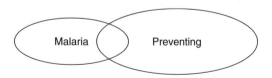

Figure 7.1   The Boolean operator 'and'

Advanced search options usually allow you to put more complex searches together by providing more than one box into which you can type your search. They will often allow you to specify exactly where in the record you want the search words to appear.

Activity 7.4

Take one of the databases you identified in Activity 7.3. Devise a question that covers your own topic area, such as the example used above (i.e. 'I want to know what causes malaria and how it can be prevented').

Develop from this the keywords you wish to use in your search.

Check the Boolean operator terms used in your search engine for the database.

From this, link two or three keywords using Boolean operators like AND, OR, NOT, etc., and see what sort of results emerge.

Note which produce the most useful results for you.

Discussion

It would be useful to discuss the results of this exercise with your supervisor or a librarian, or do this in conjunction with a library training course.

A key lesson in undertaking information searches is that there is a law of 'diminishing returns'. Getting the fullest possible answers to all your questions may take ten times longer than getting adequate answers to 80 per cent of them. Usually an adequate answer is all you need.

7.4 People and Networks

People as informants

Literature (in either paper or electronic forms) is not the only way to find out about a particular subject. Indeed, probably the quickest way to find 'where things are at' is to ask someone 'in the know'. Talking to people who are very familiar with the topic area is an excellent way to speed up finding out who has done what. This does not replace searching and analysing written sources, but it can very much help you to identify what is viewed as important work and help you to select key literature and key researchers. As has already been mentioned in Chapter 5 of this book, it helps immensely to identify the numerous people who can facilitate your research.

An example was an OU postgraduate student who, in the first few months of his PhD, sought to interview several key people in his field of study. He purposely chose a mix of researchers, practitioners and journalists in order to get varying perspectives. This aided his search of written sources. His review of the topic area thus contained both written sources and original interviews, and so added extra authority to this part of his thesis.

However, you have to be selective and careful in your use of people. This point deserves emphasis and involves an ethical issue as there is a danger of seemingly getting someone else to do your work. Your interactions with others should be part of a network of mutual support among professionals, so you should prepare yourself for talking to people. Unfocused and lengthy discussions do nothing but annoy. This does not mean that you cannot contact people from the beginning of your research when you don't know much, but you must be clear about the basis for contacting them. For example, it is perfectly acceptable to talk to even a leading expert in your field about whether the preliminary ideas for your project make sense and if they know of anyone else doing something similar.

Activity 7.5

Make a list of people in your field who you think might be interested in your research (have a look back at Activity 5.4 in Chapter 5 which asked you about this).

Sort out a set of questions that you would like to ask each of these people.

Discussion

Your list is likely to include academic and possibly industry/private researchers, but you should also think about other groups such as:

1   *Authors.*
2   *Practitioners.*
3   *Journalists*, who are a wonderful source of 'who is doing what'. Their time is often limited, so restrict yourself to a quick call unless you have a really good introduction from someone who knows them.
4   *Researchers* on 'serious' TV or radio documentary programmes.
5   *'Stakeholders'* in the subject area: people who are responsible for part of what you are studying. They should know what research and developments are under way on their patch. Such 'stakeholders' are not just sources of data once your research is under way; they can help you design and develop your research project itself. Who knows, your contacts may pave the way for a job!

Methods of contacting people

There are many ways of identifying 'people in the know' in your field. The following are just a few.

1 Conferences. **An obvious place to find key people in your subject area. This is a good way to get going as you do not have to contact anyone out of the blue. Start talking over coffee or lunch.**

2 Arrange an interview **(Offer to buy a drink or, if very important, lunch.) Also telephone interviews are increasingly acceptable, particularly for busy people.**

3 Organize a workshop **on your subject. This might sound daunting, but how about a research students' workshop initially? Your supervisor may be able to help set one up. If you are an external student, your internal supervisor should know of other research students in your field of study.**

4 Give a seminar. **This may sound very ambitious, but it can be very useful even if it is about discussing how you plan to do your research (remember, there is further guidance on presentations in Chapter 10 of this book). Furthermore, you save time as you can see several people at once rather than running around to see them. You may even end up with a 'steering group' to draw upon for advice.**

5 The internet **is a useful way to identify people. You could set up a home page on your project. People in the know might then start contacting you.**

6 Join an email or special interest discussion list. **Very often there are special interest email lists that hold discussions. Check with your supervisor. These can be well worth joining – for a while at any rate – but bear in mind the amount of emails you will generate if you decide to join a number of these. If there is no existing email list, you could set one up.**

To find people you will often need to trace the organizations for which they work. Information on the organizations themselves is often useful and may help you to select whom you approach. An internet search engine should suffice.

A further point is that 'People' sources are often the best ways to find out about the so-called 'grey literature', such as company reports, unpublished research documents and conference proceedings. As noted in Section 7.3 of this chapter, these often fail to get on to databases, and for fast-moving and emerging topic areas the less formal types of literature are often very important.

Finally, remember that you have a wealth of experience yourself and getting together with other students and sharing your research experience can help you all. This is part of the 'personal support network' mentioned in Section 5.7. Even if your project seems very different from that of other research students, tips on doing research and getting around problems can be remarkably generic! For part-time or distance students, an email network can be a useful way of keeping in touch, coupled with the occasional meal or drink at a mutually convenient location.

7.5   Keeping it Organized

Activity 7.6

Note down how you currently keep (or plan to keep) a note of anything you read.

As noted at the beginning of this section, you will end up using information on other people's research for different purposes throughout your own project and when writing up the results. Keeping records of what you have read and found, and whom you have contacted, is thus very important; if you do not have good records, you will end up having to do more or less the same work all over again!

Therefore, it is important to make notes and classify literature and other information obtained according to what it contributes to your project. You may initially be using a reference in order to review your topic field; later you may need to return to it in order to set up and focus your research question. Later still another of our purposes may emerge as you re-examine the same reference to see what method was used to gather the data it contains and how the results were analysed. Finally, you may want to compare your own results to those in the reference. It may therefore be useful to note how a reference or source contributes to:

1 information/scope of your project;

2 focusing your project;

3 method;

4 analysis;

5 conclusions.

Clearly, keeping good notes is a function for your research journal, but you will also need to have a dedicated system to record and keep track of information you have obtained. This may include keeping hard or electronic copies of key references. It is also important to record your sources of information *as you find them* so that you can easily locate them again. You also need to decide what system you are going to use for citing your sources, ensuring that you have all the information you need for that system.

Bibliographical packages

It is now very common for research students to use software packages to produce a reference list in a consistently correct form. A number of packages are available. *Endnote* is probably the most widely used package, but many others are available including *RefWorks*, *Citation*, *GetaRef*, *Papyrus*, *ProCite* and *Reference Manager*. Details can be found by searching for these products on the website of suppliers or software retailers. Many of the packages also have help desks and websites.

Find out which package or packages are recommended and supported by your university. If you have a choice, check which ones your supervisor or others in your department use. You should also be able to download a demo copy of a particular package and check it through. If your university does not supply you with a package, some retailers offer special prices or versions for students. Such deals are usually highlighted on suppliers' websites.

Basically, all these packages are databases specifically designed to store references and to produce bibliographies in a variety of specified formats. They allow you to input references from the electronic sources or enter them yourself, search for references, sort them and then generate the output in a whole variety of journal or other formats.

There are a number of web guides on bibliographic software, including Glasgow University Library and the University of Bristol. This book's website contains links to some guides.

Referencing/citations

Bibliographical packages allow you to cite references in whatever referencing system is required (so long as you enter all the appropriate details). For your thesis, some universities specify the citation system to be used (which is an issue to check with your supervisor), with many using a variant of the 'Harvard' author–date system. Whatever system you use, it needs to be consistent and provide all the information needed for somebody to be able to track down each reference.

Further details on citation methods are given in the Appendix to this chapter and are also provided, together with weblinks for advice, on this book's website.

Activity 7.7

Identify an appropriate bibliographical software package (check what is recommended and/or supported by your university) and download a demo copy.

Discuss with your supervisor the citation system you should use and how you should keep records for your literature search. Make sure you cover all sources.

7.6 Writing a Review

Students often have difficulty in starting to write their literature reviews. A real danger is the feeling that you have to collect everything first before you can write up your review. Especially when using online, internet or CD-ROM searches, the searching process itself can become almost obsessive. But it is really much better to start writing immediately. This point was emphasized at the beginning of Chapter 6, where it was noted that writing is a continuous process throughout your research degree, not a separate stage at the end. Writing is a recursive process, in which you'll find yourself cycling again and again through various drafts. This is particularly so for a literature review, which (as noted above) fulfils a number of processes, including helping you to focus on your core research question, reflect on methodology and work through how and where your work may fit into your wider subject area. Inevitably a literature review will involve the stages and cycle of writing that was covered in Chapter 6, and you will find yourself needing to apply the general principles from Section 6.4 of that chapter. Just to remind you, here is the diagram from Chapter 6 on the writing process.

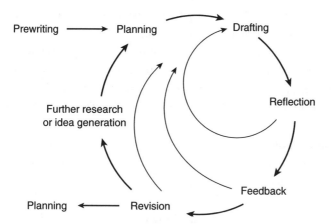

An example of this is that I got one of my full-time PhD students to write a review on just ten pieces of literature when he was two months into his PhD. These ten pieces were reasonably central to his subject area, but he did not spend ages narrowing down a vast list to 'the ten crucial works'. They were simply ten that looked promising at the time. It was surprising how drafting a review on these ten pieces developed his sense of discernment (reflection) in looking at other literature. Having completed a 'mini-review', he could judge rapidly the value to his project of subsequent articles. In consequence, doing this quick and incomplete review speeded up his whole literature review. The initial review was quickly superseded, but evolved into a series of reviews covering the different purposes needed in a literature review. This student became a professional journalist before returning to academia to become a lecturer.

Another way of getting going on your review is linked to the level and depth of knowledge needed as you focus on your core research question. Writing up the general subject area and the main issues of debate should be a relatively straightforward task. This does not require too much depth and is also something that many other researchers will have done. Try finding somebody else's general review in your subject area and examine it critically. For example, research into a detailed aspect of renewable energy sources (say, small-scale wind generators) will need to start off by discussing why renewable energy is an important issue, and the environmental concerns behind its development. This general subject is covered by many articles and books. Although you obviously must not simply appropriate another person's review for yourself (that is not ethical – see Chapter 9), a useful exercise is to work out how you might adapt this review to make it better suited to your own purposes. That can then form the basis of structuring your own general review.

The end result of your review should be a piece of written work that, like the review by Alan Woodley in the offprint at the end of this chapter, provides a story about your understanding of how research in your topic area has emerged. Look at Section 6.5 in Chapter 6. This is about crafting an argument, using citations and forging a clear argument, and all this very much applies to writing a literature review. The analysis there uses a piece of text (Extract 5) that is a literature review. You should read this as part of organizing and writing your own literature review. As well as using Extract 5 in Activity 6.5, also look at Alan Woodley's review from this chapter. This is a good example of identifying 'main paths' and 'faulty paths' to provide focus in a literature review.

There are a number of guides and sources of advice available on organizing and structuring the writing of a literature review. One useful site is CAPLITS. The address of this is on this book's website.

Finally, as this section has emphasized, you will be using information on other people's research in your subject area throughout your own research. Make sure you keep in touch with the body of research and researchers. Write up as you go along; talk to people; share your discoveries, frustrations and joys.

You are now not just studying a topic – you are *part* of the 'topic'!

References

Bruce, C.S. (1994) 'Research students' early experiences of the dissertation literature review', *Studies in Higher Education*, vol. 19 (2) pp. 217–29.

Hart, C. (2001) *Doing a Literature Search*. London: Sage.

Offprint

Reviewing the literature

Any investigation, whatever the scale, will involve reading what other people have written about your area of interest, gathering information to support or refute your arguments and writing about your findings. In a small-scale project, you will not be expected to produce a definitive account of the state of research in your selected topic area, but you will need to provide evidence that you have read a certain amount of relevant literature and that you have some awareness of the current state of knowledge on the subject.

Ideally, the bulk of your reading should come early in the investigation, though in practice a number of activities are generally in progress at the same time and reading may even spill over into the data-collecting stage of your study. You need to take care that reading does not take up more time than can be allowed, but it is rarely possible to obtain copies of all books and articles at exactly the time you need them, so there is inevitably some overlap.

Analytical and theoretical frameworks

Reading as much as time permits about your topic may give you ideas about approach and methods which had not occurred to you and may also give you ideas about how you might classify and present your own data. It may help you to devise a theoretical or analytical framework as a basis for the analysis and interpretation of data. It is not enough merely to collect facts and to describe what is. All researchers collect many facts, but then must orga-nize and classify them into a coherent pattern. Verma and Beard (1981) suggest that researchers need to

> identify and explain relevant relationships between the facts. In other words, the researchers must produce a concept or build a theoretical structure that can explain facts and the relationships between them ... The importance of theory is to help the investigator summarize previous information and guide his future course of action.

Sometimes the formulation of a theory may indicate missing ideas or links and the kinds of additional data required. Thus, a theory is an essential tool of research in stimulating the advancement of knowledge still further.

(Verma and Beard 1981: 10)

Sometimes 'model' is used instead of or interchangeably with 'theory'. Cohen and Manion explain that

both may be seen as explanatory devices or schemes having a conceptual framework, though models are often characterized by the use of analogies to give a more graphic or visual representation of a particular phenomenon. Providing they are accurate and do not misrepresent the facts, models can be of great help in achieving clarity and focusing on key issues in the nature of phenomena.

(Cohen and Manion 1989: 16)

The label is not important but the process of ordering and classifying data is.

As you read, get into the habit of examining how authors classify their finding, how they explore relationships between facts and how facts and relationships are explained. Methods used by other researchers may be unsuitable for your purposes, but they may give you ideas about how you might categorize your own data, and ways in which you may be able to draw on the work of other researchers to support or refute your own arguments and conclusions.

The critical review of the literature

An extensive study of the literature will be required in most cases for a PhD and a critical review of what has been written on the topic produced in the final thesis. A project lasting two or three months will not require anything so ambitious. You may decide to omit an initial review altogether if your reading has not been sufficiently extensive to warrant its inclusion, but if, you decide to produce a review, it is important to remember that only relevant works are mentioned and that the review is more than a list of 'what I have read'.

Writing literature reviews can be a demanding exercise. Haywood and Wragg comment wryly that critical reviews are more often then not uncritical reviews – what they describe as

the furniture sale catalogue, in which everything merits a one-paragraph entry no matter how skillfully it has been conducted: Bloggs (1975) found this, Smith (1976) found that, Jones (1977) found the other, Bloggs, Smith and Jones (1978) found happiness in heaven.

(Haywood and Wragg, 1982: 2)

They go on to say that a critical review should show 'that the writer has studied existing work in the field with insight' (p. 2). That is easier said than done, but the main point to bear in mind is that a review should provide the reader with a picture, albeit limited in a short project, of the state of knowledge and of major questions in the subject area being investigated.

Consider the following introduction to a study by Alan Woodley (1985) entitled *Taking Account of Mature Students*. You may not be familiar with their field of study, but does the introduction put you in the picture? Does it give you some idea of the work that has been done already and does it prepare you for what is to follow?

> Of the many who have looked at the relationship between age and performance in universities none has as yet produced a definite answer to the apparently simple question 'Do mature students do better or worse than younger students?'

> Harris (1940) in the United States found evidence to suggest that younger students tended to obtain better degree results.

Similar findings have been made in Britain by Malleson (1959), Howell (1962), Barnett and Lewis (1963), McCracken (1969) and Kapur (1972), in Australia by Flecker (1959) and Sanders (1961), in Canada by Fleming (1959) and in New Zealand by Small (1966). However, most of these studies were based on samples of students who were generally aged between seventeen and twenty-one and the correlation techniques employed meant that the relationship between age and performance really only concerned this narrow age band. As such, the results probably suggest that bright children admitted early to higher education fare better than those whose entry is delayed while they gain the necessary qualifications.

This view is supported by Harris (1940) who discovered that the relationship between age and performance disappeared when he controlled for intelligence. Other studies have shown that those who gain the necessary qualifications and then delay entry for a year or two are more successful than those who enter directly from school (Thomas, Beeby and Oram 1939; Derbyshire Education Committee 1966).

Where studies have involved samples containing large numbers of older students the results have indicated that the relationship between age and performance is not a linear one. Philips and Cullen (1955), for instance, found that those aged twenty-four and over tended to do better than the eighteen and nineteen-year-old age group. Sanders (1961) showed that the university success rate fell until the age of twenty or twenty-one, then from about twenty-two onwards the success rate began to rise again. The problem with these two studies is that many of the older students were returning servicemen. They were often 'normal' entrants whose entry to university had been delayed by war and many had undergone some training in science or mathematics while in the armed forces. Also, while Eaton (1980) cites nine American studies which confirm the academic superiority of veterans, there is some contradictory British evidence. Mountford (1957) found that ex-service students who entered Liverpool University between 1947 and 1949 were most likely to have to spend an extra year or more on their courses and more likely to fail to complete their course.

Some studies have shown that whether mature students fare better or worse than younger students depends upon the subject being studied. Sanders (1963) has indicated that the maturity associated with increasing age and experience seems to be a positive predictor of success for some arts and social science courses. The general finding that older students do better in arts and social science and worse in science and maths is supported by Barnett, Holder and Lewis (1968), Fagin (1971), Sharon (1971) and Flecker (1959).

Walker's (1975) study of mature students at Warwick University represents the best British attempt to unravel the relationship between age and performance. He took 240 mature undergraduates who were admitted to the university between 1965 and 1971 and compared their progress with that of all undergraduates. This gave him a reasonably large sample to work with and the timing meant that the results were not distorted by any 'returning servicemen factor'. His methodology showed certain other refinements. First, he excluded overseas students. Such students tend to be older than average and also to fare worse academically (Woodley 1979), thus influencing any age/performance relationship. Secondly, he used two measures of performance; the proportion leaving without obtaining a degree and the degree results of those taking final examinations. Finally he weighted the degree class obtained according to its rarity value in each faculty.

The following findings achieved statistical significance:

(i)   In total, mature students obtained better degrees than non-mature students.
(ii) In the arts faculty mature students obtained better degrees than non-mature students.
(iii) Mature students who did not satisfy the general entrance requirement obtained better degrees than all other students.
(iv) The degree results of mature students aged twenty-six to thirty were better than those of all other mature students.

> Several other differences were noted but they did not achieve statistical significance due to the small numbers involved. The mature student sample only contained thirty-three women, twenty-six science students and thirty-seven aged over thirty. The aim of the present study was to extend Walker's work to all British universities so that these and other relationships could be tested out on a much larger sample of mature students.

> (Woodley 1985: 152–4)

This review is more thorough than would normally be required for small projects, but the approach is much the same, whatever the exercise. Alan Woodley selects from the extensive amount of literature relating to mature students. He groups certain categories and comments on features which are of particular interest. He compares results of different investigators and discusses in some detail a study by Walker (1975) which serves as a pilot for his more extensive study of mature students in British universities.

The reader is then in the picture and has some understanding of what work has been done already in this field. Woodley no doubt omitted many publications that had been consulted during the course of his research. It is always hard to leave out publications that may have taken you many hours or even weeks to read, but the selection has to be made. That is the discipline which has to be mastered. Once you have identified possible categories from your initial reading, and have your cards in order, you will be able to group the source material, and writing the review becomes much easier.

Note: The references in this offprint are not listed as this is not necessary for its use in this book.

Source: Bell, J. (1999) *Doing Your Research Project: a Guide for First-Time Researchers in Education and Social Science* (3rd edn), chapter 6, pp. 92–6. Buckingham: Open University Press.

Appendix: Referencing style guide

(Based upon Open University Library's *Information Search Guide.*)

Bibliographical packages automatically format references in a particular style, but you do also need to pay attention to how you cite references in your text. The following provides guidance in using the frequently used Harvard author–date citation system. However, do check with your supervisor about any 'house style' used by your university or department.

The Harvard author–date system uses brief details within the text of your thesis or dissertation, which allows the reference to be identified from a fully detailed list contained either at the end of each chapter or a single list covering the thesis as a whole. This list is arranged in alphabetical order of the author's surname. If you have more than one reference by the same author, they should be arranged in date order.

In your text, citations are simply the author and date set in brackets, for example:

> Other studies have shown that those who gain the necessary qualifications and then delay for a year or two are more successful than those who enter directly from school (Thomas, Beeby and Oram 1939; Derbyshire Education Committee 1966).

The above example also shows how multiple authors and organizations are cited. When an author is directly named in your text, it is only necessary to add the date of the reference, for example: '*Sanders (1963) has indicated that ... .*'

When citing a quote within a book or a long article, the exact page number(s) should also be specified. This can be done either by using a 'p.' as shorthand for page, such as '*Sanders (1963 p. 24) has indicated that ... ', or by specifying the page number(s) after a colon, such as '*Sanders (1963: 24*).

At the end of each chapter or at the end of the whole thesis/dissertation would come your full alphabetical reference list. The following provides a guide for how this can be set out for various reference sources.

Books

Author's surname, initial(s) (year of publication) *title* (or <u>title</u>), edition, place of publication, publisher.

Flavin, C. (1999) *Power Surge: A Guide to the Coming Energy Revolution*, London, Earthscan.

Journal articles

Author's surname, initial(s) (year of publication) 'title of article', *title of journal* (or <u>title of journal</u>), volume number, issue number, date of journal, pp.· ••—••.

Watanabe, C. (2001) 'Identification of the role of renewable energy', *Renewable Energy*, vol. 8, no. 3, April, pp. 237–274.

Reports

Author's surname, initial(s) (date of report) *title* (or <u>title</u>), issuing organization, report number.

Halliday, J. (1995) *Assessment of the Accuracy of the DTI's Database of the UK Wind Speeds*, Energy Technology Support Unit, ETSU-W-11/00401/REP.

Conference papers

Author's surname, initial(s) (year of publication) *title* (or <u>title</u>), title of conference proceedings, date of conference, location of conference, pages on which the paper appears, publisher's location, publisher of proceedings.

Jones, J. (1999) *Polymer Blends Based on Compact Disc Scrap*, Proceedings of the Annual Technical Conference – Society of Plastics Engineers, May 1–5, 1999, San Francisco, pp. 2865–2867, Brookfield, CT, Society of Plastics Engineers.

Electronic journal articles

Author's surname, initial(s) (year of publication) 'title of article', *title of journal* (or <u>title of journal</u>) [online], volume number, issue number. Available from: name of service, URL of website [date the site was accessed].

Bird, R. (1999) 'You need a translator or visual communication comes of age', *Deliberations* [online]. Available from: http://www.lgu.ac.uk/deliberations/ [accessed 17 June 2005].

Web site documents

Author's surname, initial(s) (year of publication) *title of document* (or <u>title of document</u>) [online], publisher. Available from: name of service, URL of website [date the site was accessed].

Lancaster University Engineering Design Centre (2003) *Application of Schemebuilder environment for hydraulic system design focusing on concurrent engineering aspects* [online],

Lancaster University Engineering Design Centre. Available from: http://www.comp.lancs.ac.uk/edc/research/hydraulics/ [accessed 29 May 2004].

Electronic journal article

Author's surname, initial(s) (year of publication) title of article, *electronic journal name*, volume number, issue number, URL address or email contact.

Hamilton, R. (2005) 'The social geography of South Oxhey', *Human Geography Online*, 2 (3): March. email: rmt@humangeography.co.uk

Electronic mail messages

Author's surname, initial(s) (author's email address), full date of message, *subject of message* (or subject of message). Email to recipient's name and email address.

Knight, C.J. (c.j.knight@colc.ac.uk), 29 May 2005, *Teacher training for IT skill development*. Email to j.q.parker-knoll@open.ac.uk

8 Doing the Right Thing

Legal and Moral Constraints on Researchers

Martin Le Voi

LEARNING OUTCOMES

After reading this chapter and working on its associated activities you should be able to:

- Attribute ideas correctly without plagiarism.
- Understand the need for commercial and personal confidentiality.
- Understand the importance of security with computer use.
- Understand the repercussions of the Data Protection Act on your research.
- Understand basic intellectual property constraints (e.g. copyright).

8.1 Introduction

When the product of the research is going to be a public document, such as a report or a thesis which will be available to the public in a library, it is crucial to consider your legal and moral responsibilities as a writer. Your work will be exposed to public scrutiny and, as a result, may be examined to see whether it is 'legal, decent, honest and truthful', in the words of the UK Advertising Standards Authority. Moreover, the process of doing your research must take due consideration of the moral, ethical and legal standards in research, as our society currently sets them, and you must also not take unacceptable risks with health (both physical and mental): either with anyone else's or with your own.

This chapter briefly considers the important aspects of responsibilities and rights for the researcher. The early parts apply to nearly all researchers, whereas later parts get more specialized, as they deal with issues such as patents and publication rights.

8.2 Responsibilities

Academic integrity

Legal, decent, honest, truthful

Academic research is about creating a community of scholars which is sustained by both trust and scepticism. In theory, any piece of research by any professional academic should be capable of being repeated in order to test the reliability or generalizability of the results. This is one reason why in your research thesis you have to take painstaking care to describe the research methodology used, so that it may be repeated by anyone wishing to do so. Academic research proceeds by new academics treating the work of previous researchers with due scepticism, usually questioning the interpretation or theoretical constructions arrived at in previous work.

In principle, previous research can be replicated in order to test whether the findings were reliable or due to just a lucky chance. Replication and generalization apply to various enquiry methods, not just quantitative research (see Chapter 4 and below). While simple replication can and does happen, particularly in areas of research where such lucky chances may be quite common, by and large the community of scholars relies upon trust that other professional academics have done their research competently, effectively and, most important of all, honestly. For academic research to progress, this trust in the integrity of researchers is vital.

In a now infamous announcement, in 1989 Stanley Pons and Martin Fleischmann claimed to have discovered one of the Holy Grails of science, 'cold fusion'. Such a discovery could promise virtually unlimited power with none of the problems of fossil fuels (pollution), fission (radioactive waste) or some renewables (unreliability of generation, e.g. with wind or wave power). However, no other laboratory was able to confirm their results in replications. Accusations of fraud and incompetence were rife, leaving Pons and Fleischmann humiliated. But fraud was not proved; perhaps it was just that those scientists were not careful enough about checking their results or allowing for artefacts. Edmund Storms, another scientist trying to develop cold fusion, highlights what Pons and Fleishmann did wrong: 'Conventional science requires you to play by certain rules. First, thou shalt not announce thy results via a press conference. Second, thou shalt not exaggerate the results. Third, thou shalt tell other scientists precisely what thou did. They broke all of those rules' (Storms, quoted in Platt, 1998).

Much of the issue in these experiments was about the accuracy of the measurements and the adequacy of control of a myriad of potential artefacts. The output of the reaction needed high precision measuring and even had to take account of natural levels of neutron particles: one experiment was conducted under a mountain to control this adequately. The verdict of over a decade of research is that results in this area are not considered trustworthy, and even if no deliberate fraud was prosecuted, the community of scholars in this field is damaged.

In areas of the social and behavioural sciences which use inferential statistics to inform decisions about scientific theory, the situation can be worse than this. The field of inferential statistics has by design decision errors built in, and a researcher can get a positive result sometimes just by chance. It is quite easy in such circumstances for apparently interesting results to be based on experimental artefacts, sometimes leading many researchers up blind alleys.

Qualitative research methods, especially ones where a small sample is examined in depth for the light it can shed on social or psychological theory, are also very dependent on the integrity of the researcher. The analyst must take care that the analytical findings are a fair and accurate reflection of the corpus of evidence being scrutinized, and not an artificial construct imposed on the data by an analyst determined to use them for dialectic purposes which go beyond what the evidence could reasonably sustain.

You must therefore treat your research project with the utmost care. Do not succumb to the temptation to cheat and generate additional research results, or pretend that you have found something which is not there. Not only does it jeopardize the whole conception of a research community of scholars, but also it will probably do you no good as cheating is frequently found out. There are several famous cases where well-known research published by leading authorities turned out to be at least suspect, if not actually fraudulent. Highly publicized allegations were made against Professor Cyril Burt alleging the faking of results in investigations of intelligence among identical twins in order to support his theories of intelligence. Although many of these allegations proved to be false, it remains highly likely that Cyril Burt at least generated some extra cases of identical twins (which are a rare occurrence among human births) in order to boost the sample size of his studies.

There are a few other cases of scientific fraud, which are usually very notable because of the huge publicity they generate (e.g. the cloning research frauds of 2006). Fortunately, they do appear to be rare events. Scepticism regarding other researchers' work is usually not aimed at the raw data or original sources of the work, but rather at their interpretations and theoretical constructions drawn from it. This is as it should be. This chapter's Appendix gives one university's approach to defining a code of practice for academic integrity.

Activity 8.1

Obtain a copy of your own university's code of practice for academic integrity. In your own area of research, are you aware of instances where data gathering procedures and biased/exaggerated interpretations of data produced misleading results or claims? Perhaps ask your supervisors or colleagues about examples.

Plagiarism
(Adapted from the Open University's Policy on Plagiarism.)

While faking research is a case of fraud against the whole process of research, plagiarism can be described as fraudulently presenting ideas as your own when they are not. Perhaps it is more accurately described as theft, where someone else's ideas have been stolen. While this would not actually damage the progress of the research discipline, it is a serious breach of professional standards in research and one in which arguments can persist in long and bitter disputes.

It is important, therefore, that you carefully attribute all the ideas to which you refer in your work to their original authors, and any quotations you use should be accurate and appropriately referenced. For example, I have drawn upon a website to write this section, which is referenced above.

So, if your academic writing contains work that is not your own without indicating this (acknowledging your sources), you are committing 'plagiarism'. This might occur in a thesis when, without referencing a source:

1 **Using a choice phrase or sentence that you have come across.**

2 **Copying word for word directly from a text.**

3 **Paraphrasing the words from a text very closely.**

4 **Using text downloaded from the internet.**

5 **Borrowing statistics or assembled facts from another person or source.**

6 **Copying or downloading figures, photographs, pictures or diagrams without acknowledging your sources.**

7 **Copying from the notes or writing of a fellow student.**

8 **Copying from your own notes, on a text, seminar, video or lecture, that contain direct quotations.**

Plagiarism may occur inadvertently due to inexperience. So read carefully statements concerning plagiarism and how to reference your sources. Plagiarized material is often recognizable from the shifts in style, and you can expect other academics to be aware of the source.

Although you are encouraged to show the results of your reading by referring to and quoting from works on your subject, copying from such sources without acknowledgement is deemed to be plagiarism. You are encouraged to collaborate with others, but submitting for your research degree work copied from or written jointly with others is not acceptable, unless collaboration is required in the particular project. Most universities ask you to sign a statement to confirm that the thesis you have submitted is your own work, and to indicate clearly any shared components.

Submitting work that has been done by someone else and persistent borrowing of other people's work without citation are obvious instances of plagiarism and are regarded as cheating. It is intellectually dishonest to cheat, and if a case of plagiarism is proven, this is a serious offence and most universities will invoke disciplinary procedures.

Confidentiality

Commercial confidentiality
Some research nowadays is carried out with either the co-operation or the sponsorship of commercial organizations. When working with commercial organizations, you must take care not to breach any confidentiality that they expect to be maintained.

Some research studentships are funded by sponsorship from commercial or public bodies. Frequently, when these bodies commission research, they want to enter into an arrangement where they have control over the publication of the findings. This is not acceptable for research degree theses. A research degree thesis is *always* a public document, which will end up being available in the university library system for everyone to read. Sponsored research projects may occasionally result in theses which are not publicly available for a limited time, but after that time the documents will be made public. It is therefore particularly important in these cases that the thesis does not breach any other kinds of confidentiality about the research and the commercial environment in which the research was done.

Personal confidentiality and privacy

Since a thesis will be public, it is particularly important that the rights of sources are respected where necessary. Some of these issues are covered in Chapter 9 on ethics, so I will not dwell on these issues here. If you are obtaining information *about* individuals, it is clearly important that privacy is respected. If you are obtaining information *through* individuals (as informants), you may need to take steps to preserve anonymity, as journalists try to do.

If you obtain private information, you must be sure to maintain confidentiality, both in your research thesis and with your research records. You may have to keep records under lock and key. Remember, there is a substantial understanding of trust between you and your sources, and ultimately your own academic integrity, perhaps also that of your profession, needs to sustain that trust and conduct your research appropriately.

Activity 8.2

Make a note here of any personal or commercial confidentiality issues that you feel could be involved when gathering data as part of your research project. This issue will be covered further in Chapter 9 (particularly in that chapter's Activity 9.8), but it is worthwhile discussing confidentiality issues with your supervisors as part of developing your research methodology design.

Using computers

Email security, masquerading and digital signatures

Email is an inherently insecure system. In many mailers, it is trivially easy to masquerade an email such that it appears to come from someone else. Some malicious 'spam' mail does this, trying to encourage those receiving the mail to open the mail and then suffer the consequences. A typical one is a criminal who sends out email masquerading as email from a High Street bank, asking the recipient to log on to the criminal's website (which also masquerades as a bank's internet banking centre) and confirm their account details, which usually includes submitting password access details. Having received these details, the criminal can syphon off the hapless individual's money from his or her account. The original email purports to come from the bank's mail system, and the fake website often has a very convincing appearance (e.g. company logos). In an attempt to reduce this rather easy fraud, nearly all banks tell customers they will never ask for account details in this way.

If you want to send email securely, or want to be able to prove that you were the sender, the best way to do this is with Public Key Encryption. This sophisticated technology allows a user a private key which is used to encrypt a message, and there is a public key which is used to decrypt it. The user lets everyone who needs it have a copy of the public key. As the user has the only copy of the private key, which has built-in password protection, only the user can encrypt messages using it. When the recipient decodes the message, this guarantees that the message came from the authenticated user. Public Key Encryption should be used for any sensitive or confidential information you want to send by email. The keys are available from a number of sources: look for programmes that support PGP (Pretty Good Privacy) and integrate with your mail system, or contact the person with IT responsibilities in your department.

Data privacy/confidentiality

It is worth emphasizing here that there is a strong moral duty to have due consideration about confidentiality and privacy for any subjects of research you may do. Only occasionally is that moral duty reinforced with legal protection. One such case is the Data Protection Act.

The Data Protection Act

Data protection is about protecting the privacy of the individual in relation to their personal information. The Data Protection Act 1998 relates to all information about identifiable living individuals. The information can be recorded on paper as well as held on a computer. It includes simple access and display as well as more complicated data analysis techniques. The term 'information' also covers photographs and audio-visual recordings.

Organizations (data controllers) are required to register all their uses of such data with the government's Information Commissioner. Individuals (data subjects) have the right of access to data held about them. This is called subject access.

To ensure compliance with the Data Protection Acts, personal information must be:

1 **fairly and lawfully processed and only if certain conditions are met;**

2 **processed for limited purposes;**

3 **adequate, relevant and not excessive;**

4 **accurate;**

5 **not kept longer than necessary;**

6   processed in accordance with the rights of individuals;

7   secure;

8   not transferred to countries without adequate protection.

It is a criminal offence for a data user to operate outside the terms of its registered entry. Therefore, before any new application of personal data is started, it is essential that you check with whoever is responsible for data protection in your university that this application is registered.

Further information on data protection is available on the Information Commissioner website to which there is a link on this book's website.

Activity 8.3

Once you have developed your research methodology design, contact whoever is responsible for data protection in your university to see if Data Protection Act registration will be needed.

8.3   Rights

The earlier section on academic integrity links into the point made throughout this book that it is important to acknowledge any sources that you have used in undertaking your research project. Intellectual property rights (IPR) are a further consideration of properly using materials that have been produced by others. This is where you need to consider that, as well as acknowledging you are drawing upon materials produced by another person (e.g. by proper referencing), you may also need to obtain consent (and possibly pay a fee) for using their work.

As will be explained later in this section, for writing a PhD or MPhil thesis or in a Master's dissertation, you are unlikely to need permission to use copyright materials, although you should acknowledge all sources. This is because there is an exemption for works produced for examination purposes only. However, questions of copyright clearance would arise if you use any of your thesis material for other purposes, such as in a conference paper or a journal article. Certainly, as you move beyond your research degree, you will need to consider carefully issues of intellectual property rights. Consequently, it is very important to know when you can use other people's works without seeking permission and when you need to obtain copyright clearance. Furthermore, in undertaking your research project you will be creating your own intellectual property, and you therefore need to be aware of how to protect your own intellectual property rights.

Intellectual property

The UK Patent Office has an excellent website that explains Intellectual Property in simple language (IP Portal Team, UK Patent Office, 2005). I can do little better than repeat their introduction (fully acknowledged so avoiding claims of plagiarism!).

What is intellectual property or IP?

Intellectual property, often known as IP, allows people to own their creativity and innovation in the same way that they can own physical property. The owner of IP can control and be rewarded for its use, and this encourages further innovation and creativity to the benefit of us all.

In some cases IP gives rise to protection for ideas but in other areas there will have to be more elaboration of an idea before protection can arise. It will often not be possible to protect IP and gain IP rights (or IPRs) unless they have been applied for and granted, but some IP protection such as copyright arises automatically, without any registration, as soon as there is a record in some form of what has been created.

The four main types of IP are:

1   patents for inventions – new and improved products and processes that are capable of industrial application
2   trade marks for brand identity – of goods and services allowing distinctions to be made between different traders
3   designs for product appearance – of the whole or a part of a product resulting from the features of, in particular, the lines, contours, colours, shape, texture or materials of the product itself or its ornamentation
4   copyright for material – literary and artistic material, music, films, sound recordings and broadcasts, including software and multimedia

(The IP Portal Team, UK patent office, 2005)

In producing a thesis you will certainly create material in the fourth category, and could possibly also have IP in categories (1) and (3) as well.

To understand exactly what can be protected by IP, you will need to check the four main areas of copyright, designs, patents and trade marks as well as other IP. Often, more than one type of IP may apply to the same creation.

(The IP Portal Team, UK Patent Office, 2005).

Copyright and patents are the main areas that affect research students and so the rest of Section 8.3 and Section 8.4 explore these categories of IP in some detail.

Copyright

Like other forms of property in a Western capitalist society (such as land, buildings or consumer products), intellectual property can be owned, bought, sold, hired, inherited, etc. It is this ownership and those transactions that are governed by copyright law. Copyright is originated by an author. An author can keep or dispose of this property as he or she sees fit but, once it is passed on, it is gone to whoever has acquired ownership.

Much of the law is about definitions and protection of copyright from 'infringements'. Infringement of copyright could be considered a form of 'intellectual theft', and there is a small industry involved in obtaining copyright 'clearance', which is basically permission from the copyright owner to use the intellectual property they own, usually for a fee. For example, where we have used offprints in this book, we have had to obtain permission to do so from the copyright owner and, in many cases, had to pay a fee for doing so.

As important as copyright clearance are the allowable areas of use of intellectual property which do not infringe copyright protection. These allow use of intellectual property without requiring clearance from the owner (called a 'permitted act'). This is important, as you will need to consider in your research if you need permission for use of something that is someone else's copyright (such as drawing on literature or information in a database).

What is copyright?
Broadly speaking, copyright is the protection given by law (as from 1 August 1989 in The Copyright, Designs and Patents Act 1988 and subsequent statutory instruments) to an author for his or her work. Table 8.1 lists what is protected by copyright.

This list is pretty comprehensive. Generally speaking, copyright owners have the sole right to use their works or to authorize others to use them, although there are certain uses which do not constitute an infringement (see below for more details). Copyright does not last forever and, as shown by Table 8.2, varies depending on the category of work. Note that for literary, dramatic, musical and artistic works, copyright is maintained for 70 years after the death of the author, so very few academic works will be out of copyright.

Because copyright is technically a form of property, it can be split up and transferred from person to person by gift, sale or licence or on death. So, the author of a novel may grant and do separate deals with a US publisher for an American edition and with a French publisher for the French translation rights; at the same time, a film production

Table 8.1 Works protected by copyright

Original literary works including:

Articles, books, theses, prose, poetry, tables, compilations, songs, computer
 programs
Original musical works
Musical notation
Original dramatic works
Plays, scripts, screen plays, mime, choreography
Original artistic works
Painting, drawing, sculpture, jewellery, graphics, architectural designs, buildings,
 maps, charts, carvings, photographs
Films
Sound recordings
Broadcasts
Cable transmissions
Typographical arrangements
Performances
Designs

Table 8.2 Duration of copyright protection

Original literary, dramatic, musical and artistic works:

Life of the author/owner plus	70 years
Broadcasts	50 years
Sound recordings	50 years
Cable transmissions	50 years
Film: Life of authors plus	70 years
Typographical arrangements	25 years
Performances	50 years
Designs	15 years

company may have obtained film and broadcast rights. For an academic work, such as
an article, copyright may have been retained by the author or assigned by the author to
the journal in which it was published. As a result, finding the person who owns or controls the appropriate rights may sometimes be as time-consuming and difficult as negotiating the clearance that is required. The things you are not permitted to do ('restricted
acts') are listed in Table 8.3.

What copyright does not protect

Protection of ideas

There cannot be copyright in an idea or a suggestion as such (for example, the suggestion that the BBC should broadcast a *Mastermind* for teenagers). But if a suggestion takes

Table 8.3   Restricted acts

Copying
Issuing copies to the public
Performing, showing or playing to the public
Broadcasting
Adapting
Storing in any electronic medium
Rental and lending
Importing infringing copies
Dealing in infringing copies
Providing means for making infringing copies
Provision of premises or apparatus for infringing performances
Authorizing infringement

the form of a detailed format for the programme submitted in writing, then this is protected.

Who owns copyright?

As noted above, copyright can be transferred and split up. The first owner of the copyright in a work is usually the person who brought the original work into existence: for example, the author of an article or a book, the painter of a picture, the composer of a piece of music, or the author of a thesis or research article. In the case of films and sound recordings, the first copyright owner is the person who has made the arrangements to enable the recording or film to be made.

For you as a researcher, an important thing to realize is that under UK law no formalities are required to vest the copyright in the original owner and, as explained above, the owner may license various uses of the work and, indeed, may divest themselves of the copyright entirely by assignment. However, where a work is made by an employee in the course of employment, for example by a member of staff as part of their work, then the copyright belongs to the employer. Where a member of staff creates something outside the course of their employment, the rights must be acquired just as they would be from an outside contributor. So, for example, as I have written this chapter in work time, its copyright belongs to the Open University and not to me.

Many universities require students to assign copyright of their thesis to them. This is done to allow the university to use its muscle to protect the students' copyright for something that will become a public document, and also it allows the university to use the thesis for scrutiny and to send copies to other libraries on request. Universities don't restrict the use the student may wish to put their work to (e.g. production of articles, etc.).

Table 8.4   Permitted acts

Insubstantial use

Non-commercial research or private study

Fair dealing for the purposes of criticism or review – this covers reviewing
  for articles, literature review, etc.

Fair dealing for the purposes of reporting current events – e.g. in
  newspapers or journals

Bona fide examinations – so using material for a thesis/dissertation is a
  permitted act as this is produced for examination purposes

Off-air recording of broadcasts by educational establishments
  (for access from premises owned by the institution).

Photocopying under CLA licence

Instruction in the making of films or soundtracks

Recording at home for 'time-shifting' purposes

Decompilation – with caution

Redrawing – with caution

Activity 8.4

Upon registration as a research student, were you asked to assign copyright on works you produce to your university? If so, check up on what rights you have assigned to your university and your university's policy on your use of copyrightable materials and how you obtain permission to use them. This could be particularly important if, for example, you write an article for a journal that asks you to assign them copyright for that article.

If you have retained copyright on your research and its outputs, you should still check your university's policy for helping you to protect your rights.

Exceptions to copyright protection

There are certain statutory exceptions to the general protection given to the owner of copyright. Some of these are particularly useful to university (non-commercial) research and examined work (such as a PhD and M.Phil in particular). These are detailed in Table 8.4.

Undertaking work for a research degree will result in your qualifying for a number of permitted acts. The following examples deal with the use of some of these in more detail, and further guidance is provided on this book's website.

Insubstantial use

A very short extract may be used without obtaining consent. This applies, for example, when you may quote the work of another author in your thesis or in a research article.

The test for what constitutes an insubstantial part is as much a matter of quality as quantity. It would be a substantial use of a copyright work to quote the line showing whodunit in a detective story, and quotation from almost any copyright poem is likely to be substantial and therefore to require clearance; but the use of, say, one or two hundred words from a full-length non-fiction book may be viewed as insubstantial.

Fair dealing

This is the more important permitted act and may allow relatively substantial use to be made of uncleared material in specific cases:

1 **for non-commercial research or private study;**

2 **for reporting current events (except in the case of photographs);**

3 **for criticism or review of the work itself or another work, providing you identify the work and the author. This will, of course apply to reviewing the work of others in a thesis or research paper. However, the use must be for a genuine critical purpose and not for biographical or general use. This covers most situations where you are conducting a literature review or comparing your results with those of others. No hard-and-fast rule can be laid down about the length of the extract that can be used. It should be no longer than needed by the reviewer or critic for the purpose of making their point.**

These 'fair dealing' exceptions apply under the 1988 Act not only to literary, dramatic, musical and artistic works but also to films, broadcasts or sound recordings. So the BBC can use a clip of a film or an extract from an ITV programme for review purposes or for reporting current events without obtaining consent, providing the 'dealing' is fair. In the same way, you can include an extract of a work as part of your literature review or in a review article. If your research involves media clips, the same applies.

The 'fair dealing' exception is the most commonly used one in research theses. Providing the source of a work and its author are identified (hence the importance of a complete and accurate references section), academic sources can be quoted relatively freely. However, the nature of your research is crucial to the application of fair dealing. From December 2003, fair dealing may be applied only to copying and gathering materials for the purposes of non-commercial research (so this covers all academic uses).

Bona fide examinations

Another area of exemptions that is of core relevance to PhD and Master's students is the exemption of works submitted for bona fide examination purposes only. This means that you can use copyright materials in a thesis or dissertation without obtaining clearance, so long as this is the only use you will make of them. You are, of course, required to acknowledge the sources.

Although this is a very convenient permitted act for the research student, making your copyright situation a lot easier than is general, it might be better to obtain clearance or use a copyright work under another category of permitted acts. This is because you may wish to reuse material in your thesis for an article, a conference paper or presentation, or in a departmental working paper. All of these are not materials for examination and so you would then be infringing copyright. As such you need to be careful when using the examination exemption.

Photocopying

The Copyright Licensing Agency (CLA) offers a licensing scheme to universities and colleges that addresses the needs of commercial researchers. Under this, payments for photocopying are passed to the copyright holders. However, if you make photocopies elsewhere you need to ensure that the organization has a CLA licence.

Overall, the exemptions covered by these permitted acts mean that for many research and writing activities, research students do not have to obtain copyright clearance. If in doubt, contact the person or department in your university who deals with rights clearance.

Web material

Material (text or images) taken from the web has the same legal and fair use restrictions applying to it as to any other form of publishing. Perhaps more than other documents, however, is the risk involved in the original website having published the material in contravention of copyright. Unfortunately, if the original website (or document) has contravened someone's copyright, the same will be true of the next 'user' (even if fair dealing is being claimed). It is worth being sure of the legality of the originating site before reusing web materials.

Reuse of survey questionnaires

If a survey or other study is being repeated, the original source must be attributed (see above under 'plagiarism'). Sometimes there can be a breach of copyright; for example, some psychometric tests are actively copyright. This is a grey area and each case has to be examined to see what is possible without breaching copyright restrictions. Usually, academic questionnaires are available for others to use in follow-up academic studies, but this is not always the case.

Databases

Most databases are not covered by copyright unless they meet an originality criteria. The databases should state if they are so covered. Separately, there are database rights, which means that the database holder can have the right to object to abstraction from a database and restrict access to licensed users.

To clear or not to clear...

Overall, whether or not you need copyright clearance to use materials in your research can appear complex, but a useful way to think this through is to break up your decision into the various aspects of copyright discussed in this chapter, as shown in Figure 8.1.

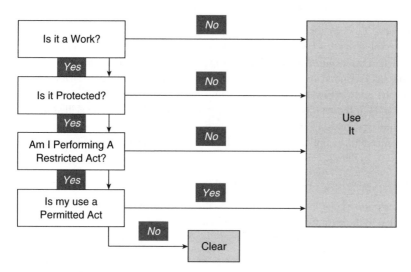

Figure 8.1   Copyright clearance decision tree Source: OU Rights Department (redrawn).

Activity 8.5

Take a piece of written work you have already produced and identify all the materials that you used in it that were authored or produced by somebody other than yourself. For each of these (or at least the main ones), work your way through the copyright clearance decision tree and identify how you are able to use these without clearance, or if clearance should have been sought.

8.4 Patents

Again, the UK Patent Office (IP Portal Team, UK Patent Office, 2005) description can hardly be improved upon:

What is a patent?

A patent gives an inventor the right for a limited period to stop others from making, using or selling an invention without the permission of the inventor. It is a deal between an inventor and the state in which the inventor is allowed a short term monopoly in return for allowing the invention to be made public.

Patents are about functional and technical aspects of products and processes. Most patents are for incremental improvements in known technology – evolution rather than revolution. The technology does not have to be complex.

Specific conditions must be fulfilled to get a patent. Major ones are that the invention must

1 be new. The invention must not form part of the 'state of the art'. The state of the art is everything that has been made available to the public before the date of applying for the patent. This includes published documents and articles, but can also include use, display, spoken description, or any other way in which information is made available to the public.
2 involve an inventive step. As well as being new, the invention must not be obvious from the state of the art. Obviousness is from the viewpoint of a person skilled in the area of technology that the invention is in.
3 be industrially applicable. This condition requires that the invention can be made or used in any kind of industry.

A patented invention is recorded in a patent document. A patent document must have

1 description of the invention, possibly with drawings, with enough detail for a person skilled in the area of technology to perform the invention.
2 claims to define the scope of the protection. The description is taken into account when interpreting the claims.

The original patent document of a patent application is published by a patent office. The application then adds to the state of the art for later applications, and anyone can comment on the application. Often the patent document needs altering or amending to meet the conditions above before a patent can be granted. The final version of the granted patent document is then republished. If more information about the state of the art is discovered after grant the patent document can be amended and republished again.

Patent rights are territorial; a UK patent does not give rights outside of the UK. Patent rights last for up to 20 years in the UK. Some patents, such as those for medicinal products, may be eligible for a further 5 years protection with a Supplementary Protection Certificate.

A patent can be of value to an inventor – as well as protecting his business, patents can be bought, sold, mortgaged, or licensed to others. They also benefit people other than the inventor since large amounts of information can be learnt from other people's patents – they can stop you from reinventing things or you can monitor what your competitors are doing. Patents also spur you or others on to develop your idea further, and once the term of the patent expires it can be freely performed by anyone which benefits the public and the economy.

The British Library has a detailed guide to the contents of patent applications.

(IP Portal Team, UK Patent Office, 2005)

A very important point in the consideration of patents is the requirement for non-disclosure prior to registration. If an invention is released on to the market or simply demonstrated publicly *before* a patent application is filed (then becoming 'pat. pending'), a patent won't be granted. This could be very unfortunate if you were hoping to make money out of an invention! Even a presentation of an idea at a conference could easily let a patent application slip out of your grasp. The best thing to do is to ask for expert advice: your university may have an Intellectual Property Management Office, or there are many patent agents who know the ins and outs of the patent application system. Remember also that many universities ask students not only to assign over to them copyright, but patent rights as well. This can help you, as your university may be able to assist you in exploiting any patentable invention, and share the returns obtained.

8.5 Summary

Academic researchers have a number of responsibilities and rights that are ingrained in the work they do. Some of these have been outlined above, and there is plenty of detailed help available on specific topics. For intellectual property, the UK Patent Office has excellent advice via its website. The UK's Data Protection Act is handled by the Information Commissioner's Office. Links to these sites are provided via this book's website.

Acknowledgement

This chapter has drawn upon material produced by the Open University Rights Department for training staff in intellectual property issues, and from the Open University document Academic Integrity: Code of Good Practice in Research.

Further Reading

For intellectual property, the UK Patent Office website is strongly recommended:

http://www.intellectual-property.gov.uk/

UK Information Commissioner (Data Protection):

http://www.informationcommissioner.gov.uk/

References

IP Portal Team, UK Patent Office (2005) Intellectual Property. http:/www.intellectual-property.gov.uk/std/fa/question1.htm, accessed July 2005.

Platt, C. (1998) 'What if cold fusion is real', *Wired Magazine,* November, issue 6.11.

Appendix: The Open University's Academic Integrity Code of Good Practice in Research

(Edited from Open University document.)

Unethical research and cases of fraud threaten the credibility of the entire national and international research community.

1 Good scientific practice (as set out in the Joint Statement by the Director General of the Research Councils and the Chief Executives of the UK Research Councils) covers the following aspects:
2 fundamentals of scientific work such as:
   maintaining professional standards;
   documenting results;
   questioning one's own findings;
   attributing honestly the contribution of others;
3 leadership and co-operation in research groups;
4 taking special account of the needs of young researchers; and
5 securing and storing primary data.

The first point on 'good scientific practice' quoted above from the joint Research Councils' statement applies to **all staff** engaged in **all aspects** of academic research in the Open University.

Irrespective of subject discipline, researchers should agree to abide by this Code of Practice and:

1 demonstrate the highest standards of integrity and professionalism in their work;
2 observe fairness and equity in their dealings with colleagues and research students;
3 agree to take advice from the appropriate ethics committees on the ethical conduct of their research;
4 participate only in work which conforms to accepted ethical standards;
5 participate only in work which they are competent to perform;
6 agree to participate in appropriate professional development and training opportunities to ensure continued competencies and develop new competencies;
7 ensure validity and accuracy in the collection and reporting of data;
8 ensure the safety of those associated with the research.

Leadership and organization

It is the responsibility of the University Research Board, Deans and Directors of Studies, Sub Deans, Heads of Departments and Research Group Leaders to ensure that a climate is created that allows research to be conducted within the principles of good scientific and good academic practice. Responsibilities for overseeing good practice in units and sub-units should be clearly allocated to named individuals.

Allegations of academic malpractice

In general terms academic malpractice/scientific misconduct can be recognized to cover two broad categories, the distinction being in terms of the focus of the dishonesty. Thus the first arises where there is fabrication or falsification of the research results; the second arises where there is plagiarism, misquoting or other misappropriation of the work of other researchers. Colluding in, or concealing, the misconduct of others is, in itself, misconduct. Honest errors do not, of course, constitute scientific misconduct.

Members of the University who do not operate in line with the Code of Good Practice in Research may be subject to disciplinary procedures where failure to comply with the provisions is serious or may damage the reputation of the University.

9 Ethical Frameworks for Research with Human Participants

John Oates

LEARNING OUTCOMES

After reading this chapter and working on its associated activities you should be able to:

- Give an account of the historical reasons why ethical conduct has become an increasingly important element of the design and conduct of research with people.
- Describe the main areas of ethical concern associated with research with humans.
- Discuss the issue of balancing research benefits with risks and harm.
- Critically evaluate an ethical protocol.
- Draft an application for ethical approval for a research project that you propose to conduct.

9.1 Introduction

This chapter provides an introduction to the ethics of research which involves collecting data from people. It does not deal with research involving animals other than humans, which is a subject in its own right. The context within which the topic is discussed is primarily that of the UK and Europe. While many of the emergent principles of sound ethical conduct in human research are, arguably, worldwide in their applicability and relevance, there is significant variation across continents in the way that ethical principles are regulated and enforced.

The main aim of this chapter is to help you to recognize that there are many ethical issues that can arise when doing research with humans, perhaps more than may at first be realized when embarking on a project of this type. The chapter also aims to help you to think about the ethical dimensions of your own research, especially if it does involve human participants, to be better equipped to plan your data collection methods in ethically justifiable ways, and to be better able to draw up an acceptable application for ethical approval if you need to.

If you are planning to carry out 'person-based' research, then you are encouraged to consider the topics that are raised in each part of this chapter by thinking about the questions that are posed at key points in relation to your own research topics and research design. If this is not the case, then there are still some ethical issues that are relevant to virtually any research. As well as with matters such as honesty and integrity in collecting and reporting data and respecting intellectual property rights that were considered in Chapter 8, there is the more general issue of having regard to the value to society of the work in which you are engaged.

Activity 9.1

Think about the area of research that you are planning to pursue.

Write a summary list of the aspects of your research that you think have an ethical dimension to them, if you think that there are any. Consider the types of data that you propose to collect: what would be ethically sound and unsound ways of collecting them?

It will be suggested later that you come back to this list and reconsider what you have written.

Why 'participants'?

It is now common practice to refer to people who serve as data sources for research as *participants*. This recognizes their active role and replaces the term 'subject', which has been viewed as possibly derogatory and certainly as portraying people as passive recipients rather than active agents. It is not so long ago that people routinely talked of 'guinea pigs' when referring to human participants, a term still heard, but now used more often in an ironic sense, recognizing the inappropriateness of this designation.

It can be argued that in some types of social research the people providing data are relatively passive, for example in completing a short multiple-choice questionnaire, while in other types of study, such as qualitative interviews, people are much more actively engaged. But the thrust of the shift to the term 'participants' is to recognize that people providing data for a study do themselves have a stake in the process, they are giving up their time and allowing an intrusion into their 'private space'. It is thus in the spirit of recognizing people's rights to have their human dignity respected that the term 'participant' is promoted.

Why 'frameworks'?

Using the word 'frameworks' in the title of this chapter suggests that the assurance of ethical conduct of research is a complex matter, needing a supporting infrastructure. However, 'Surely any reasonable person knows what's ethical and what's not?' is still one of the reactions that are encountered when research ethics are being discussed, suggesting that it can simply be left to the individual researcher to behave in an ethically sound way.

While that may have been a defensible position some years ago, the last few years have seen a massive growth in concern about and regulation of research ethics. Anyone in a university, a National Health Service trust or other institution who intends to carry out research with humans now needs to be aware of the various legal and other constraints that govern research and its conduct. There are good legal reasons for gaining proper ethics approval for a research project. Primary benefits include the protection it affords to the researcher(s), participants, host institutions and funding bodies, in that careful preparation of an application for ethical approval can reveal potential risks that might not otherwise have been considered. Evidence of proper ethical scrutiny may often also be necessary to ensure that the host institution's liability insurance provides cover for the project staff and participants.

Up to the middle of the last century, there were relatively few formal controls on the way that research with people was conducted or on the topics of research. The medical research carried out on concentration camp inmates by the Nazis caused widespread public condemnation once it became known about. In response to this, the Nuremberg Code was drawn up by lawyers in 1947 to prohibit research being carried out on people against their will. Several well-known and now somewhat notorious studies carried out by American social researchers in the 1950s, 1960s and 1970s added to the worldwide public concern about such matters and ushered in a period during which various codes of practice and legal controls were developed to regulate research.

In response to concerns such as these, research ethics committees began to be formed in the latter half of the last century, both in Europe and in America, to scrutinize and control research with humans. Initially, the focus was on medical research and the ethical governance of this area of human research is still arguably the most developed and influential. In America, since 1974, any federally funded research with humans, or any research at all that involves the use of drugs or physical intervention with humans, is legally required to have the formal approval of a recognized ethics committee.

Activity 9.2

Do you think that research ethics committees should scrutinize all research with humans or only some?

If you think that some (or all?) research does not need to go through such a process, why do you think this? How confident are you that researchers can 'police themselves'?

Comment

Some people would argue that it is patently obvious that certain types of research, for example, those involving consenting adults on non-sensitive topics, should not need to go through the inconvenience of applying for ethical approval. Some university research ethics committees (URECs) exclude very low-risk studies from the need for ethical approval. For example, one UREC states that 'where any reasonable judgement would suggest that no harm could arise to any person, living or dead' it is not necessary for ethical approval to be sought. This begs the question, however, of what is a 'reasonable judgement'. However, a counter-argument to such exclusions might be that it is a protection to all parties if an independent opinion on the ethical probity of research has been given. This chapter takes the position that all researchers gathering data from humans should at least carefully and systematically consider the ethical dimensions to their work, since these are not always immediately apparent.

9.2   The Variety of Ethical Frameworks

International frameworks

There are numerous international agreements that set out to provide frameworks for the ethical conduct of research with humans. The majority of these concern medical research, the most widely cited being the 1964 World Medical Association Helsinki Declaration, the 1997 Council of Europe Convention on Human Rights and Biomedicine, and the 1997 UNESCO Universal Declaration on the Human Genome and Human Rights.

The European Union Clinical Trials Directive of 2004 went further and set up a legal framework to support a principled ethical approach for the conduct of clinical trials in the EU.

Research in the English National Health Service

In England, research with humans within the National Health Service (NHS) is controlled by procedures developed by the Central Office for Research Ethics Committees (COREC), within the NHS Research Governance framework. Any research that involves humans or human tissue within the NHS, that is, on NHS premises or with NHS patients or staff, or where NHS staff or records are involved in identifying and recruiting participants, requires approval by a Local Research Ethics Committee (LREC) and approval by the Trust within which the research is proposed to take place. For research involving multiple sites, a somewhat different, centrally administered, MREC (Multi-Centre Research Ethics Committee) system operates.

An example of researching under the MREC was provided in Chapter 3 of this book where (in Box 3.2) Jackie Topp discussed the ethical considerations of her PhD project. The NHS system has undergone a lot of development in recent years, towards standardizing and governing the ethical scrutiny process, and now involves a nationwide standard application routine. RECs have available to them extensive manualized guidance on how to conduct their scrutiny processes (Eckstein, 2003). At the time of writing (2005) a revised set of procedures has recently been instated and extensive guidelines for applicants and LRECs have been issued by COREC. The most common forms of research governed by COREC are clinical trials of new medical treatments, and epidemiological and pathological research. The extensive set of questions asked by the new REC application forms reflect this, and other forms of research, such as qualitative investigations of health topics, can be difficult to fit within the new procedures (Hollway, 2000). This can often include research student projects which are non-clinical but require access via the NHS (as was the case for Jackie Topp in Chapter 3).

Professional organizations

Many British professional organizations have in recent years developed ethical principles and guidelines within which their members are expected to practise and conduct research. Prominent among these are the British Psychological Society, the British Educational Research Association and the British Sociological Association, all of which maintain websites carrying current versions of these codes of practice. There are links to several of these on this book's website. It is common practice for members of such bodies to state in applications for ethical approval for research that they will conduct their study in compliance with the body's ethics code.

Funding bodies

Research funding bodies are increasingly adopting equivalent sets of ethical guidelines which researchers are expected to comply with in any research funded in part or whole by these agencies. The Medical Research Council (MRC) is the undoubted leader in this respect, for obvious reasons, given the types of research that it supports. The MRC publishes an extensive body of ethical guidelines with specific documents covering particular fields of research such as in genetics. The Nuffield Foundation has been an active body in developing a Bioethics Framework which covers a wide range of medical research, and the Wellcome Trust has produced a formal statement on ethics review within which holders of its grants are required to conduct their research. The Economic and Social Research Council (ESRC) has published a Research Ethics Framework (Economic and Social Research Council, 2005), with which all researchers in receipt of ESRC support will in future be required to comply. Many funding bodies now require that applications for research funding should have already received formal ethical approval from the host institution, normally a university or other higher education establishment (HEI).

Research ethics committees in England

Formal ethical approvals for English research are given by two main stakeholders: the NHS via the COREC-regulated system of LRECs and MRECs already outlined; and by HEIs. While the NHS system has become a centrally governed one, there is no equivalent structure for HEIs. Practice varies widely in this sector, and although many HEIs have well-established research ethics committees, with clear terms of reference and operating procedures, others have less well-organized ways of maintaining ethical standards and some have none (Tinker and Coomber, 2004). An umbrella body, the Association of Research Ethics Committees (AREC), does operate as a forum for the discussion of ethical issues, but has no powers in relation to governance.

Cross-national funding of research

Increasingly, British research is being funded by bodies outside Britain, especially the European Union and the USA. This raises some complications for ethical approval of research. For example, American funding bodies are legally bound only to fund research with humans that has been ethically approved by a REC that is recognized by the American Office for Human Research Protections and that has been given what is called 'Federal Wide Assurance'. EU funding for research with humans will also require approval by an REC in the host country, although there is not at present a formal EU system for recognizing RECs as there is in the USA.

Conflict and harmony

Given the wide range of different bodies that are involved in research ethics governance affecting British researchers, it would not be surprising if there were conflicts between the different stakeholders' frameworks where more than one body is involved, as is often the case. On the whole, though, there is actually a broad agreement between all the different codes and guidelines, with only two general issues that tend to need resolution. First, different bodies have established different policies regarding the length of time for which research data on individuals should be stored, with some giving maximum times which differ, and others giving minimum times. Some funding bodies, such as ESRC, require researchers to archive data with a centralized system, the United Kingdom Data Archive, which can be difficult to reconcile with, for example, NHS or MRC guidelines on the protection and retention of patient data.

Second, the wide range of different research methodologies in the social sciences may not match up to the assumptions of what 'research' means for a particular regulatory body. An example of this is the dominance of the randomized controlled clinical trial model of research in the COREC ethical approval procedure, which can make it difficult for qualitative researchers to make an application for LREC ethical clearance that satisfactorily answers all the questions on the standard application form.

However, in general, ethical principles and guidelines do harmonize well with each other and tend to agree quite closely on the main areas in which ethical considerations apply and what counts as best practice in these areas. The sections that follow outline these areas and review the main issues in each as far as ethical practice is concerned. First, though, a brief consideration is given of the definition of 'research' and the potential for good and harm in research.

Activity 9.3

Do you think that it would be a good idea for there to be a single framework of ethical scrutiny and approval for all types of research?

If not, what different types of research do you think might need different frameworks?

Might this lead to any problems for researchers? If so, what might these be?

At this point, it is suggested that you refer to at least one set of professional research ethics guidelines, by searching the internet for a set that is appropriate for your research. You might, for example, look at the British Educational Research Association or the British Psychological Society websites. You could use the search terms 'ethics research guidelines code'. Some links are available via this book's website.

9.3   What is 'Research'?

Collecting data from humans

Before further exploring issues involved in the ethics of research, it is necessary to briefly consider what research is and, particularly, what its purpose is, since this will help to clarify what aspects of research have ethical dimensions. The general term 'research' is commonly used to describe such a wide range of activities that it would be a daunting task to try to set down a concise definition that stood any chance of meeting with general agreement and serving any useful purpose. This chapter, however, is concerned with a very specific area of research, that of collecting data from human participants, so the task is somewhat more contained and feasible.

Nevertheless, as you have seen in Chapter 4, even within this narrower ambit, there are distinctively different 'logics of enquiry' and contrasting views of what counts as knowledge.

Nevertheless, we need some sort of working definition to serve as a frame for the further consideration of research ethics. So I suggest that, in the context of the ethics of research with humans, research can be provisionally defined as:

- **An activity that aims to generate knowledge that can be trusted and valued by the researcher and others.**

To make this a concise definition, I use the term 'knowledge' in a broad sense, to include explanation and understanding, as well as explication and abduction as described in Chapter 4. So, if we accept a definition of this sort, research is crucially not just an activity in itself, it also aims to produce products of value. Research thus has a function, and assessing the functionality of a specific research design, that is, the extent to which it can deliver the products of value, is nowadays a key part of ethical scrutiny. Research that is so badly designed that it stands little or no chance of delivering any sort of valuable outcome can be considered to be lacking in ethical merit on these grounds alone.

Research as training

One specific exception to this definition, which nevertheless falls within the ambit of research ethics, is where students or trainees are practising research techniques for the purpose of improving their own knowledge and skills. The fact that this is a special case, in which the requirement of adding to a general body of knowledge can justifiably be given less weight, is recognized within the NHS REC procedures. Although all research degrees are training qualifications, one of the key criteria that are applied to research theses at examination is 'contribution to knowledge', so saying that a research degree is only about training cannot be used as an excuse for downgrading the importance of ethics in a research design. However, you might justify a training stage in your research that does not in itself produce useful results.

Activity 9.4

Consider the research that you are planning to conduct. How would you best describe yours in terms of the three main 'types' (deductive, inductive or abductive) given in Chapter 4?

If you were to decide to change your basic approach to one of the other types, do you think that the relevant ethical considerations would change? In what way?

To what extent are you expecting the data collection that you do in the early stages of your project to be more to do with training than with generating valuable knowledge?

If you have not already planned to do so, will you consider carrying out a pilot study for this training purpose? If so, and it involves collecting data from people, how will you describe to them what you are doing?

9.4   Benefits, Harm and Risk

Getting the right balance

In designing a research project, and in assessing its ethical merit, there is almost always a judgement involved which weighs up the relative balance of potential benefits and potential harms. In relation to benefits, part of this assessment should include an evaluation of the functionality of the research design. In other words, can the study deliver the benefits that it proposes? In relation to harm, there is not only the level of harm to be considered, but also, alongside this, the risks of such harm occurring. Thus, for example, it might be possible to consider a study worth conducting in a case where there is a potential harm such as personal distress if the risk of this occurring is very low. It would be easier to accept such a low risk if there were also a risk management strategy in place to deal with such a situation, should it arise. It would also be more acceptable if the expected benefits were great and the risk of these not being achieved was correspondingly low.

A good research design will have an explicit and documented risk analysis and risk management strategy in place, and good ethical scrutiny by a REC will seek assurance that this is indeed the case.

Benefits

There are quite a few different types of benefit that research might aim to deliver.

The list in Activity 9.5 gives some of the more commonly recognized of these. Add others that you may consider important. To encourage you to consider these and weigh up their relative merits, at least in your opinion, try ranking them; decide which is the most important in your view, which the least important, and how the others rank relative to each other. Separate your rankings for researchers and participants; you may find that this clarifies the differing priorities of the two groups.

(Word versions for Activities 9.5–9.7 are available on this book's website.)

Activity 9.5   Ranking Benefits of Research

Benefit	Rank for researcher	Rank for participant
Research as intrinsic good		
Contribution to knowledge		
Development of theories		
Improvements to lives		
Training researchers		
Enhancing reputation/image		
Increasing commercial success		
Entertainment and enjoyment		
Personal development		
Career advancement		

Harm

Similarly, there is a range of different types of risk and harm that might be associated with a research study. As you did for the list of benefits, consider the list of harms in Activity 9.6 and rank them in respect of the researchers and the participants' perspectives.

Activity 9.6 Ranking Risks and Harm

Risk	Rank for researcher	Rank for participant
Physical trauma/injury		
Psychological damage		
Distress		
Offence		
Coercion		
Breach of confidence		
Inconvenience		
Disrepute or litigation		
Waste of time		
Waste of resources/funds		
Failure to publish		

Clearly, the rankings of these are likely to be very much influenced by the nature of the research itself. This then highlights the point that it is almost always worth spending some time considering the likely benefits, harms and risks of proposed research studies.

Activity 9.7

For your own proposed research, consider each of the items in the 'Benefits' table and give it a score between 0 and 10, 0 being 'irrelevant or not important at all' and 10 being 'highly significant'.

Then do a similar evaluation for the 'Risks' table, this time using a percentage to estimate the risk of a harm of this type arising from your work. If you have identified a risk that is significant in your view, how might you obviate or minimize it? The advice on risk assessment in Chapter 2 may help here.

Once you have done this, go back to your answers to Activity 9.1, where you listed the ethical issues for your own work, and see if you now can add some further considerations to that list.

9.5   The 'Protocol'

Reference is often made to 'protocols' in discussions of research ethics and in applications to RECs. A protocol is, in essence, a clear, unambiguous description of how data are to be handled through the sequence of stages from the recruitment of participants from whom data will be gathered, through the processes of data gathering, analysis and write-up to the publication of findings and final contacts with participants. A protocol can often be prepared as a separate document and may contain a flowchart showing the states of data handling. Increasingly, it is expected to include a risk assessment and a strategy for dealing with problematic events that may arise under the various risk headings that may be identified. A protocol may also exist in the form of the answers to various questions in a REC proforma, but it is good practice to prepare a single document as well if this is the case.

The protocol is basically a policy guideline that all members of a research team agree to comply with, and this is usually made explicit in the signing of a REC application. Any substantive needs to deviate from a protocol that arise in the course of a research study should be notified to the REC that approved the application, before they are acted on, since they may require further formal scrutiny. Often, a REC chairperson will be prepared to approve minor changes to a protocol by Chair's action without requiring a further full application to be made.

Areas covered by typical protocols

There is a set of areas that an adequate protocol should cover. The following lists the key areas, some of which are then discussed in more detail below:

- **Names/roles of persons in the research team who will collect and handle primary (i.e. raw) data.**

- **Identity of any professional ethics code that will be followed.**

- **Procedures for the recruitment of participants.**

- **Procedures for gaining informed consent from participants and other parties such as parents and GPs.**

- **Any payment(s) or other recompense to participants.**

- **Details of data types and collection methods.**

- **Any planned deception or withholding of information.**

- **Data storage and security measures.**

- **Anonymization procedures.**

- **Scope and methods of data analysis.**

- **Debriefing of participants.**

- **Risk analysis, avoidance and management strategy.**

- **Details of liability insurance cover.**

Recruitment

Under this heading, the intended number of participants and their characteristics should be stated. This will, in effect, indicate the research methods to be employed and will be one of the factors taken into account in assessing the research functionality. If the results are intended to be generalized, the sample needs to be as representative as possible of the population to which the results are expected to apply. The mode of recruitment should be stated (for example, by advertisement, by snowballing, by random selection from a list or other means) so that an assessment can be made of the extent to which the risk of unwanted bias in participant characteristics is being minimized. You may recall that, in Box 3.2, Jackie Topp discussed the ethical issues around the recruitment of her vulnerable adult participants.

So-called 'volunteer' or 'opportunity' sampling, where participants are taken on as they come forward, or because access is easy, needs to be used with care. It is important to avoid introducing potentially distorting effects of self-selection on the sample characteristics. As a result, these sampling methods should be very carefully evaluated, even though they may seem to be efficient or easy ways to gain participants.

Informed consent

No significant data should be gathered from people who have not consented, been given a clear statement about why the information is going to be collected, or been told how it is going to be used. The extent of detail and the complexity of the process of gaining informed consent will depend on the nature of the research. At one extreme, informed consent may be considered unnecessary in the case of a study that is gathering non-personal information from unidentifiable individuals on topics that are not sensitive. A good example of this might be a study that collects time-lapse images of people passing through railway station ticket gates to investigate why queues form. Even here, though, it might be considered appropriate to post a sign which says something like 'traffic through these gates is being monitored by close-circuit television'. Another example might be a website that collects information on a non-sensitive topic, such as colour preferences, from an online questionnaire that does not ask for any personal data that would identify the persons completing the survey.

At the other extreme, where the procedure for gaining informed consent is of paramount importance, would be clinical trials of new drugs on patients with life-threatening illnesses.

Typically, consent is gained and documented by using a combination of an information sheet and a consent form. The information sheet should give sufficient detail about the research study and the data collection from the potential participant so that they can then make an informed choice as to whether or not to take part. COREC provides a checklist of points that a good information sheet will follow (based on the model of a clinical trial). This includes the following:

1   An explanatory title for the project.

2   An invitation paragraph explaining that the person is being invited to take part in a study.

3   Background, aims and duration of the study.

4   Why the invitee has been approached.

5   What contribution they would be expected to make.

6 **Possible risks or disadvantages of participating.**

7 **Possible benefits of participating.**

8 **What happens after the study ends.**

9 **How complaints or comments can be made, including giving a contact other than the researcher.**

10 **Confidentiality of data.**

11 **Any payment or recompense for participation.**

12 **What will happen with results of the study.**

13 **Who is organizing and funding the research.**

14 **Opportunities to withdraw from study and to have data provided destroyed.**

For clinical trials there would also be:

1 **Details of the drug or procedure that is being tested.**

2 **Alternative for diagnosis or treatment.**

3 **Any possible side-effects of treatment.**

Clearly, some of these points may not be necessary for particular studies, but the list nevertheless indicates the range of information that needs to be considered when drafting an information sheet. Normally, such a sheet will be on a single A4 page, possibly on both sides.

It is crucial that it is understandable by every potential participant, so it needs to be carefully worded and checked with people of a range of reading abilities. Increasingly, equal opportunities considerations are suggesting that people whose native language is not English should not be excluded from the possibility of taking part in research. This needs to be carefully thought about, and possible arrangements for translation of information sheets, consent forms and other documents, as well as the data collection itself, will need to be examined and implemented if deemed necessary.

The information sheet should be separate from the actual consent form, so that participants consenting to join the study can retain it.

In the case of children, or persons who are unable to give informed consent because of a learning difficulty or other disability, a parent, guardian or carer may give consent on the person's behalf. However, increasingly, researchers are using the principle of 'assent' to monitor whether the participant is showing any signs that they are uncomfortable with the data collection process.

The consent form itself should summarize succinctly the conditions of participation and often will include a space for a witness signature as well as that of the participant, parent, guardian or carer.

Payment(s) or other recompense to participants

It is now considered crucial to avoid any coercion or inducement to participate in a research study, and offering payments or other rewards can easily be construed as inducement. However, it is also the case that participating in a study will involve some inconvenience to those taking part, as well as possible travel costs and other expenses. It is generally recognized that reimbursing such expenses and making a small payment in recognition of inconvenience and lost time is appropriate and does not constitute inducement.

Details of data types and collection methods

So that the functionality of a research design can be evaluated, it is important in a protocol to outline the types of data that are to be collected and the ways in which they are to be collected. Without this information, the utility of the research simply cannot be judged.

Deception or withholding of information

For some studies, if the detailed hypotheses or research questions are divulged to the participants before they take part in the study, this may compromise the accuracy and validity of the data collected, or interfere with experimental or other procedures. But withholding such information at the start of a study should only be done after careful consideration and working to the principle that only essential withholding is done.

Similarly, some studies may need to involve a degree of deception to avoid compromising the data collection. For example, if the study is looking at mutual eye-contact in negotiation situations, it may be appropriate to say that it is the participants' speech that is being recorded, so that the measure of interest is not contaminated. But whenever withholding of information or deception is part of the design, it should only be done if the reasons for it have been thoroughly examined.

It is also important to debrief participants after the study in a sensitive way so that they understand the withholding or deception and why it has been done, rather than feeling that they been duped unnecessarily, since that can be very distressing to some people.

Data storage and security measures

A protocol should state how data are to be managed and stored, to show that concerns of data security have been properly considered and that procedures are in place to avoid risks of unauthorized access to data.

The Data Protection Act 1998 requires anyone collecting and storing personal data to follow a set of guidelines regarding the use of such data and providing data givers (participants) with access to data held about them. The Freedom of Information Act 2000 also gives rights to individuals to access information held in institutions. There are exceptions to these requirements in the case of research, particularly where data are anonymized. Researchers need to register their project with a Data Protection Officer in their institution to comply with the Acts. This is covered in more detail in Chapter 8.

Anonymization procedures

Increasingly, it is common practice to remove all personal identifying information from sets of data at the earliest possible opportunity after collecting them. If different sets of data from the same individuals need to be matched up, it is possible to use an encryption key technique to achieve this, by assigning each participant a unique identifier and lodging the key for this identifier–participant link with a single member of the project team, not the person who will be analysing the data. Once all data have been collected, the key can be discarded. For very sensitive data, a double-key encryption method can be used where there is an intermediate key as well, held by another person.

Activity 9.8

Draft an outline information sheet and consent form for your own research, if it involves collecting data from people, noting the things that you would cover in a single A4 information sheet and a single A4 consent form.

This activity will link to Activity 9.9 later in this chapter.

9.6   Personal Protection of Participants and Researchers

Most of the points made so far in this chapter relate to protecting the participant from harm of one sort or another. But the protection of the researcher and the sponsoring institution is also assured by complying with a properly prepared protocol. There are certain risks that can arise just from the process of meeting with and gathering data from individuals, and these need to be considered as well so that they can be minimized by careful planning. This links into the considerations of health and safety in Chapter 2 of this book.

Vulnerable groups

A common issue is the avoidance of risks associated with interviewing children, young people or other vulnerable individuals. Carrying out such research in the participant's own home, or in an unsupervised setting, lays both parties open to risks of actual inappropriate behaviour or allegations of such behaviour. One way of avoiding such risks is to ensure that a third party can observe the data collection process and that it is carried out in a relatively safe environment. In the UK, it is now common practice for employers of researchers who will be working with vulnerable individuals to require the researchers to obtain what is called a 'disclosure' from the Criminal Records Bureau (CRB). This is sent to the employer as well as the researcher and shows any records of convictions or other evidence of criminal behaviour. There are three levels of 'disclosure', 'basic', 'standard' and 'enhanced', which give increasingly detailed information and effectively cover broader ranges of information, beyond just convictions which are disclosed at the basic level. Increasingly, employers are now requiring regular updating of disclosures, for example every three years, for people routinely working with vulnerable individuals.

Children

Children represent one of a number of 'vulnerable groups' within the broad category of human participants, along with disabled people and people with learning difficulties. There are three main reasons why children are considered to be vulnerable. First, there will almost inevitably be a perceived and usually real power imbalance between child and researcher. Second, children's abilities to comprehend research and the reasons why it is done may be very different from those of adults. Third, it is reasonable to be concerned that negative experiences during childhood may have an effect on subsequent development, with the risk of long-term psychological harm.

These three aspects to children's vulnerability when participating in research each have different implications for the design of research and how it is conducted (Alderson,

2004). They are also, of course, embedded within a broader frame of socially constructed beliefs about childhood, about children and about what is right and proper conduct for adults involved in professional work with children. Perhaps the most obvious of these is a concern that adults working with children should not have any previous history of offending against children in violation of these beliefs. It is now very widely expected that anyone wishing to conduct research in an English school should have gained at least a standard level of clearance from the CRB. It is also becoming generally accepted that it is good practice for anyone engaged in any direct contact with children in the course of research to have CRB clearance.

Power imbalance

Requiring formal proof that a researcher does not have a criminal record or other evidence of potentially offending is obviously a form of protection against some of the more serious risks of harm to children, but there are other significant risks of harm which this precaution does not guard against. There are risks that children may agree to requests, suggestions or even to their perceptions of such directives, even though they may not actually be happy with these. Researchers can seem like authority figures to children, and children may feel that they have to comply with what they think the researchers want. As well as this potentially being a distressing experience for a child, because they are acquiescing to an unwelcome directive, this is also an important source of potential bias in research results.

It is worth noting that situations other than research with children can also engender power imbalance problems, for example, research carried out in developing countries where the researcher may be vastly more affluent than the participants and hence be seen as coercive. There is also an issue in relation to someone else 'recommending' participants, which can in itself lead to people feeling a sense of obligation to participate.

Competence to understand explanations of research

The second area of vulnerability relates to the difficulty that children may have in understanding what research is, why it is done and what the implications are of agreeing to participate. It is often not enough to give an explanation in terms that it is thought a child will understand, it is also often necessary to check that they have indeed understood.

Affecting children's development

The third area of ethical concern in respect of research with children is that their development itself can be seen as vulnerable to negative influences, more so than older individuals whose development may be expected to be more resilient and robust. Especially if the research has a potential for evoking negative emotional reactions and it is not always obvious what may trigger such reactions, taking part in research can be a daunting prospect for children. They may in consequence suffer heightened reactions, the memories of which may remain with them. It is important to remember how important the parents' presence can be for many children, helping them to feel secure in the presence of the unfamiliar. Although it is common for researchers to seek to collect data from children without the parents' presence, or at least with them being kept well in the background to avoid possible influence on results, the effect of this in making children feel insecure should not be underestimated.

9.7   The Broader Context

In this chapter so far, the discussion has concentrated largely on ethical issues to do with the conduct of the data gathering aspects of research, and the balancing of the requirement of minimal harm with maximum benefit from this process.

But it should not be overlooked that data collection is only one part of the research process. There are much wider ethical issues to do with researchers' conduct in a more general sense, as are discussed in Chapter 8. The ethical issues of conduct are recognized by several professional bodies. For example, the British Psychological Society not only publishes principles and guidelines for research but also guidelines for professional conduct of psychologists in a broader sense. These, for example, make it clear that it is unprofessional to claim more knowledge or skill than one actually possesses, that it is a duty to monitor one's colleagues' conduct as well as one's own, and to refrain from inappropriate relationships with clients or patients.

As was noted in Chapter 8, there are codes of conduct for academics that form a frame within which the ethics of researching with human beings needs to be viewed. These are not necessarily always clearly codified in universities' statutes and regulations, but are widely accepted by the academic community. Among the most serious offences against these codes are fabrication of evidence, falsification of analyses, plagiarism and failure to credit colleagues' contributions. Increasingly, universities are making these principles explicit and breaches of them punishable by a range of sanctions.

Activity 9.9   Evaluating a Sample Protocol

In the light of what you have read in this chapter, read through the sample application for ethical approval and the information sheet and consent form printed in Appendix 1, and critically evaluate the entries for each heading. Every entry has at least one ethical 'flaw'.

Note that this is a fictitious case, but it contains elements drawn from real applications and research projects. Once you have completed your critical analysis, turn to the comments in Appendix 2.

Finally, look back at your responses to Activity 9.1 and make notes on further ethical issues that you now consider important and that you did not note down before reading the chapter.

Web Sources

This book's website contains a number of useful links to the following: professional bodies, research funding bodies, the Central Office of Research Ethics Committees, the Criminal Records Bureau Disclosure service and the Higher Education Academy resources on research ethics.

References

Alderson, P. (2004) 'Ethics', in Fraser, S., Lewis, V., Ding, S., Kellett, M. and Robinson, C. (eds), *Doing Research with Children and Young People*. London: Sage.

Eckstein, S. (2003) *Manual for Research Ethics Committees*. Cambridge: Cambridge University Press.

Economic and Social Research Council (2005) *Research Ethics Framework*. Swindon: ESRC.

Hollway, W. (2000) 'The ethics of researching psychosocial subjects', in Hollway, W. and Jefferson, T. (eds), *Doing Qualitative Research Differently: Free Association, Narrative and the Interview Method*. London: Sage.

Tinker, A. and Coomber, V. (2004) *University Research Ethics Committees: Their Role, Remit and Conduct*. London: King's College.

Appendix 1: Sample Application for Ethical Approval

University of Middle England

HUMAN PARTICIPANTS

ETHICS APPLICATION

Title of project
The social constriction of DNR decisions in SCBUs

Schedule
2005–2006

Abstract
A summary of the main points of the research, understandable by a non-specialist.

This project will explore the semiotics employed in SCBUs as a site for negotiated mean-ing-making following decisions to not resuscitate babies who are seriously ill, abnormal or disabled. It will be an in-depth phenomenological study with parents and nursing staff in a SCBU in Central England. It will explore Uren and Wastell's conceptualization of grief as an interpretive phenomenon elicited by the loss of a primary attachment figure, thereby shat-tering core life purposes and implicating the need to reinstate meaning.

Methodology
I will be analysing the tapes to uncover underlying themes of narrative voices.

Source(s) of funding
Details of the funding body (e.g. ESRC, MRC).

Middle England University

Justification for research
What contribution to knowledge, policy, practice, and people's lives will the research make?

Having lost my newborn daughter myself some years ago when she was found to be suf-fering from Dead Gut Syndrome, I am acutely aware that deciding not to resuscitate an infant is a difficult decision for both staff and parents. The negotiation of meanings involved in reaching a collective decision and dealing with its emotional aftermath implicates repre-sentations of attachment in everyone concerned. Recent media coverage of this issue has also highlighted the need for more knowledge and understanding. As yet, there has been little research in this area and it would be helpful to people faced with these difficult life decisions and coping with them afterwards.

Investigators
Give names and units of all persons involved in the collection and handling of individual data.

Ms. Randomly Selected Surname

Published ethical guidelines to be followed
For example: BERA, BPS, BSA (see Research Ethics website for more information).

BERA

Location(s) of data collection
Give details of where and when data will be collected. If on private, corporate or institutional premises, indicate what approvals are gained/required.

Data will be collected in the SCBU in Downlands Hospital, Flintshire, Central England.

Approval will need to be given by the Ward Sister.

Participants
Give details of the population from which you will be sampling, the sample size and how this sampling will be done.

I will sample from parents whose newborn infants are taken into Downlands Hospital SCBU and are seriously ill or disabled.

Recruitment procedures
How will you identify and approach potential participants?

The Ward Sister will tell me which babies in the SCBU are seriously ill, abnormal or disabled and I will ask their parents if they are prepared to help with my research.

Consent
Give details of how informed consent will be gained and attach copies of information sheet(s) and consent form(s). Give details of how participants can withdraw consent and what will happen to the data in such a case.

I will give subjects the attached sheet and ask them to sign to show their consent. I have stated there that subjects may withdraw at any time. If they do, I will treat there data as confidential.

Data protection
Give details of registration of the project under the DP Act and the procedures to be followed re storage and disposal of data to comply with the Act.

I will store all data and the names of subjects in a database in my laptop password-protected.

Recompense to participants
Normally, recompense is only given for expenses and inconvenience, otherwise it might be seen as coercion/inducement to participate. Give details of any recompense to participants.

I will offer counselling support to any member of staff or parent who appears to be distressed by my questions.

Deception
Give details of the withholding of any information from participants, or misrepresentation or other deception that is an integral part of the research. Any such deception should be fully justified.

I will withhold any information that I am given about subjects' babies' medical condition if I feel that it may be harmful to do so.

Risks
Detail any foreseen risks to participants or researchers and steps that will be taken to minimize/counter these.

No risks

Debriefing
Give details of how information will be given to participants after data collection to inform them of the purpose of their participation and the research more broadly.

If subjects want to know more about the study I will explain it to them.

Declaration
Declare here that the research will conform to the above protocol and that any significant changes or new issues will be raised with the HPMEC before they are implemented.

I declare that I will follow this protocol and inform the HPMEC of any changes while the project is running

signature(s)

R. S. Surname

The social construction of DNR (Do Not Resuscitate) decisions in Special Care Baby Units (SCBU)

INFORMATION SHEET

My project is looking at how parents and staff deal with deciding not to resuscitate a baby who is severely ill or disabled. I am interested in the talk that goes on and how it constructs meanings that are used to justify the decisions.

If you take part in this study it will help to gain more knowledge and understanding which will benefit future parents who are faced with the same problems.

I will collect the information by tape-recording interviews with parents and staff and analysing them afterwards. All information that you give me will be treated as strictly confidential.

If you want to withdraw from the study at any time you are free to do so.

Ms. R. S. Surname
Faculty of Health Psychology
Middle England University ME1 9XX

CONSENT FORM

I consent to taking part in Ms. Surname's study and I understand that I may withdraw at any time.

NAME:

ADDRESS:

Signature:

Date:

Appendix 2: Comments on Sample Application for Ethical Approval

Title of project
Apart from the unfortunate spelling error, which is not a good start as it suggests to a committee that the document has not been carefully proof-read, this title is not sufficiently explanatory. The two acronyms are jargon and will not be understood by a lay person. A medical member of the committee would spot that DNR is an outmoded acronym for Do Not Resuscitate, and would know that the current term is Do Not Attempt Resuscitation (DNAR). This would suggest that the applicant is not up to date with current medical practice. SCBU should be expanded as Special Care Baby Unit.

Schedule
This is too vague. Normally, one should state the months during which data collection will take place. This will alert the REC to when they might expect queries or issues to arise in relation to the project.

Abstract
This is far too abstruse for any lay person to make much sense of it. It also reads as if it may have been copied from someone else's writing, which could be construed as plagiarism. No date or reference is given for Uren and Wastell, so this cannot easily be followed up. The use of the term 'abnormal' in the first sentence shows a lack of knowledge of current thinking about the appropriate use of language to describe individuals who are disabled or with other special needs. Given the sensitivity of the topic of the research, this will ring alarm bells for the REC.

Methodology
This is inadequate. More detail is required and sufficient should be given to indicate whether the methods are valid and appropriate. This is important in assessing the potential functionality of the research proposed.

Source(s) of funding
This is too general; it should state the specific fund, for example, 'Faculty of Health postgraduate studentship award fund', or, in the case of external funding, the Research Council's or other institution's grant scheme under which the award has been made.

Justification for research
The justification will also trigger 'alarm bells' for a REC; the risk here is that the researcher's personal and emotional involvement with the research topic might cloud their objectivity. There might also be a risk that in the sometimes tense atmosphere in SCBUs, the researcher might inappropriately begin to disclose her own related experiences, which could easily cause harm in an already fragile situation. It is not at all clear how and why the research might give the benefits that are claimed.

Investigators
The university and department should be stated here. For research students, it would also be appropriate to name the supervisor(s). It is good practice for supervisors to be involved in discussing the ethical elements of a planned research project and to endorse an application for ethical approval.

Published ethical guidelines to be followed
This is not an appropriate professional code, since this is not educational research. MRC would be the code of choice here, and this protocol breaches many of the MRC's guidelines.

Location(s) of data collection
The entry here displays a lack of knowledge of the proper procedures for gaining access to NHS premises for research. Both an LREC and locale approval will be required, and a lot of prior work would have had to be done investigating the possibility of such work being conducted. It is in fact highly unlikely that even a well-prepared application from a non-medical person could succeed for such a project, given the sensitivity and security issues around special care baby units. An applicant for ethical approval for such a project would also require CRB disclosure.

Participants
The sample size is not stated, nor is the selection process described. The REC would probably raise concerns about potential bias.

Recruitment procedures
This entry does not acknowledge the sensitivities of parents in such situations, for example that a significant proportion of such parents may find that such an approach adds to their distress.

Consent
It is usual to give potential participants a period of time, of at least 24 hours, to consider whether they wish to participate. This gives them time to read the information sheet, which in this case is very thin and gives little information about how the collected data might be used. It is also common practice to state that if a person withdraws consent, their data will be destroyed. It is also good practice to give contact details for a third party in the event of any queries arising that cannot be adequately dealt with by the researcher. The COREC website gives full guidance on preparing good consent forms for research in the NHS.

Data protection
This is inadequate. It should include an undertaking to register the project in compliance with the requirements of the Data Protection Act 1998.

Recompense to participants

This shows a misunderstanding of the purpose of this heading, which is to detail any payments, gifts or other remuneration for participation. However, the entry here does show an awareness of a potential risk, but since no details are given of the researcher's qualifications to deliver counselling support, this will ring another alarm bell for the REC.

Deception

This again reflects a misunderstanding of the intention of this heading. It also shows a lack of knowledge of medical ethics; no member of the medical team on a SCBU would disclose such clinical information to a third party.

Risks

Clearly, as the applicant acknowledges by implication, there are substantial risks here. A risk analysis should have been carried out and a risk management strategy planned. These should be summarized here.

Debriefing

This is rather vague. Typically, researchers will undertake to give participants some information at the conclusion of a study about the outcomes.

Declaration

The applicant should state that they will inform the REC before implementing any substantial changes that have ethical implications.

10 Research Presentations

Trevor Collins, Stephen Potter and Ann Jones

LEARNING OUTCOMES

After reading this chapter and working on its associated activities you should be able to:

- Identify the purposes of different types of presentation and the audiences involved (including disseminating results, promoting the understanding of your research field, obtaining feedback on your project and developing mutual support).
- Identify what makes a good and bad presentation.
- Work through the common fears that presenters experience.
- Structure and deliver an articulate and coherently argued presentation that summarizes and reflects on your progress and results.
- Use practical methods for selecting content and developing your material.
- Use appropriate visual materials, including the use of presentation software tools.
- Constructively defend your research in answering questions and receiving feedback.
- Make a positive contribution when responding to other people's presentations.

10.1 Introduction

This chapter considers what research presentations should achieve, the common fears that presenters experience, and the steps that can be taken to alleviate such fears and increase the value of the presentation for the researcher. Specifically, the chapter will address the concerns people have about the audience, their material and their performance.

Research presentations can take a variety of forms, from an informal talk or departmental seminar through to presenting a refereed conference paper or a presentation to a research funding agency. Being able to present research results to a variety of audiences is a necessary academic skill expected of those who have undertaken a research degree. Furthermore, presentations offer us an opportunity to receive immediate feedback on our research. We can disseminate research findings in papers and book chapters, but it is the face-to-face feedback that an oral presentation affords us that makes it an extremely valuable experience. Yet in practice many academic presentations fail to engage the audience.

This chapter explores why giving research presentations is such a valuable activity, why this may cause anxiety, and considers some of the approaches that can be used to prepare for and make effective presentations. We start by considering good and bad features of a presentation, starting with the bad.

Activity 10.1a

What can go *wrong* in a presentation? Think about presentations that you have recently attended, focusing on what went badly or didn't work so well. Make a note of these problematic features.

Activity 10.1b

The DVD programme called 'Model Lecture' contains two versions of the same lecture, both models in their own way. The first part is a short lecture by Mike Bullivant on the subject of chemical reactions. View this now; it will familiarize you with the topic and provide a comparison to the second lecture.

The second part presents the same material, but Mike has purposefully made a series of mistakes. Make a note of what you consider went wrong in the second presentation.

Using these notes and those from Activity 10.1a, draw up a list of what can go wrong and group your points into the following categories:

1   Design of visual materials
2   Use of visual materials
3   Verbal delivery
4   Structure
5   Other

Activity 10.1b (Continued)

Discussion

The second version of this lecture was put together to illustrate as many 'bad features' as possible. In reality, whilst few talks contain as many of these bad features, they are all ones that Mike and the authors have encountered in academic talks. Whilst your list may have different and/or additional features, you may also have noticed:

1 No agenda or plan (structure). Mike did not indicate what he was going to cover in his talk. Without this kind of signposting, the audience doesn't know where the talk is going and what to expect next.
2 Unreadable PowerPoint slides.
3 Insufficient time for the audience to try to read the slides (design and use of visual materials).
4 Mike talked too fast and mumbled (delivery).
5 He blocked the screen from the audience (delivery).
6 He lost his place several times (delivery).

This chapter should help you to avoid such pitfalls and to put on a good performance. As with stage performances (a metaphor used throughout the chapter), one feature that is often not apparent to the audience, but only too apparent to the speaker, is fear, and that is what is discussed next.

10.2 Fear

People are generally afraid of looking foolish or stupid in front of their peers or other people they respect. It is perfectly natural, therefore, that we get nervous about giving presentations. However, rather than suppressing or denying our nervousness, developing an awareness of the source of our fears enables us to take the necessary steps to avoid realizing those fears.

Dorothy Leeds (2003) describes four common forms of presenters' fears:

1 **Fear of embarrassment.**

2 **Fear of the audience.**

3 **Fear your material is not good enough.**

4 **Fear of performing poorly.**

In this chapter we will show you how these fears can be addressed through effective preparation and planning. We will return to this issue in the sections that follow.

10.3   Context

We start by considering the context because having a clear understanding of the context of your research presentation will help you to anticipate what might happen. First of all, you should consider your purpose, i.e. what you want to achieve by giving the presentation. Second, you should consider your audience, i.e. who will be there and what they will want from the presentation.

> 'Take every opportunity you can to share your ideas with others, however scary it seems. The act of writing a presentation is a great way to clarify arguments in your own mind.' *(Tom Heath, OU PhD student)*

Purpose

Often a presentation has more than one purpose, but it is important to establish what these may be, and which are the more important. Several different types of presentation can take place throughout the stages of a research project. For example:

1   A bid to a sponsor for funds for a project. In this case the main purpose is to show the capabilities of the research team and reassure the sponsor that they will deliver within the time available.

2   At the start of a research project, to explain and explore the broad approach of the work and to define what 'outputs' will be produced.

3   To contribute to assessment (e.g. part of a PhD transfer assessment or required as part of a postgraduate assignment).

4   To provide feedback and advice, for example from other researchers, key people and other groups interested in the project's findings.

5   To win involvement and support for the research, for example from organizations you may interview or who hold information you need.

6   To stimulate discussion or provide a forum for learning and mutual support.

7   To disseminate the results of a project.

Audience

The primary fear associated with the audience is a fear of the unknown. This is generally misplaced as the audience is rarely out to get you. As noted earlier, one of the purposes of research presentations is to get feedback, and the audience will endeavour to provide constructive criticism in order to help you. Destructive criticism is a social and professional taboo and will quickly isolate individuals from the rest of the community.

A little research can quickly cure a fear of the unknown audience. A list of the people attending may be available from the event organizers. If not, an indication of the people who may attend can be gained from the people involved in similar events in the past. For example, if you are preparing for a conference presentation you could look at the people on the programme committee or the list of accepted papers from previous years.

Such sources of information can help you answer the key questions that will shape the design of your presentation, such as:

1 **Who is likely to be in the audience?**

2 **Where in the world do they come from?**

3 **What do they know about already?**

4 **What are they interested in?**

Summary

Explicitly identifying the purpose of a presentation enables you to direct the presentation in order to ensure that you meet your objectives. The purpose and objectives you identify also provide a set of criteria for judging your own success. Audience members, like presenters, have a purpose. Finding out who the audience members are likely to be and what they may want to gain from your presentation is the first step towards making an effective presentation. Whilst you cannot completely anticipate how the audience will behave, gathering some reliable information about the audience will help you to tailor your presentation appropriately.

Activity 10.2

1   Think of a specific presentation that you may need to give in the near future and make a note of the topic of the presentation.
2   List the purpose and objectives of your presentation and order them according to importance.

Activity 10.2 (Continued)

3 Now, think of who the audience is likely to be, and write down the size and typical characteristics of your audience. Specifically, make a note of their academic background, nationality and relevant interests.

4 In order to realize your purpose, are there any specific things that your presentation needs to cover for this particular audience?

Discussion

An example of a specific presentation would be an internal seminar being given by a PhD student as part of their annual progress review, nine months into their first year of study. Such a presentation within the UK is typically used as part of the probation assessment for PhD students.

In this example, the presentation has two purposes: for the student to explain to their colleagues what they've been doing for nine months, and to demonstrate to the people on the review panel their ability to complete the PhD within the time available. Of these two purposes, demonstrating their ability to the review panel is the higher priority.

The audience in such a case will probably be fairly well known to the student. Based on the attendance at similar events in the past, the student will be able to estimate the size of the audience. The student will know the main areas of research carried out by the groups within their department, and therefore will have a reasonable idea of the topics of interest, and the level of description and suitable terminology to use.

In order to convince the review panel of the student's competency they will need to cover the problem they are tackling, the current state of the art, the work they are proposing to undertake including how they plan to complete it, and the potential contributions and anticipated outcomes of the proposed research – a tall order but certainly achievable with the right preparation.

10.4 Material

In this section we will consider some practical methods for selecting content and developing your material. Preparing a good presentation is always a challenging task and the time and effort involved should not be understated. Like writing a paper, writing a good presentation is a drafting and revision process. In order to make informed revisions, you will need to rehearse your draft presentations. Recording or asking a colleague to listen and give you feedback on your presentation will help you to gain a further insight into the audience's experience. Repeating the cycle of drafting, presenting and critiquing your presentation will help you to develop a good presentation, and improve your confidence in your own ability to deliver it within the time available.

'Practice, practice, practice! Practice in front of your friends, your mum, your dog. Anybody you trust. It's only when you stand up and try it out loud that you find out what works and what doesn't, and whether your slides make sense. Hollywood actors practice, and they've been presenting for a lifetime. So it makes sense that you need to as well.' (*Mark Gaved, OU PhD student*)

Preparing your title and abstract

A good presentation starts with a good title and abstract. These are used to advertise and promote your presentation. Chapter 6 covered preparing abstracts (in Section 6.6) and there were two activities there on abstract writing. Although they may well be written long before you think of what you are going to say, the title and abstract will influence people's decisions about whether or not to attend your presentation. An informative title will help to attract the people interested in your research and a clear, well-written abstract will provide an encouraging trailer for the feature presentation. No matter how polished the presentation is, it may still fail to achieve your objectives if given to an uninterested audience.

Activity 10.3

1   Pick five conference papers on a topic of interest to you (or search for some on the internet).
2   Have a look at the papers' titles only and order the papers according to the likelihood that you would attend the presentation.
3   Now read the papers' abstracts and reorder the papers again according to how likely it is that you would attend the presentation.
4   Finally, write down the criteria you have used for judging the titles and abstracts.

Listing your criteria should provide you with some guidelines for writing the titles and abstracts of your own papers.

Discussion

When prioritizing a set of presentations based on their title, people generally look for keywords as little else is available. When we think of the things that interest us, we are often interested not just in the phenomenon being studied but also the method of study and of course the conclusions that are being drawn. Effective titles are carefully crafted to convey the essence of the work being presented (often referred to as the 'take-home message').

Activity 10.3   (Continued)

Prioritizing by title and abstract lets us base such judgements on considerably more information than the title alone. An abstract should include the main points that you want to communicate. The cinema film trailer is a fairly useful analogy in that it will frequently show clips of the full-length presentation in order to attract an audience.

Preparing the content of your presentation

Selecting the intellectual content of a presentation is a separate stage from preparing the physical materials that will help you communicate that content. This is where we decide 'what to say' and we postpone the decision of 'how to say it' until later.

A polished presentation will carry the audience's attention through a number of connected points in order to communicate a clear and memorable take-home message. However, before the rehearsals and revisions, the initial draft is more likely to resemble a rough diamond. Deciding what to say is a reflective process where you need to consider what is important or novel in your work and why. Ultimately, you will need to impose some organization on the content, in order to present your particular perspective on the research. Exploring the potential ways of organizing the research is in itself a beneficial research activity.

People typically develop their own methods for this based on the 'what works for me' criterion. Brainstorming, concept maps and envelope sketches are just some common methods. One good start is to try and identify everything that might be relevant by simply listing or mapping the points you want to make. This is sometimes referred to as a 'brain dump', but in practice is much less drastic. When identifying the content to include, one of the things you need to consider is the time available for your presentation. All presentations should run to time and rehearsing your presentation is the best way of ensuring that this will happen. When you have identified the content you want to present and the order you want to present it in, you should consider the time available to you. There may be parts of the content where the level of detail can be expanded or reduced depending on the time available.

Some people find it useful to draw a hierarchical tree containing the points they want to make. Figure 10.1 provides an example based on the content of this chapter. Each tree node contains a point to be made, with the level of detail increasing as you go down the tree. Having a set of points allows you to look for the gaps and consider potential orderings. This can be a difficult process, but even though you may modify your initial set of points and reorder your points several times, you will eventually converge on a set that you are confident in working up into a presentation.

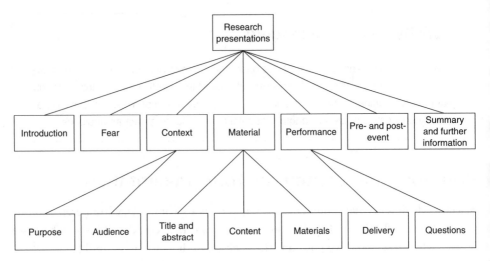

Figure 10.1   A content tree showing the main points of a talk on how to give research presentations

Hierarchical structures such as these can be useful when you have rehearsed the talk and find you need to either reduce or increase the length of the presentation. Pruning the lower branches can be an effective way of identifying what to leave out of a presentation without losing the take-home message; similarly, expanding a lower branch will help you to expand the presentation. Furthermore, when giving future presentations on the same topic you can reuse your content hierarchy, selecting only the upper branches for shorter presentations or developing the content hierarchy further to create longer presentations.

Activity 10.4

1   Think of a specific presentation that you may need to give in the near future, identifying the topic of the presentation and the likely audience.
2   Do a 'brain dump', noting all the points that you might want to mention.
3   Now draft a hierarchical tree organizing the points into an order (left to right across the tree) and detailing what needs to be covered in each point (top to bottom down each path in the tree).

Discussion

Thinking of what to say is not easy. However, rather than starting with a blank page, you can use some of the thoughts you've had about the purpose of your presentation

Activity 10.4   (Continued)

and the potential members of your audience to start identifying some of the content that you will need to cover. If you are presenting a paper that you've already written, then you have the content of the paper to help you make a start, but bear in mind that reading a paper is very different from listening to a presentation. Sketching out the main points of your argument will help you identify an order for your presentation. Deciding on the level of description that you will need to give will depend on your knowledge of your audience.

Preparing presentation materials

Having identified the intellectual content for your presentation (i.e. what to say), you are now able to start creating the narrative that will convey that content to your audience (i.e. how to say it). It is at this stage that you must bear in mind the needs of your audience. You want your presentation to be as accessible as possible. The people in the audience may not have the same cultural or academic background as you, and therefore you must take care to ensure that any assumptions you make are well justified. Effort spent on tailoring your narrative to the particular audience will make all the difference to your presentation. Although there is no substitute for great content, a poor narrative will tarnish good content whereas an excellent narrative will help the content shine.

In face-to-face conversations, we get immediate feedback on each statement and use that feedback when choosing what to say next. Presentations, particularly to large audiences, can feel a bit one-sided but this does not have to be the case. One property of a good novel is that it draws the reader into the story so that they feel part of a conversation with the narrator. If you plan the narrative of your presentation to take the form of a conversation, where you introduce interesting questions, explore evidence, explain your train of thought and draw conclusions, the audience will undoubtedly become engaged in the conversation. This is why good presentations require considerable preparation.

Whichever materials you choose to use, you should try to ensure that the materials themselves do not overshadow or detract from your message. Videos, demonstrations and animated computer slides can be used to illustrate something quickly that would be difficult to communicate in other ways, but they must be used sparingly or the lasting impression will be the form of the presentation rather than the content. The KISS mnemonic 'Keep It Simple Stupid' is good advice in this case.

Pace, clarity and terminology

Three aspects of the delivery of the presentation that will influence the preparation of your materials will be the pace, clarity and the terminology you use. It is worth assuming that there will be many audience members for whom English is not their first language. It is important therefore to speak at a pace that allows the audience time to process and understand what you say. It is also important to speak clearly. Words can easily be misunderstood because they have not been pronounced clearly and this can be an additional point to check if you are presenting in a language that is not your first language. The third factor to consider here is whether the terminology and language you are using will be understood by the audience. Is your language clear and unambiguous? Even where English is the common language, words and terms can convey quite different meanings in different contexts and countries.

Some conferences may use language translators or sign language translators to translate each presentation. If so, this has quite an impact on the presenter's pace, clarity and terminology. The golden rule here is to keep things simple. For example, use plain language as much as possible and speak clearly, in order to minimize mistranslations. If the translation is made simultaneously, those listening with headphones will hear the translation slightly after you speak, therefore you can expect some delay in part of the audience's response. If the translator is working alongside you and you are taking it in turns to speak, then you should prepare half the amount of content to allow time for you and the translator to present your talk.

Slides

Assuming your presentation is longer than five minutes, you are likely to want to create some slides to help focus the audience's attention during your presentation and to illustrate some of the points you are making. Drafting the slides will help you develop your narrative and will also help you to sort out how much you can cover in your allotted time. Remember, the golden rule is to keep things simple; therefore, try to make only one point per slide. Rehearsing the presentation will help to clarify what works and what doesn't.

The Society for Imaging Science and Technology has produced a set of guidelines for effective illustration (Walworth et al., 1999). A checklist drawn from these guidelines is given in the Appendix to this chapter. As well as using these guidelines to inform the design of your slides, you can also use them to critique a set of slides. When you get the feeling that something is not right, quickly checking through these guidelines may well reveal the source of the problem and the means for correcting it. Guidelines such as these will help to ensure that your slides are broadly accessible and easy to read.

There are many computer software tools available for producing presentation slides, such as 'PowerPoint' from Microsoft, 'Impress' from Open Office, and 'Keynote' from Apple. The default presentation settings on such systems typically meet the guidelines given in the Appendix. Presentation software, much like desktop publishing software, uses the concept of 'styles' for formatting the presentation. Setting a master slide style will help you create a consistent set of slides. The following four preparation steps are recommended for setting your slide style prior to drafting your slides:

1 *Check the page set-up.* **This involves setting the page size and orientation. Slides should use a horizontal setting (i.e. landscape).**

2 *Set the page footer.* **Set the information you want to display in the footer of each slide and whether or not the footer should be included in the title slide. Showing the date in the footer helps you keep track of what you presented and when. Including the slide number is particularly useful when using 35 mm or overhead transparency slides, as the numbers help to identify the correct slide order and orientation.**

3 *Set the master slide layout.* **The master slide layout will be applied to each slide. Adding a line or rectangle between the title and body areas of the slides will help the audience to separate them. In the master slide layout you can also edit the footer text to include the total number of slides.**

4 *Set the title slide layout.* **If you want to, you can also insert a new title master to be used for your first slide. Change the layout of your title slide as required. Adding your name, affiliation and affiliation logo to the title slide will help the audience to remember who you are and where you came from.**

You will find that separating the layout of your slides from their content requires you to maintain an element of discipline. It may be tempting to reformat individual slides in order to fit things in, but don't. Using styles ensures consistency and as a result the presentation will appear much more professional.

When providing electronic copies of your slides you should provide both the original and an HTML-based version to ensure maximum accessibility. Although several screen reader programs can deal with some proprietary presentation software formats, HTML is an international standard suitable for the majority of screen readers.

Presenter's notes

Some presenters use a script, some use note cards, and some draw on the points made in their slides as prompts. Presentation programs such as PowerPoint allow you to type in your notes and print them along with your slides. What form your notes take is a matter of experience, style and personal preference. It is well worth trying a few alternatives to see which approach suits you best.

If you are an inexperienced presenter, it can be useful to write out a full script of your talk. A script is also useful for very short presentations that need to run to a fixed time length. Note, however, that a script is delivered and understood verbally, not as a written document. A piece of text that can be understood when it is read may be too complex to follow or unintelligible when spoken. Think of it as a script for a radio or TV programme and prepare the delivery accordingly. Mark points where you want to add emphasis or a pause and change the pace and tone accordingly.

Rather than preparing a full script, many presenters use notes or note cards containing the main points they intend to make (structured around the 'bullet points' and illustrations on their slides). This approach allows a more spontaneous delivery. In order to help you manage the timing of the presentation, Gordon Rugg and Marian Petre (2004) suggest the use of a timeline where markers in your notes are used to indicate how far you should have got in the presentation. These markers can either be in terms of the time available or approximate indicators – for example, 'half way'.

Timing your presentation

In preparing your materials you will become very aware of how much you can present in the time available to you. A common rule of thumb is to allow two minutes per slide (depending on the content – diagrams, for example, can take longer). So, if you want to present for 20 minutes then your presentation should consist of no more than ten slides.

Although we may not think of ourselves as performers, when giving presentations it is a useful metaphor. Like all performers, rehearsal is essential for a polished performance, and this is particularly true for the timing of your presentation. It is only by rehearsing the presentation that you will know for sure how long it will take. It may also be useful to present to a friend, supervisor or colleagues to get feedback on your delivery. There is simply no substitute for preparation.

Handouts

Some people find it helpful to provide handouts for the audience. Following the simplicity rule, you should first ask yourself what a handout will add to the presentation. Often it leads to the audience reading the handouts instead of attending to your presentation. Given the number of things to remember on the day of the presentation, adding a set of photocopies is a significant imposition. Nonetheless, if you decide to use handouts, take care to ensure that they are easy to read. You can assume that not everyone in the audience will have perfect vision. Including a few copies in an extra-large font may well be appreciated.

Webcast presentations

Broadcasting a presentation over the web is referred to as webcasting. Increasingly there are opportunities to webcast presentations. For the presenter, the primary factor influencing their preparation will be the level of interaction with the virtual audience. This can range from the rich form of interactions available in live video conferences to the limited one-way interaction available in recorded video broadcasts. Much like face-to-face presentations, live webcasts that afford an opportunity for the presenter to interact with the virtual audience need to be structured with the form of interaction in mind. For example, if the virtual audience are to ask questions, the presenter, chairperson or facilitator will need to remind people how and when they can do this.

One of the major benefits of recording a presentation for webcasting is that it can be replayed over the web at any time in the future. This enables people unable to attend the live event to see what they missed. However, the size and speed of the connection used to access the webcast server will constrain the quality of the webcast presentation. It is reasonable to assume that the image captured by the video camera will be reduced to the size of a postcard when broadcast over the web.

As a result of the limitations of current webcasting technology, the following factors need to be considered when preparing a presentation that will be webcast:

1 **Pay extra attention to the slide guidelines referred to in the Appendix, such as using a minimum font size of 24 points, a maximum of nine lines per slide and ten words per line, and selecting colours for maximum contrast.**

2 **Use a standard font. If the presentation slides are translated into a format suitable for webcasting, then choosing a standard font will help ensure that the look and layout of your slides in the webcast are comparable to those used in the presentation.**

3 **Avoid using embedded video clips or animations. Webcasts are typically played with a relatively low frame-rate (such as five or ten frames per second), therefore, animations and videos may appear jumpy, like a flicker animation. Alternatively, rather than videoing the slides, if the slides are translated into a different format for replay over the web, embedded videos and animations may get lost or damaged. However, technology improves all the time and so this is likely to be less of a concern in the future.**

4 **Avoid animated slide transitions. Like embedded video clips and animations, animated slide transitions that involve a lot of movement are to be avoided (such as spiral, blinds, swivel, dissolve, stretch, checkerboard and zoom transitions).**

Activity 10.5

Pick a conference presentation on a topic of interest to you (or search for one online using a search engine and download it).

Using the guidelines from the Society for Imaging Science and Technology (see Appendix), critique the design of the slides. Take care to critique the form of the slides' design rather than the academic content.

Discussion

Focusing on a conference presentation that is not your own should have helped you to gain some distance from the content and to consider the design. As well as making you more aware of design features to avoid, in reviewing other people's slides you may also find good design features that you can adopt for your own purpose.

Summary

Choosing an expressive title and writing a clear abstract will encourage people interested in your research area to attend your presentation. Bearing in mind what you know about the audience and the time available will help you choose the content that you will be able to cover. Drafting your presentation materials, such as the slides, will enable you to develop your narrative. There is no substitute for preparing and rehearsing your presentation. As with drafting a paper, you should plan to go through several iterations of preparing, rehearsing and revising your presentation.

10.5   Performance

'It is so rewarding when people come to talk to you after a presentation saying they really enjoyed it!' (*Andreia Santos, OU PhD student*)

The theatrical metaphor is particularly appropriate for academic presentations. When it comes to show-time you are in the spotlight performing to an audience of your peers. All good performances will engage the audience's attention. Classic characteristics of poor performances include: running over time, little or no eye-contact with the audience, distracting body movement or clothing, and inaudible speech.

On the day of the presentation you need to keep a cool head, consider the sources of your nerves and recognize the steps you have taken to address them. This may not fully alleviate the nerves, but it will help you to maintain control of the situation. Your presentation can be considered to be a performance in two acts: act one is the delivery of the presentation, and act two is your response to the audience's questions. Considering how to answer questions about your talk will also help you to consider appropriate questions to ask in other people's presentations. We'll consider each of these in turn.

Delivering the presentation

To some extent nervousness is to be expected; you are, after all, putting yourself in the spotlight. However, when the time comes to give the presentation, you should already have some idea of who will be in the audience, you will have prepared what you are going to say and how you are going to say it, so the remaining fears will be in relation to your performance and delivery. Again, preparation will help alleviate your anxieties.

Attendance

Try to encourage people to attend your presentation, especially any friends and other people you would like to impress. Catching sight of a friendly face can often help to reassure you during the presentation. You can also ask a friend in the audience to take a note of any questions you are asked, so that you can reflect on them after the event. Similarly, you can ask a colleague to critique your presentation and give you constructive feedback afterwards.

Appearance

A large part of the impression you give people will be drawn from their initial impression; therefore, your appearance is worth considering. Don't wear things that will distract the audience from what you have to say. Think of the purpose of your presentation and the audience involved, and try to dress in a way that conveys the image you want to project. Is it a 'jeans and jumpers' or a 'suits and skirts' event? It is usually safer to wear more formal rather than informal clothes. Having said that, wear something that you feel comfortable in as well as meeting the expectations of your audience. If you are uncomfortable your delivery may suffer.

Check the venue

Rugg and Petre (2004, p. 140) emphasize the value of reconnaissance of where you will deliver your presentation. You should certainly check the presentation equipment and how it works. For example, you will want to know beforehand that you can read your files on the presentation computer, that your portable USB drive (if you are using one) works and how your presentation will be controlled on the particular computer you will be using. You may also need particular software on the computer or access to the web. There can be problems if the computer you are to use has an older version of the operating system than you have. If you plan to use any additional equipment, other than that provided by the organizers, try it out in the room you will be presenting in. If you have any accessibility requirements, for example if you use a wheelchair or audio fre-quency induction loop, contact the organizers as early as possible to ensure that any nec-essary arrangements can be made. It is also worth thinking about the venue's layout and where you will stand (so as not to block the screen). If there is no drinking water supplied in the room, make a note to bring a bottle with you for your presentation. Finally, if you are presenting a seminar or academic paper you may be introduced by a chairperson, and if this is the case, go out of your way to meet that person before your presentation.

Your delivery

When you give a presentation the increased adrenaline that results from your nerves will make you think faster than normal. Taking slow even breaths will help you to remain calm and to control your nerves. Drinking water will help to balance your breathing, relieve your dry mouth, and can be used subtly to create pauses between slides, allowing the audience to consider what you have just told them. Maintaining eye-contact with your audience will keep them engaged in your conversation. If you do tend to get nervous, an open body posture will help to mask your nervousness (e.g. avoid crossing your arms and legs, or clenching your fists). Although everyone feels nervous, it is very rarely detectable by the audience.

Some people tend to speak more quickly or mumble when they feel nervous. As sug-gested in the previous section, make a conscious effort to attend to the pace, clarity and terminology you use in your presentation. If you are using a microphone, try to keep it at a constant distance from your mouth and if possible try it out before your presenta-tion. Given the choice, clip-on microphones are often easier to deal with than hand-held microphones. If you are not using a microphone you will need to project your voice to the people at the back of the room. To project your voice you need to breathe a little deeper than usual and control the power of your voice with your diaphragm. Finally, enjoy your performance. Provided you are well prepared, you will have every reason to be confident in your material and your enthusiasm for your work will shine through.

Questions

You may feel that this is the most intimidating part of a presentation. However, as noted in Chapter 11, building up experience in dealing with questions about your research will be invaluable when your viva arrives. If you would rather deal with people's ques-tions at the end of the presentation, you should tell your audience that this is your pref-erence. If an audience member interrupts when you are not expecting them to do so, you can easily lose your train of thought. Taking questions during a presentation has the benefit of addressing any misconceptions or queries as they arise, but you need to be prepared to adapt the pace of your presentation in order to ensure that your presentation does not overrun as a result.

Preparation also helps with questions. Being aware of the likely questions not only enables you to prepare a set of good answers, but it can also inform how you present your chosen content. An awareness of the issues that your audience will be attuned to enables you to tailor the content in such a way that the obvious questions are already addressed in the presentation, allowing more of the available time to be used for the unanticipated, insightful questions.

The approach to answering questions should be the same in any presentation, whether a student seminar or your PhD viva. Therefore, the key points here are similar to those for dealing with viva questions, specifically:

1 **Give straight answers to straight questions. Resist the temptation to wander off the point, so that your time and the audience's time are not to be wasted.**

2 **If you feel a question indicates that your talk was unclear, briefly restate the relevant points and check that the problem is resolved.**

3 **If you feel a question is unclear, always ask for clarification: 'I'm not sure what you mean, could you explain it further please?'**

4 **If you think a question is based on a doubtful premise, challenge it (for example, if you think the questioner has missed the point).**

Note the points made in the discussion of Activity 10.6 above about complicated or multi-part questions. These points are also covered in the text on the viva (Chapter 11), but you will hit this situation first in presenting your research in other ways.

Asking insightful questions is a skill to be developed, much the same as answering questions or delivering the presentation. Research does not occur in isolation, the development of any research field is dependent on the research discourse. Asking and responding to questions in research presentations is one of the most immediate opportunities we have for engaging in the research discourse.

People ask questions for a number of reasons; for example, to clarify a point made, to learn more, or to bring some additional work to the presenter's attention that they may not have been aware of or considered. Asking questions in order to show how much you know is a cheap trick and rarely respected, but engaging in the discussion and exploring the issues raised in a presentation is a highly valued contribution.

Activity 10.6

1 Now watch the second part of the DVD clip of the 'Model Lecture' where Mike is asked a series of questions. You are shown Mike giving *different* answers to the same questions.
2 Make a note of the good and bad responses that he gives to each question.

Discussion

Question 1. This question seeks further information. The poor answer is evasive, even rude, and doesn't answer the question. The good answer explains why the information was missing (Mike had to be selective in what he presented in only ten minutes) and explains that his work had covered neutral nucleophiles.

Question 2. This is an example of a complex, ill-informed question. The good answer recognizes this and, without being rude, Mike identifies the separate questions and answers them in turn. His bad answer simply picks up the last part of the question and fails to cover the rest adequately, if at all, as well as being just plain rude and patronizing. Even the answer he gives is broadly uninformative.

Question 3. This is an example of where it looks like there is a genuine mistake in the presentations. In his good reply, Mike works this through and concludes that there is something wrong. He then agrees to check it out and let the questioner know the result. In the poor answer, although he admits an error, he quickly tries to blame someone else, and makes no attempt to resolve the problem.

Question 4. This is a question about the limitations of the research. Very often questions at conferences are about what the researcher has not done. The good answer recognizes that the further research suggested would be a good idea and suggests meeting up later to discuss how this might be carried forward. The bad answer only grudgingly acknowledges that the questioner has a valid point. It's a rather defensive 'I know better than you' response.

You might also like to repeat this activity for the questions asked in the video programme on the viva, which is associated with the next chapter. These were in a genuine discussion, with no prior knowledge of what the questions would be.

The next and final activity below asks you to apply what you have learnt about asking questions to your own research presentations.

Activity 10.7

Using the content hierarchy you drafted in Activity 10.4, identify a set of four questions you think your audience might ask. The questions should be:

1 Questions requiring *further information or clarification*, e.g. 'can you say more about the framework that you said you adapted for your work?', or 'can you clarify the differences between the two types of condition?'
2 Complicated or ill-formed questions that might have several parts.
3 Questions or comments that indicate a fundamental disagreement, e.g. 'Doesn't this integrated transport policy that you discussed depend on a very high level of government funding for public transport?' (from a speaker who does not believe that it should be funded in this way …)
4 Questions that might suggest a genuine gap or flaw (that you had not noticed!) in your research.

For each question, prepare an answer that draws on the content of your presentation or, if necessary, additional content that you did not include in your presentation.

Finally, draft a few stock phrases to be used when you are unable to answer a question – remember, honesty is the best policy. Questions that you cannot yet answer can be used to form the goals of your future research. They can also provide excellent opportunities for further discussions with individuals after your presentation.

Discussion

The questions that are generally asked at research presentations are often about the rigour of the work done, the interpretation of the findings and the consequences of the research. As a general tactic, the five Ws and one H methodology can be used for generating questions: Who, What, Where, Why, When and How. For example, How did you do X? What does Y mean? Who would use the outcomes of this research?

As noted above, questions that you cannot answer are opportunities for future research projects; however, answering questions with something other than an answer can be tricky. Honesty is always the best policy. Here are some potential situations and stock responses:

1 If someone suggests something you've never considered: 'That's a nice suggestion, thank you very much.'

Activity 10.7 (Continued)

2 If the answer requires more than a few sentences: 'I haven't got time to answer that now, but I'd be happy to discuss it later.'

3 If you disagree with someone: 'Thank you. I don't agree with you. I think...' (always refer evidence to support your claims).

4 If the question makes no sense to you: 'I'm not sure what you mean, could you explain it further please?'

Summary

The analogy drawn with a theatrical performance is not intended to imply that you put on an act. Your presentation should be a strictly non-fictional account of your research. However, stage techniques can improve the experience for both the performer and the audience. When a presentation goes well the end result appears effortless, even though a great deal of hard work will have gone into it. The narration of your presentation will be easy to follow and your answers to the audience's questions will be clear and complete.

With experience you will become more aware of the sources of your nerves and the steps you need to take to alleviate them. Feeling nervous is a very important self-protection system that helps us avoid making fools of ourselves in public. In this chapter we have discussed several practical approaches for authoring and delivering presentations. These approaches can be used to help you appreciate and manage your nerves but hopefully not eradicate them.

10.6   Pre- and Post-Event Preparation

While attending a conference or seminar presentation you can either ask questions as part of the presentation in order to facilitate public discussion, or after the presentation as part of a private or select group discussion. If you did not get your questions answered during the conference you can certainly raise the issues later via email or telephone.

Also, prior to attending a conference or workshop you can identify the people with whom you would like to discuss your research. A list of the accepted papers will give you a good idea of who will be there, and if there are people you would like to spend some time with you can read up on their current work before you go to the conference so that you find it easier to engage them in a conversation. You can even email or telephone people before the event to check if they'll be there, introduce yourself and your interests, and to arrange to meet them at the conference.

Making effective research presentations requires a significant amount of hard work. The act of preparing and presenting your research helps you reflect on the work you have done. Matching your preparation and performance skills with your networking skills will help to ensure that you maximize the rewards of giving a good presentation.

10.7   Further Advice

There are a number of websites providing further information and advice. Links to these are provided on this book's website. These include:

'PowerPoint Accessibility Techniques.' Set of accessibility guidelines from WebAIM: Web Accessibility in Mind. Available at webaim.org

Presentations.com – Presentation information resources. Available at presentations.com

'Tech4Speakers – Helping speakers use technology more effectively.' Available at tech4speakers.com

Webcasts from the Open University. A series of example webcasts held at the Open University, UK. Available from stadium.open.ac.uk

References

Leeds, D. (2003) *PowerSpeak: Engage, Inspire and Stimulate your Audience.* Career Press Inc., Franklin Lakes NJ.

Rugg, G. and Petre, M. (2004) *The Unwritten Rules of PhD Research.* Buckingham: Open University Press.

Walworth, V., McCann, M., McCann, J. and Rosenblum, L. (1999) *Guide to Effective Illustration: Images for Presentation and Publication.* Report from the Society for Imaging Science and Technology, May 1999. Available at: http://www.imaging.org/resources/vcguide (last accessed May 2005).

Appendix: A Checklist of Design Guidelines

Here is a checklist of design guidelines drawn from the Society for Imaging Science and Technology's *Guide to Effective Illustration: Images for Presentation and Publication.*

1   Always use a horizontal layout (i.e. landscape).
2   Use an easy to read clear font (e.g. Arial or Times).

3 As a minimum use 36 point type for titles, 30 point and 24 point for text.
4 Have a maximum of 9 lines of type or equations per slide.
5 And a maximum of 10 words per line.
6 When using colours select colours with a high contrast.
7 Graph curves should be bold, encoded by a line pattern or simple labels.
8 Do not use grid lines on your graphs.
9 Clearly label all of your graph axes.
10 Your slides when printed on A4 size sheets should be readable at 8 feet.
11 35 mm slides should be readable at arm's length (use dots to identify the lower left-hand corners of your slides).

11 The Examination Process and the Viva

Stephen Potter

with contributions from Professor John Swift

LEARNING OUTCOMES

Other chapters in this book have covered the preparation of a written thesis. Here we look at the examination process and the oral examination – the viva voce (usually shortened to 'viva'). All research degrees in the UK have a viva. For taught post-graduate dissertations (part of an MA or MSc), a viva or a presentation with questions may occasionally be involved.

After reading this chapter and working on its associated activities you should be able to:

- Effectively prepare for your viva.
- Constructively defend your research outcome, listen, receive feedback and respond perceptively.
- Understand how your examiners are appointed and what they are required to do.
- Understand what is involved in evaluating postgraduate and PhD research.
- Demonstrate to your examiners your ability to critically analyse and evaluate both the findings of others and your own findings.
- Demonstrate that you have fulfilled the core competencies required for your research degree.
- Demonstrate your overall willingness and ability to learn and acquire knowledge.

11.1 Why a Viva?

Having written a thesis, you may well ask why you have to be put through the ritual of an oral examination. This is because a viva performs three crucial functions.

First, the viva is a check that the thesis is really the candidate's own work. Answering questions and discussing the content of a thesis shows that you have not got another person to do the work for you or lifted large sections from somebody else's work. Such fraud is very rare, but not unknown.

Second, the viva examines your ability to discuss and defend your research. This is part of being a professional researcher.

The third reason applies to every thesis and is a very important one. An examiner will have questions about how your research was designed, how it was undertaken, the conclusions drawn, or virtually any aspect of the work. A viva is where such matters can be raised, and it is your opportunity to further explain, justify and defend the way in which the research work was done.

There is a real danger that, if the award of a research degree depended only on marking a written text, an examiner may misunderstand what you had done. The viva is the chance for both the examiner to raise points of discussion and for you to clarify the situation. If an examiner asked for modifications or a rewrite on the basis of the written text alone, you might feel aggrieved if, in your view, such requirements were based on a misunderstanding or a genuine professional difference in opinion. In this respect, the viva is to your advantage. In many ways not having a viva is a less fair examination process.

In addition, the viva gives you the opportunity to meet and debate with an expert from another institution. There is a good chance that the examiners will find your work intrinsically interesting. In some cases, ideas for publications and even further collaborative work and jobs have resulted from a viva.

11.2 The Examination Panel

It is normal for a UK examination panel to consist of one external and one internal examiner. However, particularly if the candidate's subject is multidisciplinary, or if an inexperienced examiner is involved, it is often possible to appoint a third examiner.

The role of supervisors can vary. In some universities a supervisor can be an examiner. However, this is generally not permitted, but one or more supervisors may attend the viva as an 'observer'. The supervisor/observer is not a member of the examination panel and does not participate in the examination, but can be called upon by the examiners for advice and points of clarification. Their presence can also be very reassuring for a candidate. In some cases there may also be a separate chairperson to manage the viva.

Procedures for appointing an examination panel vary between universities, although they all follow a fairly similar pattern. Your own university's rules will specify the number of examiners, if a chairperson is required and whether there can be a supervisor/ observer. In all cases, examiners are required to be independent of the candidate and to be qualified in the subject area, and it is required that the panel contains adequate experience in examining or supervising students.

Do check up on the procedures and rules of your own university and/or discuss this process with your supervisor(s). This is something that should not be left to when you are about to submit your thesis, but should be clarified considerably earlier. This is because, although examiners are not formally appointed until shortly before a thesis is submitted, there is an informal process that leads up to this. For example, at the Open University the formal process is that, when a student gives notice of submission, the Research School asks the Head of Department to nominate a panel for the oral examination (viva). In practice, your supervisor is the key person in approaching potential external and internal examiners. The Head of Discipline usually depends on a supervisor's advice to nominate the examiners, so supervisors will first make an informal approach to potential examiners to check whether they are willing and available to examine a thesis. Although the practice of supervisors varies, once you are putting together the first draft of your thesis, the question of who might be your external examiner should arise.

The crucial choice is that of the external examiner, who usually has the upper hand in both examining the thesis and in the viva. It is up to your supervisor if they consult you about the choice of examiners. A student cannot have the right to choose an examiner, but some discussion of the subject is acceptable and normal. However, it is crucial that the examination panel is entirely independent and unbiased. For example, the OU guidelines state that examiners have to declare an interest if they are:

1 **planning to employ the candidate;**

2 **planning to co-publish with the candidate;**

3 **a past student of the supervisor;**

4 **a 'regular' examiner for a particular supervisor or department;**

5 **involved, or have been involved, with the candidate in a close personal relationship of any kind.**

One additional point is that an examiner cannot be someone who has had a significant influence on the way you have designed and conducted your research, or who has collaborated closely with you. It is perfectly in order for your examiners to know you and be aware of your work, but they need essentially to be separate from it in order to be able to examine it.

In discussing with your supervisor the sort of person who could be a suitable examiner, some people think that only a 'big name' external examiner would be appropriate, but 'big names' are not necessarily good examiners. It is important that an examiner is sympathetic, understanding and has the right attitude towards your research. The last thing that you need is an examiner who enjoys belittling others, even if they are a 'big name'. The examiner needs to be able to judge your thesis at an appropriate level and not have unrealistic expectations of what is achievable in a PhD. If they have these characteristics and are also a 'big name', that's great, but not all 'big names' are good examiners!

Activity 11.1

Check with your own university regulations about the composition of an examination panel and the procedure and criteria for appointing examiners.

Having done this, then consider what are you looking for in an examiner. Write down the sort of areas of expertise, abilities and characteristics that your(s) examiners should have.

This list could be helpful in discussing with your supervisor(s) the sort of people to be your examiners.

11.3   What Happens in a Viva?

There is no standard viva. A viva is usually completed in between two and three hours. You, of course, should take a copy of your thesis to refer to (and do not forget a pen and paper as you may need to take notes on questions). If you have any background material not in the thesis that might be useful in answering questions (for example, interview transcripts or experiment print-outs), it is perfectly acceptable to bring such material along.

One person will chair the viva. The chairperson is responsible for the examination being conducted according to your university's regulations and procedures, and is also responsible for completing the paperwork. The chairperson should also explain to you how the viva is organized, so if anything is unclear it is quite reasonable to ask about it.

Examiners usually meet just before the viva to compare their preliminary impressions and to agree the main areas for discussion. A number of universities require the examiners to submit an initial report on the written thesis before they meet. These reports are then compared and agreement made about who will ask what questions. Your supervisor/observer may also attend this meeting, although the regulations of some universities specifically forbid it.

Examiners may already have agreed informally on an initial recommendation and they might tell you at the beginning of their viva. For example, they may say, 'Based upon the thesis, we feel that it is PhD standard, but we may require a few minor amendments to be made. We will discuss these with you.' However, don't necessarily expect this to happen.

Where appropriate, and with the agreement of both the candidate and examiners, a viva may include the inspection of experimental apparatus, demonstration of software, viewing of original data sources or any other reasonable request. As an external examiner I have known several viva examinations to include a short verbal presentation. I found these to be very helpful in introducing me to the candidates and their work.

The examiners will, obviously, have read the thesis and will have prepared a set of questions to ask. These questions may be strategic (relating, for example, to the whole approach adopted, what 'contribution to knowledge' it represents or key ways in which the results have been interpreted) or tactical (for example, detailed aspects of the research method or points of clarification). You must be prepared for examiners to largely ask questions about aspects they feel are unsatisfactory or unclear. If your work relates to a current controversy or debate in your subject area, the examiners are also likely to ask questions to make you address this. The upshot of such an approach is that you can get a rather negative impression of what is happening. The phrase 'defending a thesis' is often used and is an appropriate term. Many students feel they had been 'grilled' at their viva and were expecting the worst, only at the end to be congratulated on their work and told they had passed with no more than some minor corrections needed!

> Copies of the OU recommendation forms for a PhD and MPhil are in the Appendix to this chapter. See if you can obtain a copy of the forms that your own examiners will use and the criteria involved.

At the end of the viva, the examiners have to complete a report recommending a result. For the Open University, there is a form used that specifically asks for comments on how the thesis displayed evidence of the competencies required. These were discussed in Chapter 2 (section 2.2), which went through the competencies required for a research degree. These include originality, critically evaluating existing knowledge, proficiency in research methods, presentation, etc. At the viva, these are the core academic criteria that your examiners will use. At universities that require an initial report before the viva, the examiners will have covered these points already, so the post-viva report is consequently shorter and concentrates on the candidate's 'defence of the thesis'.

At the end of the viva, you will be asked to leave the room while the examiners discuss the outcome. Most of this time is usually taken up sorting out what to write on the paperwork involved. You may be thinking that a great debate must be taking place as to whether your work is 'worthy' or not. In truth the examiners are probably trying to think up a suitable phrase to express how well you answered their questions and whether 'good' is an acceptable comment for its presentation and style. If any amendments are needed it can also take a while for the examiners to agree upon exactly what these should be and to write down what is required.

Possible results

It is worthwhile checking your own regulations, but in general, among UK universities, the following are the usual possible results from a viva.[1] These are a recommendation that:

1 *The degree be awarded.* In this case it is a simple matter of opening the bottles of fizz (or some other form of celebratory activity).

2 *The degree be awarded subject to corrections and minor modifications.* Corrections of minor typographical errors or minor editorial amendments are required. These need to be specified together with a maximum time period in which to make them. The bottles of fizz are still very appropriate.

3 *The degree be awarded subject to substantial amendments (without re-examination).* The thesis is considered to contain limited deficiencies that the examination panel is confident can be corrected satisfactorily by the student. No re-examination is needed, but a time period is specified in which to make the substantial amendments. This result is still worth a bottle or two, but hold some back for after the amendments have been made.

4 *Major revision and resubmission with re-examination.* This result (sometimes called a 'referral') means that, in the examiners' view, the candidate's work is essentially on the right lines, but needs some improvement before it can be finally accepted. The candidate is given the opportunity to make major specified revisions and resubmit for examination and viva by the same panel. Again there is a time limit (typically up to two years) for resubmission. A referral is often viewed as rather traumatic, but in fact it is far from a disaster. However, it is probably best to keep the fizz back for the moment. Further advice on such a situation is given in Section 11.5 of this chapter.

---

1 Again you should check your own university's regulations as the categories may differ (for example, in some universities there is no category 3) and the time periods set for the submission of corrections can also vary.

5 *Award as a lower degree than the one submitted.* In exceptional circumstances, many universities permit the examination panel to recommend that a thesis submitted for a PhD merits only the award of a Master's. This may also be subject to minor modifications or amendments. It would be hard to recommend the fizz under these circumstances.

Typically, about 20 per cent of research degrees are awarded with no changes needed; about 50 per cent are awarded subject to corrections and minor modifications; about 20 per cent are awarded subject to substantial amendment; 5 per cent require resubmission; and 5 per cent are awarded a lower degree than the one submitted.

6 *Fail: no degree to be awarded.* This is an extremely rare recommendation. The examiners have to state as fully as possible why they were unable to make any other recommendation. If this happens, open the fizz anyway[2] but make sure you know why this decision was made.

Remember that categories 1, 2 and 3 are all passes and that the most common recommendation is 2.

When will I know the result?

Check with your supervisor about this. The usual process is for the examination panel to inform the candidate of their recommendation after they have adjourned for a short discussion. If the candidate has to leave the premises, the procedure is usually to inform the internal supervisor who lets the candidate know.

11.4 Preparing for Your Viva

Having described the sort of things that happen in a viva, how is it best to prepare? Several weeks will have elapsed between submitting your thesis and the viva (most UK universities now specify that a viva should be within six weeks to two months of a thesis being submitted). Consequently, you will have probably been busy with other things and so you need to consciously get back 'up to speed' on your thesis.

NOTE: Your own university may have a website or guidance notes on viva preparation. Do check. Web links are also provided on this book's website.

The following real, but anonymous, quote from a PhD student is, perhaps, a typical experience:

---

2 The appropriateness of the advice to 'open the fizz anyway' has been the subject of debate within the course team. My view is that you are perfectly sensible people and we shouldn't be too prudish.

In my own case I was busy with a new job during the weeks before my viva so I didn't consciously prepare much apart from rereading the thesis the day before. However, I did feel pretty well prepared though: presenting conference papers and giving seminars over the years of the research; knowing a bit about my examiners (knowing two of them slightly myself and my supervisor knew the third one well); and being very familiar with my data.

On the day, the viva basically felt like a searching interview for a job which I felt I had a pretty good chance of getting. (Something which younger students may not have experienced, perhaps!) The chair set a constructive tone and everyone was friendly, if a bit formal. I was glad my supervisor was there as he backed me up a couple of times, for instance by explaining that certain things in the rather lengthy thesis were included for the benefit of readers such as himself who were not very familiar with the field (e.g. the technicalities of NHS planning systems). At the end it was definitely a case of 'open the fizz'; they didn't even want me to correct the typos!

Now that I am an examiner myself, I value the memory of my own viva, and feel it should not be necessary to be hostile or confrontational. It should be a constructive event, particularly if the result is 'more work to be done'. One can still find out the candidate's weak points as a researcher without intimidating them as a human being! If they have the misfortune to be very arrogant, they may be inviting more difficult and relentless questions (I have seen this happen!), but most candidates' behaviour will reflect nervousness rather than arrogance or over-confidence.

Activity 11.2

Watch the programme 'The Viva Experience' on the DVD. This 30-minute programme explores a number of real-life viva experiences by students who had recently undertaken a viva, together with viva examiners.

The students had mixed experiences and one had had a particularly tough viva. Make a note of what you feel are the key lessons that would help you in preparing for your own viva.

Discussion

In this programme, the students were asked how they prepared for the viva and how useful these preparations proved to be in practice and the examiners were asked how they prepared for examining a PhD and why they agreed to viva particular PhD candidates. You may find the examiner's interest and enthusiasm for the students' work very encouraging. The examiners also discussed what they expect a viva to do, both in general terms and concerning the specific questions they asked. The lessons and 'top tips' covered in this programme are picked up and developed in the following sections of this chapter.

Preparation strategies

This section picks up the theme of effective preparations that was explored on the DVD programme.

Preparation for a viva can be seen in two ways, consisting of:

1 **experience preparation;**

2 **specific preparation.**

Experience preparation
Experience preparation alerts you to the type of experience you will have in the viva.

One preparation method is to have a 'mock viva', as was mentioned in the DVD programme. This is where a candidate has a dry run, with unfamiliar tutors acting as examiners, followed by feedback on the candidate's performance. A mock viva is considered in more detail later in this chapter.

The sort of experiences provided in a mock viva can be obtained in other ways, which include:

1 **A series of discussions between you and your supervisor(s) in the months leading up to the viva on what areas of the thesis you both think will attract the examiners' attention, what sort of questions they could ask and how these might be answered. You might have a special tutorial on this a week or so before the viva. In this, take on board the 'Know thy examiner' tip from the DVD programme. What are the sort of issues that your examiners go on about in their papers and at conferences? They are likely to concentrate on the same areas in your viva.**

2 **Practice discussing your work and answering questions on it. For example, arrange seminars on your work in your final year, so as to build up experience on dealing with questions. An example of this is that one student arranged a departmental seminar where a couple of chapters of her PhD had been circulated in advance and everybody asked questions about them. She viewed this as a pretty good way of preparing for her viva. However, do remember that questions in a viva are likely to be rather different. For example, in a seminar a speaker is unlikely to ask you what original contribution your research has made to a field of study.**

The section below on viva questions will help you and your supervisor work through such experience practice.

Specific preparation

Moving on to consider the specific content of your thesis, there are a number of methods to help you prepare for your viva.

One idea is to create a 'road map' of your thesis. As you read through your thesis, make a short note of what is on every page or group of pages. For example:

pp. 33–34 Craik and Lockhart model discussed

pp. 47–50 Wolfram's ontological theory debunked

The result is a four- to six-page 'road map' of your thesis. This is valuable because:

1 **It gives a point and focus to the re-reading process, which makes it more effective.**

2 **It makes sure you know what you have written.**

3 **Commonly in a viva, an examiner asks a question which you are sure has been addressed. It is perfectly possible that the examiner has missed a point or (even though they are not supposed to) has 'skim read' parts of your thesis. So, instead of (unconvincingly) saying that you have covered the point somewhere and spending five minutes scrabbling through the pages (usually unsuccessfully), you can quickly scan down your notes and say: 'Ah yes, I debunked Wolfram on page 47.' This is enormously impressive to examiners (and could save you from being asked to do amendments to something you have already covered).**

An external part-time PhD student whom I supervised said he found making 'road map' notes particularly useful. At his viva he was asked more than once whether an issue had been covered; I was rather impressed by the way he glanced at his set of 'road map' notes and then immediately turned to the page in his thesis where the point was covered. I think it impressed the external examiner as well!

An alternative to the 'road map' is 'indexing' the important parts of the thesis with 'Post-it', notes (perhaps using a colour code); again, this allows you to turn immediately to the right section of your thesis when needed.

Another preparation strategy is to imagine yourself in the place of your examiner and filling in something like the OU's recommendation form. Look at the form in the Appendix to this chapter and consider:

1 **What sort of questions would you ask to check out the criteria for your degree?**

2 **How would you try to create a constructive dialogue?**

3 **How would you try to put the candidate at ease?**

4 **How would you organize the order of points, of the questions and the discussion?**

(If you know anything about your examiners this can be useful. Certainly, you should find out something about their own research, if possible.)

To help you, ask any readers who are commenting on the thesis draft whether they have any examiner's questions they can give you.

Often, having submitted a thesis, a candidate reads it again and realizes that, with the benefit of hindsight, they can see better its strengths and weaknesses. So re-read your thesis carefully. If you think some parts might have been done better, be prepared to say that you now recognize this and how you would improve it.

Activity 11.3

Imagine yourself in the place of the examiner who, having read your thesis, is filling in the EX33 form recommending a result (if you have obtained the documentation used by your own university, use that).

Look at the form and write down a list of questions that, were you your own examiner, you would need to ask about your thesis in order to fill in Sections 5.2, 5.3 and 5.4.

A mock viva

A mock viva combines experience and specific preparation by asking one or two people to read your thesis and then ask you questions as if they were your actual examiners. This is usually done reasonably close to the actual viva, something like a week or two beforehand.

A student in the Open University's Institute of Educational Technology had a mock viva where two colleagues acted as internal and external examiners and were given the thesis to read four weeks before the viva. The candidate said that one of the main advantages was that the mock viva made him think about his thesis from the point of view of other people and it was especially useful for the parts he had taken for granted that people could understand. The mock examiners asked the candidate for some items (records of research) that he had not considered bringing with him to the viva. He consequently decided to do this and it improved his confidence. Interestingly, the mock viva examiners came up with only one question that was asked by the real examiners. The sort of specific questions asked will very much depend on the individual examiners.

It takes a lot of effort to set up a mock viva, and to be fully beneficial it must be taken seriously. It can provide an experience of a viva-like situation and give you an opportunity to discuss problematic areas and where you did not field questions well. However, a danger of a mock viva is, if the actual viva ends up running in a totally different way, you could have had a misleading experience. As mentioned above, the questions will not be the same as in the mock viva (although one or two may be). As long as you are aware of how individual a viva can be, a mock viva can be helpful. It can give you a very good feel of what the process is like and how to deal with questions on your work.

Possible PhD viva questions

Rugg and Petre (2004) have a very useful section on the nature of questions asked in a viva. This is included in the offprint at the end of this chapter. Read this offprint now. It usefully covers both benign questioning and what to do when you face more difficult questions.

Activity 11.4

Listen now to the DVD audio interview with Marian Petre on types of viva questions and how to respond to them. She is particularly concentrating on dealing with more difficult questions. This will help you consider the type of questions you may get in your viva and how to deal with them. In this programme Marian emphasizes that, with preparation, it is always possible to deal with 'killer questions', but the real danger concerns 'suicidal answers'.

The following general questions could be used in a mock viva or another activity in which you work out answers. These, of course, do not cover questions specific to your research topic, findings or method.

In one sentence, what is your thesis?

Why were you interested in this research topic?

Summarize your key findings. What was the most interesting to you?

What is your original contribution to knowledge in your subject area?

What are the main achievements of your research?

What would you do differently if you could do your thesis again?

Why did you use the particular research methodology in your thesis?

What are the alternatives to the approach or method you used?

What did you gain by the approach or method you used?

How do you know that your findings are correct?

Which are the three most important papers which relate to your thesis?

Who has had the strongest influence in the development of your subject area in theory and practice?

Were there any ethical implications relating to your research? How did you deal with them?

What were the crucial research decisions you made?

If you were given £X thousand tomorrow to continue your research, what would you do?

What have you done that merits a PhD?

Whom do you think would be most interested in your work?

What are the main issues and debates in this subject area? How does your research relate to these?

Has your view of your research topic changed during the course of the research?

What have you learnt from your research experience?

What advice would you give to a new research student entering this topic area?

What would you have gained by using approach X?

How have you evaluated your work?

What published work is closest to what you have done? How is your work different?

What are the most recent major developments in your area?

How long-term is your contribution, given the anticipated future developments in X?

How do your findings relate to the literature on the subject?

Have you thought about publications? Which journals are appropriate?

What do you see as the next steps in this research?

Based upon: City University website, Rugg and Petre (2004, pp. 180–1) and course team inputs.

Activity 11.5

Using the above list (plus other ideas of your own from Activity 11.3 or otherwise), develop some questions on your own research based on Rugg and Petre's reading involving:

- Warm-up questions
- Confirmatory questions
- Calibration questions
- Scholarship questions
- Pushing the envelope questions

Would any of these questions expose a weakness in your thesis (killer questions)?

The questions that you generate could be used in preparation or a mock viva.

What might impress examiners

A good viva should be one where both the candidate and the examiners feel they have been enriched by the experience. So, impressing the examiner is really a matter of getting this good, symbiotic relationship going. The following list is based upon comments by examiners on what really impresses them:

1 **Well-considered replies that answer (and do not dodge or drift away from) the question asked.**

2 **Flexible and agile thinking in response to unanticipated questions, backed up by argument and/or evidence.**

3 **Good understanding of appropriate research methods.**

4 **Critical awareness of the field of enquiry which demonstrates knowledge beyond that shown in the thesis alone.**

5 **Clear reasons for what is included and excluded from the research, and how this affects the results and conclusions drawn (e.g. 'to fully explore your question would have taken the research in a rather different direction, requiring a different methodology').**

6 **Self-critical assessment showing honesty in what has been achieved, partly achieved or not achieved at all.**

7   Awareness of what remains to be researched and any key developments since the thesis was submitted (i.e. keeping up with the subject).

8   A sense of your personal desire to undertake the research, your search for answers, and your integrity and thoroughness.

During a viva you may have to choose between defending your ground and giving way. This relates to Rugg and Petre's comments on dealing with where there may be a weakness in your research. If the examiner has got it wrong, and you have every reason to defend what you did, then say so. However, over-energetic defence, especially if a question is raised in more than one way, is usually counter-productive, as it suggests you are unable to recognize the critique being made. In such cases, show you understand the critique, check with the examiner that you understand their point and, if necessary, go for Rugg and Petre's three-point plan.

What to wear

One other question that can arise is what to wear to your viva. As is mentioned in Chapter 10 on presentations, your clothes should not be a distraction – either to you or your examiners. Smart clothes seem to be the norm, but make sure they are comfortable (not too tight or likely to be hot). A few universities actually specify a dress code. For example, when I was an examiner for a viva at the University of Oxford, both the candidate and his internal examiner had to wear formal academic dress.

Helping your examiners

The anticipation and experience of a viva is almost certain to involve some degree of nervousness. A sympathetic panel of examiners will expect this. Remember that the purpose of the viva is to examine you at your best and not to create difficulties or inhibit your performance. This was one point made in the DVD viva programme. It is therefore important for you to help your examiners. Also it is possible for the examiners to be nervous. The following series of points may help you to help them to help you!

1   Give straight answers to straight questions – resist the temptation to wander off the point (especially if you know you have a tendency to do so).

2   If you feel unsure whether you have answered a question fully or in the manner expected, ask the examiner if the answer is what they sought. This is not a sign of weakness, but an indication that you want to offer a full and reasoned answer. Remember, the examiner does not know the thought processes you have gone through to arrive at your results or conclusions.

3 Similarly, if an examiner returns to the same point, ask them why they are doing so or in what way they feel you have not answered their question.

4 If you feel an examiner's question is unclear (as an examiner, I know I have asked some awfully vague questions!), always ask for clarification. The examiners will respect your need for accuracy – it reveals precision in your thinking.

5 Quite often what appears to be a single question actually contains two or more interdependent questions. Watch out for this. Point out that the question is of this nature, break it down and deal with the questions or issues in a stated order. Do not be worried about asking an examiner to remind you of the second or third part of their question.

6 If you think a question is based on a doubtful premise, challenge it (for example, if you think the examiner has missed the point).

7 In the face of a different explanation or interpretation to the one you have drawn, consider your response carefully. Examiners often do this to stimulate a discussion.

8 If it is an explanation you have considered and rejected, say so and why. If the examiner's explanation or perspective is new to you, think about its strengths and weaknesses and comment on these. For example, if you feel it misses the point of what your research explores, say so.

9 Examiners will not normally expect you just to accept their position. They welcome a discussion. Remember that an error of fact is unarguable, but an 'error' of explanation or interpretation is arguable.

10 If you make a mess of an answer, lose the point, or simply dry up, acknowledge this and start again. Everyone knows these occasions can be nerve-racking. Do not be afraid to ask for time to think about a question. For example, 'That's a good point which I hadn't considered. Can I think about that for a moment?' If you are still stuck, admit you do not have an answer (you may be able to go back to it later).

11 Things that give out wrong signals to examiners are:

- false modesty;

- exaggerated claims you cannot sustain;

- distortion of facts to fit what you want;

- 'flannel' to try to hide something.

12 Be friendly, honest, alert and interested and (difficult as it may seem) be your-self, not an image you have of the perfect candidate.

Activity 11.6

Having looked at the checklists above, are there any areas that you feel require particular attention? Discuss these with your supervisor(s).

Finally, be prepared to *enjoy* your viva. It is a wonderful opportunity to discuss your research with a group of people who actually want to know what you have to say. Relish this!

11.5   After the Viva – Handling Revisions

For some reason, most books providing training advice for research students fail to mention the possibilities of food and drink following a viva. This may be because little training is needed on this subject. Rugg and Petre do mention the possibility of a hangover, but more practically they consider what to do if any amendments are needed.

If amendments are needed, your examiners will be required to provide you with a written list and/or annotated copy of your thesis specifying precisely what is wanted and the date by which amendments have to be submitted. Make sure the examiner's requirements are specific and that your clearly understand what is needed. You should not accept vague phrases such as 'develop', 'rephrase' or 'make clearer'. Your supervisor should pay particular attention to getting precise amendment requirements. If you feel there is any ambiguity, then raise this with your supervisor.

It is best to get any amendments out of the way as soon as possible. Rugg and Petre (p. 174) note:

Doing the revisions can produce surprising feelings of revulsion for some students – it's a bit like washing up greasy plates in cold water the morning after a wild party when you have a massive hangover – or so we are reliably informed by friends who attend wild parties. It's worth knowing about this so that if you find yourself engaged in displacement activities rather than doing the corrections, then you can spot this and do something about it.

Particularly if large amendments are needed, it is important to meet up with your supervisor as soon as possible, work through precisely what the examiners have asked for and prepare a schedule for the tasks involved to complete the amendments. It is very important that you do not simply hide away, prepare the amendments in isolation and shove them in without meeting and discussing them with your supervisor. The guidance provided by your supervisor is needed, possibly more than ever – so provide them with draft amendments and arrange a tutorial to check that the amendments do fulfil the examiners' requirements.

Acknowledgement

Section 11.4 draws upon John Swift's 'The viva voce', in D. Newbury (ed.), *The Research Training Initiative*, vol. 7, 1997, pp. 7–19. Birmingham: University of Central England.

Reference

Rugg, G. and Petre, M. (2004) *The Unwritten Rules of PhD Research*. Buckingham: Open University Press.

Offprint

Questions examiners ask

- **Warm-up questions** to calm you down. Often of the form, 'So how did you come to research this subject?' Or, 'Can you summarize your core thesis for us?'
- **Confirmatory questions** to let you demonstrate your knowledge. Often of the form of asking you to reiterate or define something in your dissertation.
- **Deep confirmatory questions** to let you demonstrate that your knowledge is more than skin deep. These are usually follow-ups to confirmatory questions that take up some point in your answer. Just keep your head and continue to address the questions.
- **Calibration questions** to help the examiner check their own understanding of your work.

- **Scholarship questions** to let you demonstrate that you know the field as well as your own research.
- **Salvaging questions,** when you've written something badly, to let you show you do know what you're talking about after all.
- **Pushing the envelope questions** to see how far your knowledge goes.
- **'This is neat' questions** to give the examiner a chance to discuss your interesting ideas.
- **Redemptive, 'lesson learned' questions** to give you a chance to admit some awful blunder in your work so that the examiner can 'let you off' without worrying that you'll make it again. A typical example is, 'Would you take this approach again if you were pursuing this issue?' when a student has applied an inappropriate method that yielded little.
- **'This is a good student; how good?' questions** – a little 'sparring' to let you really show your stuff.
- **'Give me a reason to pass you' questions** – often, if the examiners continue asking about the same topic, it's because they're interested; if so, then co-operate actively with them, rather than trying to change the topic.

These are all moderately benign questions. If you arouse the examiners' anger or a suspicion that there is something wrong with your work, however, you may be asked some hard, sharp questions. The next section lists some classic 'killer' questions and suggests some ways of responding effectively to them.

Killer questions and how to survive them

In this section, Q = question, A = suggested answer, C = our comments on the question and/or answer.

Q: *How does your work relate to Jim Bloggs' recent paper?* (when you've never heard of Bloggs)

A: 'I'm not familiar with that paper. Does he take an X approach or a Y approach?'

C: Show something you do know that's relevant; then, when the examiner offers a précis: 'Ah, so it's like so-and-so's work?'

Q: *Isn't this obvious?*

A: Well, it may appear that way with hindsight, but there was surprisingly little work on this topic in the literature, and the question needed to be properly answered.

C: Many dissertations codify what people think they already know but which has never been properly established. 'Obvious' can be good; it can make a contribution. Marian's *external* examiner asked her this and, fortunately, her internal examiner answered him that it was only obvious because he'd read her dissertation. You might try a modestly phrased version of this answer yourself if nobody offers it for you.

Q: *Isn't this just like Brown's work?*

A: It differs from Brown's work because …

C: Everyone worries that someone else is going to 'gazump' them and publish exactly their work just before they do. Forget it. There will be something – a difference of approach, of technique, of sample – that distinguishes your work and protects your contribution. If you know Brown's work already, then you should have already identified how it differs from yours; if you don't, ask about Brown's work until the answers reveal a difference.

Q: *You use the term X in two different ways in Chapters 4 and 6. What do you mean?*

A: In Chapter 4, I was using Smith's definition, which was most appropriate for that part of the thesis. In Chapter 6, I was using Brown's …

C: Answer the question, giving a concise clarification. Make a note of what you say because you'll probably be asked to amend the text with the clarification when you do your corrections.

Q: *Why didn't you … ?*

A: Because …

C: This is why you reread your thesis and have a mock viva. Rereading your thesis will remind you of why you did things the way you did (and, conversely, tell you why you didn't use the other options). This will also give a sanity check that you haven't missed anything obvious. If the suggestion is something little known in your field, then you can reply along the lines of, 'That's interesting, and it sounds as if it should be more widely known in this field'. You can then turn this into a discussion of methods in the field and an opportunity to talk about the things you *do* know about.

Some ways of addressing weakness

Sometimes, you just have to admit that you were wrong. Occasionally, just making the admission with humour is effective. (As with the student who, when asked if she would use the same (fruitless) survey technique again, said with feeling: 'Hell, no'.)

Mote often, it's safer to follow the three-point plan:

1 Reiterate why whatever you did was a justified choice at the outset.
2 Explain, as simply as possible and without apology, that you understand why it failed.
3 Make some alternative suggestions about what you'd do instead next time that would improve your chances of getting it right.

No one expects doctoral research to flow smoothly without errors or hitches. Indeed, it is rare for any research to do so – research is opportunistic and (happily) full of surprises. What examiners expect is that students will respond to the errors and hitches with intelligence and by learning from them.

Source: 'Questions examiners ask', 'Killer questions and how to survive them' and 'Some ways of addressing weakness' pp. 178–80 of Rugg, G. and Petre, M. (2004) *The Unwritten Rules of PhD Research*. Buckingham: Open University Press.

Appendix: EX33 Research Degree Examination – Examiner's Joint Recommendation and Report Forms

The first page of the EX33 form is the same for all research degrees, so only one example of it is included in this Appendix. This is followed by the pages for the PhD, and MPhil versions of the form. The comments and names are fictitious, but are based on the author's experience of the sort of things examiners write about candidates' theses and their viva.

THIS PAGE COMMON TO ALL RESEARCH DEGREES	SPECIMEN	EX33 (PhD) (August 2000)

Examination Panel Report Form

This form should be completed by the examination panel and returned by the internal examiner to the Research School on the day following the oral examination. At least one copy of the thesis must be returned with this form. Please indicate in Section 4 if a copy of the thesis is retained by the examiner(s) and/or candidate.

1. Candidate Details

Candidate name:......ROBIN COX...
Personal identifier: ...RO542850.......Discipline:...SOCIAL GEOGRAPHY...........................
Thesis title:......EMISSION REDUCTION FROM CITY TRAFFIC:...............................
........................OPPORTUNITIES AND SCOPE..
Degree for which submitted: **PhD**   Resubmission: Yes or (No) Date of oral: 25.6.98

FOR COMPLETION BY RESEARCH SCHOOL
Date of registration:.. Date of Submission: ....
Scheme of study: Full-time   ⟨Part-time external⟩   Part-time internal
Highest qualification on entry:..

2. Examiner Details

Internal examiner/assessor..........:......J.E. PRESTON...
Post held   :......PROFESSOR OF TRANSPORT STUDIES........................
External examiner   :......K. HAMILTON..
Post held   :......READER, URBAN STUDIES..................................
External examiner   :..
Post held   :..
Observer at oral   :......J. BROWNING...

3. Recommendation (see section 10.0 of the examination guidelines EX10)

We recommend: Tick one box

i)   the candidate be awarded the degree for which the thesis has been submitted   ☑

ii) the candidate be awarded the degree for which the thesis has been submitted   ☑
     after satisfactory completion of corrections and minor modifications specified overleaf*

iii) the candidate be awarded the degree for which the thesis has been submitted after   ☐
     satisfactory completion of substantial amendment specified overleaf but for which
     resubmission is not required*

iv) the candidate be permitted to resubmit the thesis for re-examination for the degree for   ☐
     which it has been examined after major revision

v)   another recommendation as specified below (see 10.5 of the examination   ☐
     guidelines EX10)

vi) that no degree is awarded   ☐

Open University form Ex33: the PhD version, pp. 2–3

SPECIMEN

4. **Copies of Thesis Returned**

    Number of copies of thesis returned with this form: ___2_____

    Number of copies of thesis taken by student: _____1_____

    Number of copies of thesis retained by examiner(s) (please give details and reasons): ___1_____

    RETAINED IN ORDER TO COMPARE WITH CORRECTED VERSION_____

    At least one copy of the thesis must be returned to the Research School after the examination.

5. **Report on PhD Thesis**

    The examination panel is asked to provide comments about how the thesis satisfies the criteria for the degree (see section 9.3 of the examination guidelines EX10).

    (i) **Please comment on the presentation and style of the thesis.**

    GENERALLY WELL PRESENTED, BUT WITH SOME MINOR ERRORS OF GRAMMAR.

    FIG 4.2 UNCLEAR AND NEEDS TO BE REDRAWN

    (ii) **In what way does the thesis show evidence of being a significant contribution to knowledge?**

    THE CANDIDATE PROVIDED NEW AND DETAILED INFORMATION
    ON EMISSIONS AND REDUCTIONS FROM A RANGE OF POSSIBLE
    PUBLIC TRANSPORT DEVELOPMENTS AND SHOWED CURRENT VIEWS
    OF THE LINKS BETWEEN THE TWO ARE OVERSIMPLIFIED. FURTHERMORE
    HE EXPLORED THE LIMITS OF EXISTING MODELLING TECHNIQUES,
    INDICATING WHERE THEY ARE UNSUITED TO TAKING INTO ACCOUNT
    KEY VARIABLES

    (iii) **In what way does the thesis show evidence of the candidate's capacity to pursue further research without supervision?**

    THE RESEARCH INVOLVED SEVERAL STRANDS WHICH REQUIRED
    CAREFUL CO-ORDINATION. THIS WAS SUCCESSFULLY ACHIEVED
    AND INDICATES THAT THE CANDIDATE IS NOW A CAPABLE RESEARCHER.

SPECIMEN

(iv) **How much material worthy of publication does the thesis contain? Please indicate how much, if any, has already been published or accepted for publication.**

THE CANDIDATE HAS ALREADY PUBLISHED FOUR PAPERS BASED ON THE EARLIER PART OF HIS THESIS. TWO ARE IN REFEREED JOURNALS. WE DISCUSSED POSSIBLE PUBLICATIONS BASED UPON THE CONCLUDING CHAPTERS WHICH THE CANDIDATE WILL PURSUE.

6. **Please comment on the candidate's defence of the thesis at the oral examination.**

THE CANDIDATE WAS ARTICULATE AND RECEPTIVE TO THE CRITICISMS AND COMMENTS MADE BY THE EXAMINERS. HOWEVER SOME POINTS COULD HAVE BEEN DEVELOPED MORE VIGOUROUSLY.

7. **Please give any other comments on the thesis.**

In the case of recommendation 3(ii), 3(iii) or 3(iv) please provide detailed information about the corrections and minor modification, substantial amendment or major revision that the candidate is required to undertake. Continue overleaf and/or attach an additional sheet as necessary.

CORRECTIONS AND MINOR MODIFICATIONS HAVE BEEN REQUESTED, WHICH ARE DETAILED IN A SEPARATE SHEET SUPPLIED TO THE CANDIDATE.

The Research Degrees Committee will formally ratify the recommended result on the basis of this report. Please ensure that detailed comments are provided in each relevant section, since a request from the Committee for clarification or elaboration will delay formal notification to the student of the ratified result. Please ensure that a copy of the thesis is returned with this form and that comprehensive details of any changes required by the examination panel are provided.

Signed: Internal examiner / assessor: ____J.E. Preston_____

               External examiner: ____K. Hamilton_____

               External examiner: _____

               Date: ____25.6.98_____

Open University form Ex33: the MPhil version, pp. 2–3

SPECIMEN

4. Copies of Thesis Returned

Number of copies of thesis returned with this form: ___4_____

Number of copies of thesis taken by student: _____

Number of copies of thesis retained by examiner(s) (please give details and reasons):_____

At least one copy of the thesis must be returned to the Research School after the examination.

5. Report on MPhil Thesis

The examination panel is asked to provide comments about how the thesis satisfies the criteria for the degree (see section 9.2 of the examination guidelines EX10).

(i)   Please comment on the presentation and style of the thesis.

THE THESIS WAS WELL WRITTEN AND EXCELLENTLY ILLUSTRATED. THE READER WAS GUIDED WELL THROUGH THE STUDENT'S RESEARCH, WITH EACH STAGE EXPLAINED CLEARLY.

(ii)   In what way does the thesis show evidence of candidate's proficiency in the methods and techniques of research?

THE CANDIDATE EXPLORED HOW PRODUCT BRANDING TOOLS AND PROCESSES THAT HAVE BEEN DEVELOPED FOR SALES IN SHOPS NEED TO BE ADAPTED FOR SELLING VIA THE INTERNET. SHE EXPLORED THIS ISSUE VIA A LITERATURE SEARCH AND THEN CONSIDERED THREE POSSIBLE RESEARCH METHODS BEFORE CHOOSING IN-DEPTH INTERVIEWS OF BRANDING MANAGERS IN STORES MOVING TO INTERNET SALES. THE METHODS AND TECHNIQUES WERE APPROPRIATE AND WELL CONDUCTED.

(iii)   In what way does the thesis show evidence of an adequate knowledge and discussion of the literature in the specified field of study?

THE CANDIDATE CONDUCTED A THOROUGH LITERATURE SEARCH OF THE BRANDING LITERATURE, USING SPECIALIST DATABASES/CD ROMS AND ALSO CROSS-CHECKED THIS BY CONSULTING SPECIALISTS IN THE SUBJECT.

SPECIMEN

(iv)   **Does the thesis demonstrate initiative, independence of thought and a distinct contribution to scholarship?**

THE CENTRAL QUESTION OF THE THESIS WAS ORIGINAL AND THIS ISSUE HAD NOT PREVIOUSLY BEEN STUDIED SYSTEMATICALLY OR FROM AN ACADEMIC PERSPECTIVE. IT IS A DISTINCT CONTRIBUTION TO SCHOLARSHIP.

6. Please comment on the candidate's defence of the thesis at the oral examination.

THE CANDIDATE RESPONDED WELL TO THE QUESTIONS AND INITIATED A LIVELY DISCUSSION!

7. Please give any other comments on the thesis.

In the case of recommendation 3(ii), 3(iii) or 3(iv) please provide detailed information about the corrections and minor modifications, substantial amendment or major revision that the candidate is required to undertake. Continue overleaf and/or attach an additional sheet as necessary.

NO AMENDMENTS OR CORRECTIONS WERE REQUIRED. THIS WAS AN EXCELLENT PIECE OF WORK WHICH DESERVES AN UNQUALIFIED PASS.

The Research Degrees Committee will formally ratify the recommended result on the basis of this report. Please ensure that detailed comments are provided in each relevant section, since a request from the Committee for clarification or elaboration will delay formal notification to the student of the ratified result. Please ensure that a copy of the thesis is returned with this form and that comprehensive details of any changes required by the examination panel are provided.

Signed: Internal examiner / assessor: .M.Y. Quin..

External examiner: .A. Ismail..

External examiner: ....

Date: .14.11.98...

12 Developing your Career

Verina Waights

LEARNING OUTCOMES

After reading this chapter and working on its associated activities you should be able to:

- Explore opportunities to develop your career.
- Identify the skills that you can offer a prospective employer.
- Write job applications and CVs that promote your knowledge, experience and suitability.
- Prepare for interviews effectively.

12.1   Introduction

There is no such thing as a career path – it's crazy paving and you have to lay it yourself.

(Robert Linnecar, quoted in Association of Graduate Recruiters, 1995)

This chapter aims to help you to build the crazy paving – using the skills and experiences that you have already acquired to put your feet firmly on to the next slab of concrete and to determine where the following slab may be. I really like this metaphor rather than the traditional one of 'rungs on a ladder' because much of your progress will be serendipitous – being in the right place at the right time; maybe it is serendipity that has brought you thus far already! But even if this is the case, there is much that you can do to make the most of opportunities that come your way. Serendipity will not work for you if you are a passive recipient – you need to actively pursue your goals. As Louis Pasteur said in 1854, 'Chance favours only the prepared mind'. Ideally you will be reading this during the early months of your studies towards a research

Figure 12.1   Crazy paving path through flowerbed

degree, while there is time for you to act on the ideas in the beginning of the chapter. It is more likely though that you have nearly completed your research degree and are busy looking for a job to make you feel that being an impoverished student or spending much of your leisure time working towards your degree was worth it. If this is the case, you may wish to move directly to Section 12.6, 'I've finished! Get me successfully out of here'. You can always go back to the earlier sections later.

So first things first. Do you know where the next slab of concrete is likely to lie?

12.2   When I Finish My Research Degree I Want to …

Some people are fortunate enough to decide on a career at an early age and never deviate from that path. One past OU PhD student was given a book on astronomy for his seventh birthday and was determined to study astronomy. He is now a lecturer in astronomy at the University of Amsterdam. But not everyone is so certain of their career path. You are studying for a research degree at the moment, which probably reflects that you enjoyed research during your undergraduate studies. You may be totally passionate about your subject, wanting to talk about it with anyone who will listen, your colleagues, friends, people you meet in the café. Or maybe research is just not for you, at least not full-time, day in, day out. Whatever your thoughts, this chapter is designed to help you plan your career. We are talking long-term strategies as well as the fairly imminent problem of what you are going to do next.

Career planning can be described as a circular process that continues through your life (Hawkins, 1999). You need to establish *where you are now*; *where you want to go*; and *how you are going to get there*. Some time after you have '*got there*' you will need to *review and improve your career* and so the cycle begins again. In fact, you entered this cycle when you chose your subjects to secure university entry. You reviewed your career when you finished your first degree and now you are reviewing it again.

First try Activities 12.1 and 12.2. These will help you to focus on your career, and to work out the issues that are important to you. The first activity builds on Activity 2.1 which you undertook in Chapter 2, 'Getting going'.

Activity 12.1   What I Want to Do Next

Just take two minutes. Don't dwell on your answers, if you answer spontaneously you are more likely to get a realistic perspective.

I registered for a PhD because . . . . and now I want to . . . . (still do the same/do something completely different/don't know).

I want to do this because I . . . . (find the new research area more interesting/am passionate about XXXX/would like to earn a high salary so I'm going to train as an accountant or lawyer).

It is important that you acknowledge your true feelings. I have worked with students who have felt they are letting their supervisor down by not wishing to continue in research. Consequently, they have been unwilling to discuss their career plans with them. But in my view, it takes a mature and strong person to admit to changing their mind, so don't feel you owe anybody anything and just be true to yourself. Ali and Graham (2000) suggest that there are three possible ways forward: continuing in your research field, developing existing expertise or taking a new direction. If you don't know which direction you would like your career to take, you may find Activity 12.2 helpful.

Activity 12.2   What I Need from My Career

Listed here are some of the main factors that affect people's satisfaction in their work and their life. Mark each one on a scale from 1 (not very important to you) to 5 (very important to you). Allow 10 minutes for this activity; again, don't dwell on your answers as your gut feeling is probably more trustworthy than your intellectual analysis. When you reach the end of the list, you may like to add others that you feel should be included in 'your' list. For example, you might wish to include particular skills or personal 'strengths' that are important characteristics of your career.

	Not important ⟶			Very important	
	1	2	3	4	5
Challenging work using my abilities and skills fully					
Contact with people					
Control over my work					
Feeling appreciated					
Flexible working					
Good income					
Good work/life balance					
High level of responsibility					
Job security					
Managing major projects					
Managing people					
Opportunity for promotion					
Opportunity to be creative and take risks					
Opportunity to develop skills					
Pursuing excellence					
Specific geographic location					
Status outside the organization					
Status within the organization					
Using the skills and knowledge that I have gained during my research degree					
Variety					
Work which helps others or benefits the wider community					
Working in a team					

Taken from the EPSRC Career Development Training Pack, based on an extract from M. Mitchell and Z. Gruhn, *Making Headway*. CRAC, Cambridge (UK) 1995.

Did you find this activity useful? You may have found that thinking about these factors has enabled you to identify directions that you don't want to pursue even if you are unsure of your next destination. For example, you may be aware that museum conservation work is poorly paid, so if earning a high salary is important to you this would not make a good career option. Once you are clear about the factors that matter most to you, you need to identify career options that offer those opportunities. The best way to start is to consider the range of jobs on offer. Browse the websites linked to this chapter on this book's website, current newspapers and publications relevant to your field. Ask members of your department about the destinations of previous students. If particular positions sound interesting, determine whether they would satisfy at least the top three or four factors in the previous activity that you identified as important to you. If you have decided not to pursue an academic career, move on to Section 12.4.

12.3   Staying in/Entering Academia

If you love the challenge of academic life – both the pleasure from researching and of teaching others about your field – the most likely next step is a postdoctoral position or a lectureship. In some disciplines, especially within science and technology, you are unlikely to secure a lectureship until you have served an apprenticeship of one or two postdoctoral fellowships. These fellowships enable you to build up your research profile and to gain further teaching experience. In arts, humanities and social sciences, however, doctoral graduates are more likely to move straight to a junior lectureship.

So how do you secure a postdoctoral position?

There are two main sources of postdoctoral fellowships. Primary investigators may have research funding for people to carry out specific projects that may vary in length from six months to three years. These positions are advertised in a variety of ways, in *The Guardian*, *TES*, discipline-specific publications, on noticeboards at major conferences in your field, or on websites, such as jobs.ac.uk. There is a list of job-related sites on this book's website.

Alternatively, if you wish to work in a specific area, you can try proposing your own project. You are not eligible to apply for funding in your own name, so you need to work with an established academic who will include you as the 'named person' in the proposal. This identifies you as the person who will undertake the project if the bid is successful. If this approach appeals to you, you need to research the topic thoroughly and write an outline proposal. It is also useful to look at the requirements of Research Councils, charities, etc., who are likely to support your area of research. You then need to interest an academic in your proposal, who will 'work it up' with you so that it has a good chance of being successful. You may like to do this with your current supervisor, although many academics will advise you to move on from the institution where you completed your PhD so that you gain more experience. Indeed, Blaxter et al. (2001) identified three strategies for developing academic careers effectively: to move between institutions, or between countries or out into industry and perhaps back into academia. If you wish to move departments, your supervisor should be able to suggest academics who may be interested in your proposal. If your supervisor is very keen for you to continue with them and to develop the ideas arising from your thesis, you may find that option very attractive. If this is your preferred route, the best way forward is to talk to your supervisor, other academics in your field and the postdoctoral fellows already in your department.

Networking

As mentioned in earlier chapters, networking is essential when undertaking many aspects of your research project. However, it will also increase your chances of finding your next position and may lead to some new angles on your research. A good supervisor will introduce you to colleagues in your field but you can also network for yourself. Most researchers really enjoy talking to researchers just entering the field. They find new researchers' enthusiasm and fresh perspectives both exciting and invigorating. So before you attend a conference, take time to read through the list of delegates and identify the researchers that you would most like to meet. Read the abstracts of their conference papers and their latest publications so that you can discuss their research intelligently. Then, after listening to their presentation, you can approach them with a related question to start the conversation. You will most probably find that the conversation soon turns to your own research, and often some good ideas for your research will follow. Another way to network, especially if you wish to work with researchers abroad, is to email them, either with a question about their research or asking advice about a problem that you have encountered. Most researchers enjoy problem-solving and will be pleased to give their expert opinion. Then, when you apply for a postdoctoral position in their research group they will hopefully remember your interest in their research and call you for interview.

But maybe you have already decided that you don't wish to pursue an academic career, so what other options are open to you?

12.4   Continuing to Research Outside Academia

You may be able to continue in your research field at a research institution such as CancerResearchUK, or in a library, government department or museum. Much of the advice in the previous section about networking may be helpful as many researchers from other backgrounds attend conferences in your field. You will also find the next section helpful as you will need to emphasize your transferable skills as well as your research skills when you apply for such positions.

Help! I only know how to research

Some full-time students are concerned that they will have spent three or more years on their research and have nothing to offer a prospective employer beyond knowledge and skills related to their research. The *Research Councils' Joint Statement of Skills Requirements*, which indicates the skills you should have by the time you complete your PhD, came into being to ensure that students have the necessary skills to pursue a career of their choice. Although these requirements were drawn up for PhD students, many of these skills can be readily acquired through study towards an MPhil or a Master's degree.

You may be familiar with the Joint Statement but still be unsure that you have the appropriate skills. The best place to start evaluating your skills is to consider the skills employers are looking for. You may be surprised to find that knowledge of your subject area is not necessarily the most important factor:

> We like PhDs in our business sector – they never take anything at face value. That is a real bonus in a business compliance function. Their philosophical training and critical judgement have direct application in business services, whatever the topic of their research.
>
> (Head of Graduate Recruitment, 'Big 4' Accountancy firm, quoted in 'What do PhD's do', UKGRAD Programme, 2004)

In fact, it is the ability to critically analyse situations, identify actual or possible problems and conceive novel solutions that often, but not always, sets research degree students apart from recent graduates. If you would like to develop these skills further, there are many thought-provoking books available such as *Stop Working and Start Thinking* (Cohen et al., 2000). You may find it interesting to try some of the activities related to critical thinking on this book's website.

Hawkins (1999) summarizes skills that employers desired from graduates in 1998. This skills base has hardly changed in the intervening years. In Table 12.1, Hawkins' description of the characteristics of someone displaying each skill is given against a list of graduate skills obtained from employers in response to a survey in 2002.

Clearly, as a successful Master's or PhD graduate you are even more likely to have these skills on offer! Do you agree with this, or do you feel that your skills have become more limited as you have focused on such a narrow field over the last few years? Several full-time students with whom I have worked have worried that their skills base has reduced

Table 12.1   Skills sought by graduate employers (in ascending order, although the precise order of desirability will depend on the employer in question)

Skill	Characteristics of someone displaying this skill
Motivation and enthusiasm	Inquisitive, purposeful, focused, self-belief, realistic, resourceful, drive
Interpersonal skills	Listener, adviser, co-operative, assertive
Team working	Supportive, organized, co-ordinator, deliverer
Oral communication	Communicator, presenter, influencer
Flexibility and adaptability	Versatile, willing, multi-skilled, resourceful
Problem-solving	Practical, logical, results orientated, critical thinker, analyser
Planning and organization	Decision-maker, planner, able to prioritize
Managing your own development	Self-reliant, positive, persistent, ambitious
Written communication	Clear, concise, persuasive
Customer orientation	Friendly, caring, diplomatic
Time management	Dedicated, conscientious, efficient
Business awareness	Competent, market aware
Numeracy	Accurate, quick-thinker, methodical
Leadership	Initiator, motivator, energetic, visionary
Cultural sensitivity	Aware of diversity, appropriate use of language
General IT/computing skills	Office skills, keyboard skills, software packages, PowerPoint
Risk-taking/entrepreneurship	Competitive, flare, creative,
Foreign languages	Oral and writing skills
Specialist knowledge and skills	e.g. journalism, engineering, accounting

Source: Association of Graduate Recruiters (1995) Hawkins (1999).

during their PhD. If you have been studying towards your research part-time you are less likely to be concerned about your skills base as you probably have developed a broad range of skills during your employment. However, you may still look at advertisements for positions that interest you and wonder whether you can meet the criteria. It could be argued that your transferable skills set has actually broadened even though you have been researching in a narrow area. Activity 12.3 will help you to see this more clearly.

Activity 12.3   What Skills Do I Have to Offer?

Take each skill listed in Table 12.1 and identify an example from your studies towards a research degree where you have exhibited this skill. For example, working in a research group demonstrates that you can work co-operatively, and applying for funding to attend a conference indicates that you are resourceful and self-reliant.

Doing this activity may have highlighted skills that you cannot demonstrate through your academic studies to date. If you are in the early stages of your studies you have time to develop these skills; for example, presenting and defending a paper at a conference will demonstrate your communication skills as well as disseminate your research to a broad audience. All is not lost, however, if you are applying for positions now. Remember that you have a life apart from being a student and you can draw on these experiences to fill in the gaps. As mentioned earlier, this is relatively easy for part-time students, but with a little thought should be possible for full-time students also. For example, if you have worked as a barperson you have needed to be diplomatic to prevent people from queue-jumping and upsetting other customers. Or you may have shown leadership qualities by taking a scout group camping for a week. This activity also highlights the importance of continuing to pursue interests outside your studies. Not only will this give you a broader range of skills, it also demonstrates to future employers that you are a well-rounded interesting person who will fit in well with the rest of the team. There are not many opportunities for the lone individual who only wishes to be involved in their research. Even if you aspire to stay in/enter academia, you will be expected to engage with undergraduates and to contribute to departmental administration.

But you need to decide if you require evidence of all these skills, as some of them may not be relevant for your preferred career. For example, you may not be required to build relationships with customers or to be fluent in another language. From this activity you may be more certain about whether you wish to develop an existing expertise or pursue a new direction.

12.5 Personal Development Planning

Many students find personal development planning (personal development planning (PDP) was introduced in Section 12.2) tedious, but it can be a valuable tool for planning your future. If undertaking the previous activity led you to identify areas in which you would like to develop your skills, you have already embarked on a personal development plan. The other stages in planning skills development are:

1 deciding on a course of action;

2 determining the time scale for development;

3 ascertaining the criteria for successful acquisition of the skill(s).

This record is also invaluable when you come to write your CV as you will have the information that you need at your fingertips. PDPs are in use widely in industry. Visit this book's website to explore other ways to develop your PDP.

Activity 12.4   Personal Development Planning and Keeping a Portfolio

Take a few minutes to fill in this plan, based on your assessment of skills that you would like to acquire. Keep a portfolio of any training that you undertake with your PDP to help you to prepare your CV.

Skill needed	Action to be taken	Success criteria	Time-scale
e.g. leadership …	Run the department seminar programme	All sessions filled and programme running smoothly	Autumn term

You may be unable to acquire certain skills through your studies, your employment, or through your hobbies and interests, so you will need to search for other opportunities. For example, you could gain some classroom experience through talking about your research with local schoolchildren, or gain undergraduate teaching experience through demonstrating or leading seminars. You could contact organizations of interest to you and ask to shadow relevant employees for a few days or volunteer with a charity or other voluntary organization to expand your range of skills. You could take a short course to enable you to acquire additional knowledge and skills such as business management or a foreign language, especially if you would like to change direction.

So far we have looked at the general principles underlying developing your career. In this last section we will explore the practicalities of moving on.

12.6   I've Finished! Get Me Successfully Out of Here

Job-hunting

Hopefully you are reading this early enough so you can plan to apply for jobs in the few months preceding submission. However, if you are in your final year you may have been too focused on drafting your thesis to worry about the future. But now, suddenly, it is all over. You have successfully defended your thesis in your viva, and enjoyed a well-earned celebration. All you have left to do are a few minor corrections and to send the copies to the library. Whatever your reasons for studying, now is the time to seriously look for a job. In addition to looking on websites (see the list on this book's website) and in relevant publications, you can use your network to seek out suitable positions. Let it be known that you are job-hunting, especially if you would like to join a particular research group. These researchers may know of positions that you hadn't heard about, and may put in a good word for you when they meet with their colleagues.

If you are a full-time student planning to leave academia, let your family or friends know the type of position you are looking for. If you would like a position that is similar to any of those in your institution, for example in administration or finance, ask the incumbents for an short appointment (say 30 minutes) to discuss your options. Make it clear that you are seeking advice and don't expect to be offered a job, and most people will be willing to talk to you. You will find this is also true for people in other organizations. Many firms have a website, so use this to identify the correct person to contact and write to them directly, including why you believe talking to them is beneficial. Research their organization so that your reasons for wishing to see them link both to the organization and to their own expertise within it.

Speculative letters

You can write to organizations that interest you, stating the kind of position you are seeking and asking if they are likely to have vacancies in the foreseeable future. Covering letters are discussed later in this chapter, but you need to research each organization thoroughly for this approach to have any chance of being successful.

Most importantly, don't give up. Finding the next step on the crazy paving may take time as it may not lie directly in front of you. You have just spent three or so years completing your research degree, so it is worth holding out for an appropriate job. You may have come to the end of your studentship, in which case temporary employment through an agency will keep you in the manner to which you are accustomed – after all, a research degree stipend is not a fortune! If you find the work unrewarding, as you most probably will, this will give you the motivation to keep searching. If you have undertaken a research degree part-time to further an established career, now is the time to check out the promotion criteria within your organization, although you may need to move to another organization to progress your career. Home-grown talent is not always recognized!

Writing your CV

As soon as you start job-hunting it is important to have a suitable CV. You may not have looked at your CV since applying for your current position, so it may take you longer than you think to bring it up to date. Also, you will probably have to complete an application form when you apply for a position and so you may not have time to simultaneously polish your CV.

General points

Your CV should be well presented on good-quality paper and sent to prospective employers in an A4 envelope so that it is kept flat. If you send it by email, include it as an attachment so that when it is printed out the header is not the email header. Also, follow the email immediately with a hard copy in the post.

Many organizations prefer a CV to be no longer than two sides of A4, although academic CVs can be as long as necessary. Your CV needs to be aesthetically pleasing and effortless to read, which can be achieved very easily using word processing. It is important that your CV makes good use of white space and is consistent in its use of fonts, heading sizes and tabs. Also, active language is more inviting to read than the passive voice (you might like to consult the table of forceful and persuasive language in this chapter's appendices). Avoid acronyms and jargon as members of the panel may not be familiar with these terms. Small tightly packed print with small margins is difficult to read, so keep within the page limit. You need to give concise details that carry a wealth of information.

Always remember that the purpose of a CV is to secure an interview, so don't be ambiguous or mention things that may be detrimental to your application. Tailoring your CV to each application is a skill worth developing. When applying for academic positions, you need to give high priority to your publications and papers you have presented and to conferences that you have attended. When applying for non-academic positions, these academic indices will be less important than the other skills you have acquired. However, if you are changing from an academic to a non-academic environment it is important to show that you were successful in academia and to list any publications (examples of both types of CV are given on this book's website).

CVs are usually in reverse chronological order, beginning with your current position and working backwards to your schooldays. The academic CV will focus on your academic positions and qualifications first and list any other work experience later. Typically, a non-academic CV will begin with a personal profile that summarizes your major skills and will then highlight the skills that you have developed during your education and employment experience, either paid or voluntary. The non-academic CV allows the prospective employer to determine at a glance that you have the skills they are seeking.

Your CV does not need to be headed Curriculum Vitae, but does need to include the following.

1 **Personal details.**

2 **Employment experience.**

3 **Educational qualifications.**

4 **Training courses you have attended.**

5 **Additional skills.**

6 **Interests.**

7 **References.**

This is a typical order for presenting a CV, but apart from your personal details coming first, the layout is up to you. You may change the layout to emphasize different aspects of your CV, depending on the requirements of the position you are seeking.

Personal details. Include your name, date of birth, home or institutional address, email address and daytime phone number. You do not need to include your gender, marital status, number of children, nationality, or any disabilities unless you believe these will help your application, such as stating you are Japanese because the organization has offices in Japan. This is an example of tailoring your CV to match the position that you are applying for and we will look at this tactic in more detail later.

Employment experience. This will probably be the next section if you are applying for a non-academic post. If you have very limited work experience you may prefer to highlight the skills acquired during your education next.

In this section include any relevant experience, either paid or unpaid. It doesn't matter if you only have a few weeks experience as an unpaid volunteer. What is important is that you highlight your responsibilities and your achievements in each position so that your prospective employer can readily see that you have relevant experience.

Educational qualifications. Start with your research or Master's degree and work backwards to include your first degree and qualifications you were awarded at school. Include a brief description of your research project, emphasizing the major skills you have developed.

Give the title and class of your first degree and outline the major topics studied. Don't list every module, but group similar topics together to give a concise synopsis. If you are applying for an academic position, give a brief outline of your third-year dissertation. Again, you should emphasize the main skills that you acquired through your studies.

Include your grades for the qualifications that enabled you to study at university such as A levels, BTech, GNVQs or the International Baccalaureate. If you have non-UK qualifications, for example the Nigerian Certificate of Education, give the UK equivalent so that the qualifications are meaningful to the employer. There are several websites that will give the UK equivalent of your qualification if you don't know this already.

You don't need to give the specific results for your qualifications at the end of compulsory schooling. For example, a general statement, such as 'I gained 10 GCSEs, grades A* to C, including English A, Maths C and Science C', will suffice. It is always useful to highlight maths, English and any other subject that is not apparent from your further education, such as science, technology or a foreign language. These help to build a broader picture of your capabilities. Again, if you were at school outside the UK, perhaps in Greece and gained the Apolytirio Gymnasiou (Technical Secondary) certificate, give the UK equivalent.

Make sure that your education and employment details account for the period from when you finished compulsory schooling to date. If you took a gap year, either before or after your first degree, say so. If you had a period of unemployment, state this, but try to make something positive from the experience such as you used the time to analyse your future direction, to take a short course or to spend more time with your children, parents, etc. It is important that you don't leave any unexplained gaps as some employers may reject your application out of hand. Other employers may decide to ask you about the gaps at interview, but relying on this may be a risky strategy.

Training. Part-time students have an advantage here as you have probably undertaken continuing professional development with your organization. For PhD and MPhil students this is where your graduate training programme to meet the skills requirements of the Joint Statement comes into its own. By now you should have a wealth of generic skills that will vastly enhance your employability or career progression. Don't just list the courses but use them to demonstrate your range of skills. For example, 'attending the course on health and safety has enabled me to identify hazards in the workplace and to avoid risks when I undertake field work'.

Additional skills. Here you can include anything else that might be helpful. It is usual to indicate if you have a driving licence, or proficiency in another language (with level of competence), or IT. As a research degree student you are very computer literate. You are probably familiar with spreadsheets, statistical packages and reference managers in addition to word processing, which are sought-after skills in both academia and non-academic organizations.

Interests. Including these in your CV fulfils several functions. They show you are a well-rounded individual. Your interests also give you an opportunity to mention skills that you have acquired in addition to those from your education and employment.

References. You will need at least two referees, three if you are applying for an academic position. They should include your supervisor and your present or last employer, even if the work was only temporary. Give their names, addresses, their status, telephone numbers and email addresses. You should also identify their relationship with you, e.g. Supervisor, Head of Department, Training Co-ordinator. Don't forget to ask your referees for permission to give their names. They are unlikely to refuse you but it is impolite to assume. Always let them know if you have an application in the pipeline so that they can respond quickly to a request. It may be useful to pass on details of the positions to help them to write an appropriate reference.

Examples of academic and non-academic CVs can be found on this book's website.

Making your application relevant

When you see a position of interest, you need to secure an interview. Analyse the advertisement to see if the position is right for you and if you are a likely candidate. Use the following headings to assist you.

1   **Qualifications – do you have these or equivalent qualifications?**

2   **Experience – do you have relevant experience?**

3   **Personal qualities – do you have the qualities they are seeking?**

4   **Style – do you like the sound of the organization?**

5   **Prospects – will this position be sufficiently challenging and enable you to progress?**

6   **Location – is this suitable geographically, or for ease of access?**

7   Salary – is the salary competitive? Don't sell yourself short. If you don't know the 'going rate' for a particular position, consult an online salary comparator (see this book's website for a link).

8   Your expectations – think back to activity 1. Does this position meet the top four or five factors that you identified as important in your career?

If the advert includes a contact number, ring the person for an informal chat. You can then refer to the conversation in your covering letter which helps keep you in the interviewer's memory. Before you ring them, research the position and make a list of points for discussion. If you are ill-prepared you may lose the job before you have even completed the application form! Also, you need to send for the further particulars. These will include a job description and the essential and desirable skills that the employer is seeking. If you can satisfy the majority of the essential skills and a high proportion of the desirable ones, and the position is still appealing, continue with your application. If you cannot offer most of the skills required, you may be wasting your time as you will not make the shortlist. Shortlisting is carried out by scoring the skills offered by each candidate against the criteria and only candidates with a high score will be asked for interview.

Application forms

Many organizations and all educational establishments ask you to complete an application form. Sometimes this will be online, which is easier to fill in as you can type and amend your answers as necessary. If you are required to submit a handwritten form you will need to take a lot of care. It is worth photocopying the form and using the copy to draft your responses. Each answer must fit the space allocated, so make every word count. It may take several drafts before you are happy with the result. Check that your grammar is correct and that there are no spelling mistakes. When you fill in the form make sure you comply with any instructions, such as 'use black ink', 'write in block capitals', 'do not attach additional sheets'. Failure to do so may result in your application being rejected even if you are a good candidate. You may be surprised to learn that a past OU PhD student failed to secure an interview because her application form included both handwriting and block capitals, which led the panel to conclude that she did not pay sufficient attention to detail.

You may be asked to submit your CV, so the application form should not just repeat your CV but should be tailored to fit the position. Use the advert, the job description and the further particulars to identify the relevant skills, and to show how you meet these requirements. Make sure you use the employer's keywords in this process. Sometimes applications are screened electronically prior to the panel seeing them. If you haven't included the keywords, your application will be rejected.

Activity 12.5 Analysing the Requirements of the Position

Find an advert for a position that interests you and obtain the job description and further particulars. Alternatively, use those on this book's website.

List the main requirements in the skills column below. Next to each requirement give evidence from your education, employment or life experience to demonstrate that you have the necessary skills or knowledge.

Skill/knowledge	Evidence
e.g. manage projects	During my studies I ensured the different aspects of my research progressed concurrently, at an appropriate pace. I also met deadlines to successfully submit an outline of my proposed fieldwork and gain funding from the British Council.

Submit a covering letter with your application form, and include your CV if requested. You may be asked to submit other documents at this stage such as samples of your work, which you should choose carefully to reflect the range of your abilities, or a letter outlining why you are suitable for the position.

Covering letters

Your covering letter introduces you to your prospective employer and acts as an ambassador for you. Limit it to one side of A4. It should state:

1 The name and the address of the employer.

2 Your name, address, telephone number and email address.

3 Any dates when you will not be available.

4 The title of the position and the employer's reference number.

5 The documents that you are enclosing, application form, CV, etc.

6 **Your major skills and key reasons for your application for this particular position in this particular organization – to encourage the employer to look at your application straight away (kept this brief but pertinent).**

If appropriate you should state the reasons for moving from an academic to a non-academic environment, such as 'I would like to develop my career by moving to a research institution' or 'having managed research projects I know that my main interest lies in project management'.

If English is your second language, ask a native speaker to read your CV, application form and covering letter. This may help you to demonstrate a good command of English.

Interviews

Congratulations! You have secured an interview. Soon you will be tackling the most challenging part of the process. You need to convince the panel that you are the right candidate for the job.

Pre-interview

It is vital that you continue to target the specific position. The pre-interview pack may include details of materials that you need to prepare. These details usually indicate the specific skills, capabilities and characteristics your prospective employers are seeking. It is worth spending time analysing the requirements in the pre-interview information, and also revisiting the job advert and further particulars of the position, to ensure that your materials (and/or answers to interview questions) demonstrate these attributes directly.

You may be asked to give an oral presentation on either your research or a topic that your prospective employers select, or to prepare some materials, for example teaching materials for a seminar or a portfolio as evidence of your abilities. You may be asked to present a business plan for a new product or an outline proposal for a book for publication. This is your chance to show your creativity, research prowess, teaching abilities, etc., but don't spoil it by overrunning your presentation slot or producing overlength materials. Practice your presentation until you are confident that you can deliver it in the time available; people are less than impressed if you read your script, whether English is your first or second language, but they are happy if you have a crib sheet. Refer back to the guidance in Chapter 10 on presentations to help you to prepare for this important occasion. Ask a few of your friends or trusted colleagues to listen to your presentation, and to give feedback on the content, delivery and timing. Similarly, ask colleagues to comment on any written materials you prepare. If English is your second language, ask a native speaker to give feedback on your presentation or written materials.

If you are isolated from your research group, send the documents by email. This is the time for full-time students to call in favours; after all, you will be doing this for them when they are called for interview.

If you are given details of the panel, look them up on the organization's or institution's website. Background information about each member will help you to anticipate and prepare for likely questions. If the members are researchers, read their latest publications. Use the website to find out more about the policies, research and course profile of your prospective department in academia.

Researching employers

Research the organization that you are trying to enter to determine whether it has good career prospects. For example, it will be useful to know whether:

1   **Your prospective organization is a key player in its field.**

2   **The services/products of this organization are profitable.**

3   **This is a growth area with prospects for expansion.**

Then read up about the background of the organization. You may like to ascertain:

1   **The organization's specific services or products.**

2   **Their main customers and competitors.**

3   **Their structure, policy and mission statement.**

4   **If the organization appears to be financially sound.**

5   **The role of the division, unit or group that you would be joining.**

From this research, make a list of a few pertinent questions to ask at the end of the interview to confirm your interest in the position and the organization.

Travel

Plan your journey so that you arrive in plenty of time, and be sure of your destination. Some universities and businesses have more than one site in a town, which can lead to confusion, and won't help your nerves at all. If necessary, go a day early and stay over. If you ask the organization to recommend a nearby hotel or guest house so that you can attend the interview, they may pay your expenses, but you should not expect this. The convention is that they will pay your travelling expenses. Don't let your nerves get the better of you. You have done really well to get to the interview. Often only five or six candidates are interviewed so you have every chance of success.

Difficult questions

Some people dread interviews and worry they will be asked difficult questions that they will not be able to answer. The following activity will help you to prepare for the interview.

Activity 12.6   Interview Role Play

Ask one or several of your colleagues to play the role of the interviewer(s). They don't need to have done this before, although if do you have friends who are experienced interviewers, get them involved! Find a quiet room where you are unlikely to be interrupted and place chairs so that the candidate's chair is facing the other(s). Set a timer for 30 or 40 minutes, which are typical interview periods. Give your interviewers the questions in the appendices, which have been asked in actual interview situations, and let them fire away. They should select one or two questions from each group to give you a representative experience. Try to give an interesting answer, based on your experience and skills. You may find it helpful to use the structure CARAs as recommended by the OU Careers service. CARA is:

1   Context 20 per cent – what the objective or situation was.
2   Action 50 per cent – your part in it, the problems you had to solve, or the actions that you took.
3   Result 20 per cent – what the outcome was.
4   After 10 per cent – what you learned from the experience.

Don't say anything derogatory about yourself – it does happen!

When the time is up, discuss with your interviewers ways in which you could improve your performance. Also, make bullet points of your answers so that you feel prepared to cope with these types of questions. Ask other postdoctoral fellows in your discipline, verbally or by email, to suggest other possible interview questions so that you can prepare answers to these too. Don't learn answers by rote as you will probably forget them under the pressure of the interview.

Dress

Despite the typically casual approach to dress in universities, people usually dress more formally for interviews, as you did for your viva. Generally, this is not the time for personal statements about dress but the time to dress professionally, which for men includes a tie. This demonstrates you can act the part when the occasion arises, such as when representatives from the Research Council decide to visit your department.

Professional dress is even more crucial in the business world. Dress codes for positions that interact with customers or clients are usually very conservative and you will be expected to adhere to the dress code at all times.

Some university departments or creative organizations, however, expect you to express yourself through your own style, but if you are not sure of the organization's attitude it may be safer to opt for a conservative approach.

On the day

Research has shown that first impressions are very important. So how do you make a good first impression? We have already discussed dress, but now body language plays a larger role. You need to appear confident, even if you are quaking inside – after all, as one professor said to me years ago:

> You are being considered for employment because they think you are capable of doing the job. Don't forget no one wants surgery from a consultant who isn't confident that he can carry out the necessary operation. Go in and show them they were right to shortlist you.

So enter the room with confidence. As each member of the panel is introduced to you, shake their hand and look them in the eye and say you are pleased to meet them. Sit down and try to appear relaxed. You are here to sell yourself, not in a flamboyant way but calmly and sincerely. The interviewers are looking for someone who will fit in with the team. They liked the impression of you that they gleaned from your application and are keen to meet you. They also want evidence that you can think on your feet. If you are uncertain of the meaning of a question, ask. Don't rush your answers, take time to think by saying, 'That is a good question' or 'I hadn't considered that, I need a moment to think about it'.

As the interview draws to a close, make sure you take the opportunity to ask questions. If they have already been covered, say so, rather than appear unprepared. You may be asked if you are still interested in the position, how soon you could start and the salary you are expecting. It is common for the salary quoted in the advert to cover a range, so have a starting point in mind. As you leave, thank the panel for their time. Even if they don't appoint you, they may call you for interview if you apply again, so leaving on a good note may be crucial to your long-term aims.

After the interview you need to weigh up whether you will take the position if offered. An interview is a two-way process and it is important you feel both excited by the position and comfortable with your future employer. I have known students return from an interview feeling uncomfortable with the place, their prospective employer or the actual position. If you feel this, don't take it. Alternatively, you may wish for further information, or realize you have forgotten to ask something that may influence your decision. You can rectify this if they offer you the position. Either talk to the interview chair on the phone or ask for a further appointment to clarify issues. Most people are happy to talk to you again. If they are unwilling to do this, do you really want to join them!

If you are not offered the position, and it was one that you particularly wanted, write to the panel asking for a de-brief. State in your letter that you were disappointed not to be selected and you would like some feedback to assist you to apply again in the future. Most interview chairs will be willing to talk to you over the phone for a few minutes.

Other types of selection processes

Telephone interviews

If you have applied for a position in a country other than where you are living, you may be interviewed by telephone. This may be from a single interviewer, or a panel using a conference call. Sometimes the call is pre-arranged, but several of our students have received a call unexpectedly. This can really catch you unprepared – one student was still in bed! But it is amazing how quickly you can wake up in response to an adrenaline surge – she secured a three-year postdoctoral fellowship in Australia. So my advice is, prepare thoroughly for a position in another country. Research the organization, practice those difficult questions, maybe even ask a friend to interview you over the phone. You never know, the next phone call that you receive could be a career-changing one.

Psychometric tests

These tests wax and wane in popularity, but you might wish to join an organization that relies on them. Often you will be told this prior to your interview, so you will have time to prepare. There are two main types of test:

1 **Aptitude, ability, intelligence and cognitive tests, which assess the level and nature of your reasoning abilities. These are usually multiple choice, timed, and designed so that you cannot answer all the questions in the time allowed. It is worth practising these tests beforehand. Always leave more difficult questions to last as it is the number of questions that you get right that counts.**

2 **Personality tests, which assess your behaviour in different situations, your attitudes and preferences.**

If you would like more information, then Prospects and SDLdirect are useful websites. These tests have questions to check for consistency, so don't try to bluff or to give answers that you think they are looking for. If your replies show inconsistency you won't have a chance of the position. Sometimes not fitting their profile may be an advantage. I know of one student who received feedback which stated they were unsuccessful because they were clearly seeking a position with more responsibility and use of initiative.

Sight-unseen activities

These can run the whole gamut from discussion groups, business simulations, timed written activities, presentations, to problem-solving tasks. If you know that you might have to complete this kind of activity, ask advice from other people who have undergone similar experiences. On the day, make sure you read or listen to all the instructions carefully because when you are nervous it is easy to misread or misunderstand. If appropriate, brainstorm a plan of action for a couple of minutes and then get started. Usually it is easier once you become absorbed in the task – you are too engrossed to be nervous.

So finally, best of luck. There is a position out there that is just right for you, you just need to find it. And remember the golden rule of job-hunting. You may get rejection after rejection, but then you are called for three interviews in the same week and offered all three positions. But deciding between offers … now that's another story.

Acknowledgements

This chapter was developed from workshops for PhD students at the Open University. The workshops were led by the author, Dr Melanie Hanna and Professor Wendy Stainton-Rogers. Thanks also to the Open University Careers Service for the use of the structure CARA.

References

Ali, L. and Graham, B. (2000) *Moving on in Your Career: A Guide for Academic Researchers and Postgraduates*. London, RoutledgeFalmer.

Association of Graduate Recruiters (1995) *Skills for Graduates in the 21st Century*. London: Association of Graduate Recruiters.

Blaxter, L., Hughes, C. and Tight, M. (2001) *The Academic Career Handbook*. Buckingham: Open University Press.

Cohen, J., Medley, G. and Stewart, I. (2000) *Stop Working and Start Thinking: A Guide to Becoming a Scientist*. London: BIOS Scientific Publishers.

EPSRC Contract Researchers Career Development Training Pack, available from www.epsrc.ac.uk

Hawkins, P. (1999) *The Art of Building Windmills: Career Tactics for the 21st Century*. Graduate in Employment Unit, University of Liverpool, UK.

The UKGRAD Programme (2004) *What Do PhD's Do?*, analysis of first destinations for PhD graduates available from www.grad.ac.uk

Appendix 1: Useful Words to Describe Your Skills

Management	Communication	Financial	Leadership
achieved	arbitrated	accounted	facilitated
analysed	communicated	accuracy	guided
arranged	created	administered	implemented
contracted	influenced	allocated	launched
controlled	interacted	audited	led
co-ordinated	interpreted	budgeted	listened
delegated	liaised	calculated	maturity
developed	mediated	increased	mentored
directed	motivated	maintained	referred
effected	negotiated	managed	related
eliminated	persuaded	planned	responsibility
established	presented	solved	sensitivity
expedited	proposed		supported
improved	reasoned		teamwork
organized	recommended		understood
prioritized	reconciled		
produced	recruited		
reduced	simplified		
reinforced	translated		
reorganized			
revamped			
revised			
scheduled			
selected			
streamlined			
structured			
supervised			

Creative	Research	Teaching	Attention to detail
adapted	analysed	advised	approved
conceived	conducted	briefed	arranged
conceptualized	contributed	coached	compiled
created	controlled	demonstrated	completed
designed	critiqued	encouraged	enforced
developed	diagnosed	explained	executed
expanded	evaluated	informed	implemented
generated	identified	instructed	pinpointed
initiated	interviewed	lectured	responded
innovated	investigated	stimulated	retained
integrated	produced	trained	validated
invented	programmed		
modified	proved		
originated	provided		
	set up		
	surveyed		
	synthesized		
	tested		
Personal			
accomplished			
achieved			
decided			
handled			
mastered			
operated			
participated			
performed			
proficient in			
utilized			

Appendix 2:   Interview Questions
(Supplied by Interviewers)

Academic

What publication are you most proud of and why?

Why haven't you published anything during your PhD?

Why haven't you published anything with your supervisor?

What do you see as the main benefits of your research?

Tell me about your PhD research assuming that I have no background knowledge.

What do you anticipate that you would find easy in teaching undergraduates and what would be challenging?

Where will you apply for research funding?

What skills can you bring to the department?

What do you anticipate gaining professionally from your research?

What are you looking for in terms of continuing professional development?

Why are you interested in this research project?

Non-academic

What dealings have you had with the commercial applications of your research?

Who do you see as our main competitors?

What qualities can you offer our organization?

Why have you chosen to join our organization?

What key points would you include in a business plan to develop a new product?

What are the key points to bear in mind when you sub-contract?

Where do you see the market in two years' time?

How do you think the strong/weak pound will affect our organization?

General
Where do you see yourself in five years' time?

Can you describe a time when you had to work to a tight deadline?

Can you describe a situation where you needed to pay attention to detail?

Can you describe a situation where you experienced pressure in a job?

Most jobs involve some financial management, can you give an example of managing a budget?

What do you see as your main weaknesses?

Why do you want this job?

How do you respond to challenging situations?

Can you talk about a situation where you demonstrated oral communication skills?

Can you give an example of where you influenced a group of people?

What do you think is the most important consideration when co-ordinating a team?

What do you think is the most important aspect of written communication?

What do you find most challenging about working in a team?

What salary are you looking for?

What are your strengths?

How do you establish priorities in your current job?

What is it about a career in XXX that interests you?

Index